The Complete Idiot's Quick Steps Guide

Copying an Audio or a Data CD

1. Click Start, Programs, Roxio Easy CD Creator 4, Create CD.
2. Select CD Copier.
3. Select the source CD-ROM drive and destination CD-RW drive in the drop-down menus. Insert your source disc in your CD-ROM drive and your recordable CD in your CD-RW drive.
4. Use the Advanced tab if you want to change any settings, such as the speed at which the disc gets recorded or the number of copies to be burned.
5. Click the Copy button.

Creating an Audio CD from Other CDs, MP3 Files, and WAV Files

1. Click Start, Programs, Roxio Easy CD Creator 4, Features, Easy CD Creator.
2. Click File, New CD Layout, and then Audio CD.
3. Use the Explorer pane to locate CDs in your CD-ROM drive or audio files on your hard disk.
4. Click and drag files to the layout pane. Alternatively, highlight the file(s) and click the Add button.
5. Watch the time indicator bar at the bottom to be sure you don't try to copy more than the CD will hold (usually 74 minutes).
6. If you want to copy music from more than one CD, insert each CD and repeat steps 4 and 5.
7. Click the Record button when you're ready to start burning.
8. Make any selections you want in the CD Creation Setup dialog box (write speed, close disc, and so on).
9. Insert a blank recordable CD in your CD-RW drive.
10. Click the Record button.

Creating a Data CD

1. Click Start, Programs, Roxio Easy CD Creator 4, Features, Easy CD Creator.
2. Click File, New CD Layout, and then Data CD.
3. Use the Explorer pane to locate files and folders you want to copy to the CD.
4. Drag files to the layout pane. Alternatively, highlight the file(s) and click the Add button.
5. Watch the space indicator bar at the bottom to be sure you don't try to copy more than the CD will hold (usually 650MB).
6. Click the Record button when you're ready to start burning.
7. Make any selections you want in the CD Creation Setup dialog box (write speed, close disc, and so on).
8. Insert blank a CD in your CD-RW drive.
9. Click the Record button.

Creating an Audio C...

1. Click Start, Programs, Adaptec Easy CD C... ...pin Doctor.
2. Click the 1 button in the first pane to select the source of the audio.
3. Select a source: CD, LP, Tape, other input device, or files on your hard drive.
4. Click the 2 button in the second pane. Select the audio destination (CD-R drive, hard disk, or audio playback).

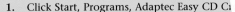

D1444931

Creating an Audio CD Using the Spin Doctor   Continued

5. Use the Options dialog box in the Options menu to clean up the pops and scratches in your source, or modify the audio with special effects.
6. Click the Record button. If recording from LP or cassette tape, be sure to start the source playing.
7. When using an LP or a cassette tape, use the Pause button when it's time to flip the record or tape to the other side.
8. If using digital CD or audio files as the source, recording stops when finished. Click Stop Recording when a record or tape is finished playing.

Adding Song Titles to Music CDs in Easy CD Creator

You can add this information automatically if you are connected to the Internet:
1. Insert the source CD in the CD-ROM drive.
2. Select this CD-ROM drive in the explorer pane of the Easy CD Creator as the source drive.
3. Click the Internet button on the toolbar.
4. If the information is available on the Internet database, it is downloaded in a few seconds and displayed on the screen. For future use, the information is stored on your computer.

Formatting a Disc for DirectCD Use

1. Insert the CD-R or CD-RW disc into the CD recorder drive.
2. Click Start, Programs, Roxio Easy CD Creator 4, Create CD.
3. From the first menu, select Data. From the second menu, select DirectCD.
4. Click Next when the DirectCD wizard dialog box appears.
5. In the Format window, select Quick if the disc has been used before or Full if it is a new blank. The new blank takes about an hour to format. Click Next.
6. Enter a name for the disc and then click Finish. From then on, when you insert it into your CD-RW drive it will be recognized by DirectCD and can be used just like your hard disk.

Times Required to Record a Disc

Recording Speed	Approximate Time	
	74-Min/650MB Discs	80-Min/700MB Discs
1x	74 minutes	80 minutes
2x	37 minutes	40 minutes
4x	19 minutes	20 minutes
8x	10 minutes	10 minutes
12x	7 minutes	7 minutes

Trademarks

Warning and Disclaimer

Associate Publisher
Greg Wiegand

Acquisitions Editor
Jenny L. Watson

Development Editor
Todd Brakke

Managing Editor
Thomas F. Hayes

Project Editor
Karen S. Shields

Copy Editor
Megan Wade

Indexer
Aamir Burki

Proofreader
Benjamin Berg

Technical Editor
Dwight L. Torlay, Jr.

Illustrator
Judd Winick

Team Coordinator
Sharry Lee Gregory

Media Developer
Aaron Price

Interior Designer
Nathan Clement

Cover Designer
Michael Freeland

Production
Brad Lenser
Steve Geiselman
Gloria Schurick

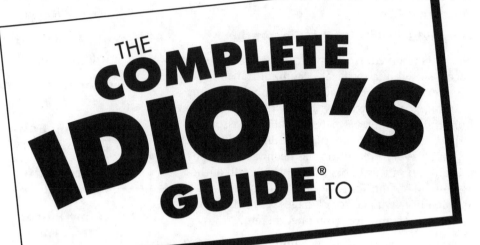

THE COMPLETE IDIOT'S GUIDE® TO

Creating Your Own CDs

by Terry William Ogletree

201 W. 103rd Street, Indianapolis, IN 46290

Contents at a Glance

Contents

About the Author

Terry W. Ogletree is a con artist who has, so far, made a great living fooling multi-national companies out of large sums of money by working in the "consulting" business. If you will recall, the definition of "consultant" is one who borrows your watch to tell you what time it is. These past four years he has managed to demand huge advances for such successful titles as *Practical Firewalls* and *Upgrading and Repairing Networks, Second Edition*. He has worked with many operating systems, including OpenVMS, UNIX, and all flavors of Windows NT. It has been said that the delays in Microsoft's releasing new versions of NT and Windows 2000 were because Terry has been on their beta list for the past five years.

Currently, he is performing consulting services at Bristol-Myers Squibb in Princeton, NJ. When finished with that assignment, he expects to be able to find a large corporation in New York City from which he can suck sufficient funds to live quite comfortably. If not, he may retire to his home in Marietta, Georgia, and go back to the only job he was ever proficient at—bagging groceries at the local store.

You can contact Terry at his Web site www.twoinc.com.

Dedication

Dedicated to Charles, Billie Jean, Gordon, Susan, Heather, Holly, Mitsey, Blackberry, Joey, Ritchie, and Zira.

Acknowledgments

This book is my first Complete Idiot's Guide. When I first took on this project, it seemed to me that it would be much easier than the other books I have worked on. However, that turned out not to be the case. The special involvement of Jenny Watson, Que's senior acquisitions editor, and Todd Brakke made the process a lot easier. Jenny is always a joy to work with and one of the most professional persons I know. Todd has worked on my last two books, and this time I must give him a lot more credit than in the past. As development editor, he came up with much of the design of this book and also contributed very specific suggestions about CD burners and applications that use them. If he hadn't been so busy working his regular job at Que, he could have been a coauthor of this book and you'd have gotten it earlier! It's easier to write a book of this kind when the development editor knows the topic so well.

The technical editor, Dwight Torlay, also contributed much to the information you'll find in this book. Dwight has been working with CD burners for several years now and knows just about all the tricks of the trade. Of course, Dwight, who puts together his own PCs, would be a welcome addition to any book writing team in this field. I thank him for both his suggestions and for catching my errors when writing this.

I would like to acknowledge several people once again for their support during the writing of this book. First, Robert G. Venard and Tom Crayner, for whom I currently am working at Bristol-Myers Squibb. If you're not having a good time at work, it's hard to go home and write! Of course, I couldn't have gotten this job without the help of John Rogue and Angelo Simeo of The Computer Merchant. Special thanks to James Garrett, Steve McGuire, and the rest of the Devereux Street Gang—always a fun place to escape to for relaxation. A very special thanks again to Michael D. Parrott and his wonderful wife Brenda for keeping the finances straight, a topic about which I am a total idiot. And a very very special thanks to Jo, who seems to have gotten married between my book projects. So instead, thanks to Jo and Jeff Johnson!

A very special thanks to Andy Jones and Jordan Scoggins for showing me around New York City when I could find time to squeeze in a quick trip here and there.

And, of course, as always, my parents, Charles and Billie Jean Ogletree, to whom I owe everything good I have ever received in this lifetime

Tell Us What You Think!

As the reader of this book, *you* are our most important critic and commentator. We value your opinion and want to know what we're doing right, what we could do better, what areas you'd like to see us publish in, and any other words of wisdom you're willing to pass our way.

As an associate publisher for Que, I welcome your comments. You can fax, email, or write me directly to let me know what you did or didn't like about this book—as well as what we can do to make our books stronger.

Please note that I cannot help you with technical problems related to the topic of this book, and that due to the high volume of mail I receive, I might not be able to reply to every message.

When you write, please be sure to include this book's title and author as well as your name and phone or fax number. I will carefully review your comments and share them with the author and editors who worked on the book.

Fax: 317-581-4666

Email: quefeedback@macmillanusa.com

Mail: Associate Publisher
           Que
           201 West 103rd Street
           Indianapolis, IN 46290 USA

Introduction

Things come and go. Here today, gone tomorrow. For those who have a huge collection of vinyl phonograph records or cassette tapes, those words have an ominous meaning: It's time to buy all your favorite music all over again on CD. You can still buy a phonograph player, or supplies such as a needle or cartridge, at stores that sell higher-quality audio equipment. However, this does not solve the problem of the slow degradation of the record or tape over time as it is played or as it succumbs to the elements.

While the phonograph record has been replaced by the CD, cassette tapes have endured. I would suspect this has been due to the fact that cassettes are convenient (especially in a car), and you can always put together a tape of your own design by recording on a blank cassette tape. Until very recently, tape was the only way to go if you wanted to "copy" music.

Tape allows you to make a complete copy of your favorite album (and now CD). It also enables you to pick and choose which songs you want and the order in which you want to hear them. If it weren't for the fact that cassette tapes are analog in nature, most people would be satisfied using them to back up their audio collections.

In the computer world, don't forget that tape has been, and in some circles still is, the method of choice for backing up large amounts of computer data. Heck, in those olden days of yore, tape was a primary method of storing any kind of data. Anyone remember using the Commodore PET?

Now that the digital revolution has taken off, the price of a CD recorder drive has dropped dramatically, along with the price of blank recordable CDs. Instead of the slow, tedious process of recovering computer data off a tape drive backup, backup CD-Rs offer nearly instant access to their data. A quick click and drag in Windows and it's right back on your hard drive!

Instead of having to settle for a second- or third-generation tape copy of your favorite songs, you can now create almost perfect copies using digital recording. CD recording provides the same capabilities that tape does when it comes to mixing and matching songs from various sources to create your own dream sequence. It gives you the same crystal clarity that you'd get if you were playing the source itself.

To make matters even better, this book shows you how to use Roxio's Easy CD Creator's Spin Doctor to record not just from other CDs, but also from your collection of vinyl records and tapes.

Note that Roxio is a subsidiary of Adaptec, so depending on your version of the software, you might see Adaptec in the figure title bars instead of Roxio.

Thanks to the CD-RW drive going mainstream, no piece of data is unsafe and no song from a one-hit wonder must wallow on a disc with lesser music (just copy it to your own custom compilation disc)!

Different Tracks: What's in the Book

This book starts out with a brief introduction to CD recording. I would have written more, but, as my editor points out, readers of this book will be more interested in jumping into the fray and starting to create CDs than worrying about photoreflective layering and other words that can't be pronounced without the aid of a physics professor. We'll still touch on some of that stuff in the first part of this book, though, because it can help you understand some of the basic necessities. Certain concepts such as the differences between recordable discs, how a CD-Writer writes discs differently from a disc you would buy at your local music shop, and much more can ease you safely into those shark-infested CD burning waters. To help you find out where to start in this book, and it doesn't have to be at the beginning, I offer the following summaries of the various parts you'll find herein.

Part 1: So You Want to Create Some CDs, Do You? An Essential CD Technology Primer

Recording audio and video has progressed over the last hundred years to a point that, with digital recording techniques, it is possible to preserve a particular audio or video event forever. Digital recordings can be transferred bit by bit to your computer, to CDs, and even to portable devices. Chapter 1, "The Digital Revolution!" talks about how far we've come.

If you've ever wondered how a CD is actually manufactured, or how recordable and rewritable discs you can burn on your computer differ, then you'll like Chapter 2, "The Machine Behind the Curtain: How CDs and Recordable CDs Work."

Part 2: Creating an Audio or a Data CD

In this book, we use Roxio's Easy CD Creator 4 Deluxe as the application for most examples. In this section, you'll find chapters on creating and copying CDs. If you want to burn a CD with tracks from other CDs, MP3 files, and WAV files, you can become a music CD producer by reading Chapter 3, "Using Easy CD Creator to Make Audio CDs."

Chapter 4, "Using Easy CD Creator to Make Data CDs," shows you how to copy files from your computer to CDs. You can use the CD recorder to back up important files for long-term storage.

From there, we dig into more advanced methods you can use to record to CDs. If you want to take your audio further, such as extracting music from other sources (for example, vinyl records, cassettes, radio, or almost any other source that uses standard audio jacks), then check out Chapter 5, "Your Very Own Record Studio: Using the CD Spin Doctor."

Aspiring video producers should check out Chapter 6, "Toss Your VCR: Using Video CD Creator to Create Video CDs," while Chapter 7, "Using Your CD Recorder Like a Hard Disk," shows you how to use your CD recorder almost as if it were a hard drive. You can use it as a target for save operations from Windows applications such as Word and Excel. If you use rewritable discs (CD-RW), you can even erase the disc and start over again.

The last chapter in this section is for those who simply want to copy CDs. Chapter 8, "The Easiest Way to Pillage—Copying CDs Using Easy CD Copier," shows you how to make copies of both audio and data CDs. The first thing you might want to do when buying a new, expensive software application is to use this chapter to make a backup copy of the application CD.

Part 3: Entering Murky Waters: Creating Multisession CDs

Multisession CDs enable you to write data to CDs over time without having to burn the whole thing at once. Chapter 9, "Understanding and Using Multisession CDs," as the name implies, talks about what a multisession CD is and how it compares to other types of CDs.

Chapter 10, "Best of Both Worlds: Creating CDs with Both Audio and Data," discusses the standard multisession formats used to create CDs. With these discs, you can store both songs and an artist's video on the same CD. Do you have no idea why you'd want to do that? Take a gander at this chapter, and it could give you some ideas for things you'd never even thought of trying!

Part 4: It's Always Better to Look Good: Creating the Jewel Case Covers and Disc Labels

This section covers the Jewel Case Creator that comes with the Roxio software. In Chapter 11, "Using Jewel Case Creator to Create Labels and Inserts," we step through the basics of creating a simple CD label and the inserts for the jewel case. In Chapter 12, "You've Got the Look: Using Graphics and Other Advanced Stuff with Jewel Case Creator," we go further and look at adding graphics to your creations.

Part 5: Other Nifty Programs and Tools for Your CD Recorder

Roxio includes several other programs with Easy CD Creator 4 Deluxe. In Chapter 13, "Other Roxio Utilities," you'll find out how to put your family photographs on CD and how to use the Session Changer to change sessions when using multisession CDs. Chapter 14, "Extra Delivery! Using PhotoRelay," covers in a little more depth a photo-editing program.

No matter how well you prepare, there is always the possibility that something will go wrong. That's what Chapter 15, "We're Gonna Need a Bigger Boat: Troubleshooting CD Recording," is all about. If you run into trouble spots in your CD burning adventure, this is your survival guide.

Chapter 16, "Other Neat Software," talks about two other popular applications you can use to burn CDs. The first is MusicMatch Jukebox 5.0, and the second is Microsoft's newest Media Player 7. Both of these enable you to do far more than just burn CDs, however, so be sure to check out these easily attainable alternatives.

Other Junk You'll Find Herein

Similar to a child, I like to write in the margins and all over the page. In this book, you'll find some examples of this in the following forms.

Between Tracks

These small bits of text are inserted here and there to provide tips, notes, and extra information that aren't in the main body of the text. You might find a shortcut, or possibly a topic you may want to explore further in another chapter of the book.

Arcane CD Speak

Sometimes words just say too much. So much that they don't make sense. In these little text bites, I explain some of this terminology. You don't need to know these words to get the job done, but they'll make you sound smarter when you're spouting off to friends about how clever you are.

Don't Get Burned!

Caution! Caution! Caution! Can I make it any plainer? These notes point you away from potential pitfalls and help you keep from spending hours working on your pet project only to have something go wrong in the process.

Start Having Fun!

Read this book fast! Why? Because the Internet and the music industry are moving faster than you are! Make backups of your precious CDs. Put your family photographs on CD for long-term digital storage. Scour the Internet for new songs, new files, and new programs. After you get started with your CD recorder, you'll wonder how you ever got along without it. CD recording for the home user really is a *digital revolution!*

Part 1

So You Want to Create Some CDs, Do You? An Essential CD Technology Primer

I know that most of you reading this book are mostly interested in just getting right to the fun part—burning CDs! Here in this first section, though, we will first take a quick look at CDs and the technology behind them. If you understand how digital recording differs from analog recording and if you understand how CDs are mastered and manufactured, as discussed in Chapter 1, "The Digital Revolution!" then some of the actions you go through when you burn CDs will make more sense. The second chapter in this section talks about how recordable CDs work. Although they produce the same results as mass-produced CDs, they are written much differently from a disc you'd buy in a store.

After you've read these two really exciting chapters, you'll be ready to use Easy CD Creator to start burning plastic!

Chapter 1

The Digital Revolution!

In This Chapter

➤ Analog is out! Digital is in!

➤ Digital methods provide superior audio and video quality.

➤ Digital methods allow you to transfer information from fragile and decaying media to something more stable.

➤ You can store computer files and programs, as well as audio files, on a CD using a CD burner.

➤ Roxio's Easy CD Creator is a comprehensive package that can do what it might take several other products to do.

If you're one of those whippersnappers born in the 1980s or sometime after that, you will never know the time that some people devoted to protecting their music collection before CDs came along. Analog phonograph records were fragile platforms to hold music and—other than various forms of magnetic tape, such as cassettes or reel-to-reel—there was no alternative. Music was recorded as an audio signal that was laid down onto tape by magnetically manipulating atoms on the tape, or it was etched into the surface of the master that would eventually lead to stamped phonograph records.

Such fragile things are subject to quick deterioration. All you have to do is walk across the floor not-too-softly and the needle might skip across the record. There's the first scratch. And it will show up in the playback. When the compact disc was finally released, its capability to store audio digitally was heralded as a great leap forward in the music industry. And, indeed, it has come to prove itself to be just that.

CDs and DVDs: A Revolution in Data Storage

Digitally recording music on a CD improves on the analog record in two major areas. First, the actual sound quality is much better on the CD than on the record. The digital recording method used to sample music at thousands and thousands of times per second almost guarantees you won't miss a beat.

The 74-Minute Myth

You might wonder why CDs were developed first to store 74 minutes of audio information. The "urban folklore" answer is that it was selected because it could hold the entire performance of Beethoven's Ninth Symphony. This is, however, not true, at least as far as this author has been able to determine. The amount of audio data was more likely determined by the technological capabilities available at the time the compact disc was first introduced. As technologies are further developed, we are able to fit more and more information in a much smaller amount of disc (or disk) real estate. Thus, we now have 80-minute CDs and, even more importantly, DVDs that can hold much more information than CDs can—even though both are the same physical size.

The second area that CDs can be said to excel is in their durability. Now, I'm not saying you can take your CDs and use them to play Frisbee with your dog. However, in normal everyday use, CDs are much more durable than records. Record needles continually scratch away a small amount of the surface each time a record is played. Basically, you damage your precious music collection just by listening to it! With audio tape, a similar process of deterioration occurs as the magnetic surface of the tape is passed over the tape head when it is played. You might say that with vinyl and tape, it's downhill from the very start!

The laser used in audio playback devices for CDs does no damage to speak of to the CD itself. It simply points the laser at the disc and processes the amount of light reflected back. Nothing touches the surface of the CD other than a clamping device, which holds the CD in the drive by clamping onto the very center of the disc, where there is no recording surface. The wear and tear factor for CDs, when compared to vinyl and tape, is almost nonexistent.

DVDs are pretty much an evolution of the CDs. These discs, however, can hold a lot more information. Up to this point, DVD has mostly served to replace your videotape collection, and comparing the advantages of DVD movies over videotape isn't much different from the advantage of CDs over vinyl records. DVDs give you a much clearer picture and better sound, and, because of the large amount of space available for data, DVDs also allow for other options that videotape cannot provide, such as the capability to select from multiple languages or use subtitles.

What Does DVD Stand For?

As you already know, CD stands for compact disc. So what is this DVD thing? Originally, the term was considered an acronym for digital video disc. Later, when it was realized that the DVD, like the CD, could have other uses, such as in the computer industry, many began referring to them as digital versatile discs. In the end, no one really agreed on one name, meaning that DVD doesn't really stand for anything anymore (depending on who you talk to).

After you get past the physical advantages of the CD itself, the digital method used for recording audio needs to be considered. Vinyl and older tape machines used analog methods to encode sound. When a copy was made, the sound quality was degraded a little each time. Lost sound quality comes about partly because of the wear and tear on the original and the condition of the recording equipment. And let's not even get into making copies of copies with analog music. Have you ever made a photocopy and then tried to copy that copy, and copy the copy after that, and so on? The same gradual demise of the image you see in a photocopy also happens to your music when making copies of copies using a cassette tape. Major bummer! Of course, it makes one wonder if, when it comes to cloning human beings (something that is not far away), can we expect the same results?

Digital recording writes audio on the CD in a digital format that is similar to the way your computer stores its data. As a matter of fact, you can, using the right program, extract songs from your favorite CDs and store them as files on your hard drive. Because the music is stored in a digital format, it is even possible to do a little error correction to help ensure that the sound quality is up to par.

When using CDs to store computer data, the error correction scheme used is even more powerful than that used on audio CDs. This is because there is less tolerance for a mistake in a computer program or the data it uses than there is in an audio file. You probably wouldn't even notice if one zillionth of a second of music got screwed up while burning your favorite CD. Having your CD-RW drive flub those few bits when burning a computer program or word processor file, however, could cause disaster!

Duplicating and Creating Your Own CDs

As this digital revolution has progressed forward in time from the 1980s when CDs were first introduced, we've come to a sort of mini-revolution: recordable CDs. The terms generally applied to these discs are *CD-R*, which are blank CDs you can burn once (and only once), and *CD-RW*, which are discs that can be used and erased and used many more times.

CD-R technology, with high prices, started to take off around 1996, and prices have since dropped dramatically. More significantly, the price of the blank media—the blank CDs—has dropped a lot, too. You can expect to pay around a buck a disc, or less if you find them on sale. At the expense of just a dollar, you can make a copy of your favorite CD so that you have one for the car and one for home. Or, use only the copy for listening and put the original away for safekeeping.

Because CD burners can also be used to store not just audio information, but computer data files also, their use is becoming more widespread. Using a program such as DirectCD, which is discussed later in this book, you can write to a CD-RW disc just as if it were a hard disk on your system.

For Computer Nerds as Well as Aspiring Musicians!

As you can see, buying a CD burner gives you the chance to get a lot more out of your computer. If you follow this book's lead and use Roxio's Easy CD Creator 4.0 for your CD burning pleasure, the sky is very nearly the limit. If, for example, you happen to be someone who has a large collection of LPs just sitting around the house, you're going to find it impossible not to use Spin Doctor to clean up the sound and make CDs from those LPs. After waiting all these years, you could even put the songs in the order in which *you* think they should be. To heck with those dopey record producers!

When you're finished copying all your LPs and making backup copies of your CDs, you can get started scanning and storing all your family photographs on CD. Want to annoy relatives and friends? Create video CDs or video postcards and send everyone the family movies you so excellently produced over the last holiday.

And for those of us who are also computer nerds, there are even more reasons for using a CD burner. All your software CDs can be backed up so you don't have to repurchase them or wait weeks to receive a new copy from the vendor when one screws up or gets played with by the cat. Important data can be stored on CDs, again at less than a buck a disc. If you are a programmer, you can distribute copies of your software using a CD burner and make professional-looking labels and jewel box cases to go with them.

And, at the risk of sounding like a poorly produced infomercial, there's more, more, *more*!

The Copyright Zoo

One thing I should make perfectly clear here at the beginning of this book is that, as president, I am not a crook. Oh, sorry, my mind is slipping again. What I meant to say is that *you* should not be a crook. The Internet, much less new computer technology such as recordable CDs, has made a quagmire of existing copyright laws, even though they've been updated during the past few years to try to cover new technology.

As this author understands it, you are allowed "fair use" copying privileges to make backups of CDs or other recordings you already own—for your own use. This means you can't, legally, make copies and sell them. Whether you can give away copies to friends is a hot topic of debate. Of course, those "people" who run the Hollywood media machine have introduced copy protection encryption on DVDs and have fought others in court who have merely tried to give us the tools to make copies of what we already own! In my opinion, what they are trying to do is judge you a criminal just because you want to make a copy. This situation did not exist when home tape recording came along. Of course, people were a lot friendlier back then!

The point here is that you shouldn't get yourself in trouble until all these legal arguments settle down and the government (at least in the U.S.) can tell you what you really can and cannot do—which they can't right now. So, when reading this book please note that **this author and Que** do in no way mean to encourage the breaking of any laws, no matter how silly or ambiguous they are.

For the record, I'm holding on to my Napster stock. From here on out, you're on your own!

What to Look for in a CD Burner

So, how do we get to this wonderful world in which we can copy most anything and store it on a CD? Well, if you haven't already, go buy yourself a CD burner. Today, you can get a very good one for under $200 (watch for the sales and rebates). Things to look for include:

➤ The drive should support CD-RW discs as well as CD-R discs that can be burned only once.

➤ The drive should support packet-mode writing so that you can use software such as DirectCD.

➤ The drive should support multisessions.

Cross Reference

Packet Writing? Multisessions? It's Already Confusing!

If you don't know what the word *multisession* means or what *packet writing* is, don't worry. Just make sure any new drive you buy supports it (pretty much all of them do). If you want to know more now, check out Chapter 7, "Using Your CD Recorder Like a Hard Disk," for the scoop on packet writing. Or, for the dish on multisession CDs, see Chapter 9, "Understanding and Using Multisession CDs."

Quite frankly, the speed at which the drive records shouldn't concern you too much. At 1x speed, recording a CD will take a little longer than 74 minutes. At 2x, that drops to 37 minutes, more or less. For drives that claim to burn at higher than 4x rates, you must carefully choose which media you use for your CD-R blanks. Sometimes bigger and faster isn't better. One of the main troubleshooting tips you'll find throughout this book is this: If you're having problems, drop back to 1x and see whether that works. So, unless you're just a very impatient person, don't worry about the speed too much. Heck, you might end up creating a disc in 10 minutes and then find it's unusable. Do this a few times and you could have successfully created the CD at 1x speed the first time through!

If you buy a new drive today, it will most likely meet the previously mentioned requirements, so don't worry about this stuff too much. Just don't go buy a bargain somewhere like a flea market and expect it to perform up to the standards set by today's products. Besides, for the price, you might as well get a good one. A poorly made drive will ruin so many discs trying to record properly that you'll end up spending more money on blank CDs than you did on the drive itself!

If you got your CD burner with a new computer, it should be installed and set up already. If you have just purchased—or are about to purchase—a new drive, you need to follow the drive's instructions to install it properly. If you're just terrified of popping open that computer case of yours, call that computer nerd friend in your speed dial or see whether the place you bought your drive can install it for you (for a price).

Software Applications Used in This Book

Every CD burner I've ever purchased came with one version or another of Roxio's Easy CD Creator. Because it's the most common one out there, that's what this book uses in teaching you how to get the most from your CD burning experience.

Unfortunately, what you get with a CD burner is usually an older version of the software. It's still just fine for creating music or data CDs, or for making copies of them. However, the examples in this book are based on Easy CD Creator 4.0 Deluxe. For those of you using the 3.0 version, all is not lost! This is not to say that this book is of no use to you; the majority of programs covered here look and work the same way in version 3 as they do in version 4. There will just be some features, such as Spin Doctor and Video CD Creator, that you won't have.

However, if you're looking to upgrade or start fresh with Easy CD Creator 4.0, you can find it in most every computer store. If you are thorough, you can find it with a rebate coupon or on sale, as well.

Easy CD Creator is by no means the only player in the CD burning market. We use it here because, again, it's the most common and generally has the broadest array of features. In addition to the Roxio software, we do talk a little about a few other programs you can use to burn CDs. These you'll find in Chapter 16, "Other Neat Software."

Roxio's Easy CD Creator 4 Deluxe

The first thing you should do with this software is to install it and make a copy!

To install Easy CD Creator 4.0 Deluxe, first exit all other programs just in case one of them doesn't play nice with the other kiddies. Then, insert the installation CD into one of your computer's CD drives. In just a short time, the installation dialog box, shown in Figure 1.1, pops up asking you which products to install.

Between Tracks

No Menu?

If you find that the installation menu does not pop up when you insert the installation CD, you might not have your computer set to use the autorun feature. In that case, double-click My Computer on your desktop and then the icon for your CD drive. Look for an icon for the program's Setup application. Double-click it and you're off and running!

Figure 1.1

The installation main menu enables you to select which applications to install.

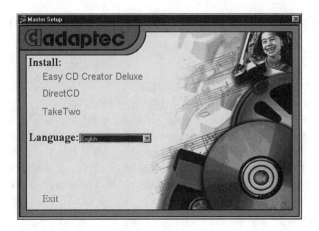

You can install, one at a time, any of the following:

➤ **Easy CD Creator Deluxe**—This is the program that enables you to create CDs from various sources, or to copy CDs.

➤ **DirectCD**—This application enables you to use specially formatted recordable CD-R or CD-RW discs as if they were ordinary hard disks on your system.

➤ **TakeTwo**—You can use this program to make a backup of a few drives, or your entire system, and also to create floppy disk that can be used to restore your system.

DirectCD and TakeTwo each have a chapter devoted to them. Easy CD Creator, because it can perform many kinds of tasks, is covered in several chapters. If you want to follow the examples in this book as we proceed from chapter to chapter, you should go ahead and install all three of these options. You can always go back and remove any program you don't end up needing.

Between Tracks

Getting Rid of Programs

To remove an installed program, open the Control Panel by clicking Start, Settings, Control Panel on your desktop. Double-click the Add/Remove Programs icon. The dialog box that appears next has a list of all the stuff installed on your computer. Look for the Roxio program you want tossed off your system, click it once and then click the Uninstall button.

To install Easy CD Creator Deluxe, click its button on the menu shown in the Figure 1.1. The next dialog box is the warning urging you to close any other applications before proceeding with the installation. Do so and then click Next. Another familiar dialog box, the Software License Agreement dialog box, then pops up. Read all 400,000 words of this agreement if that's your thing, and then click the Yes button if you agree to it. If you don't, well you'll need to get yourself another program.

If you agreed to the license agreement, the next dialog box you get, as shown in Figure 1.2, is the Personalization dialog box. The manufacturer wants your name and, to ensure you're not a thief, they want the Tech Support ID (TSID) that is printed on a label that comes with the package. You are supposed to place this label, for safekeeping, in a spot designated for it inside the software manual. That's probably a good idea because the odds are that you'll probably reinstall one or more of these products.

Figure 1.2

Enter your name and the technical support ID number that came with the software.

To complete this dialog box, just click inside the field you want to fill out and type in the correct information. When you're finished, click Next.

Next, you are prompted for where you want to install the program files on you hard drive. Unless you have a better place to put them, just go with the default folder and click Next.

The Setup Type dialog box prompts you to perform a typical, compact, or custom installation. For the purposes of this book, use the Custom option so that all the product's capabilities are installed. After you make this selection, the Select

Careful!

Make sure, when entering the TSID number, that you enter exactly what is shown on the label. Even one incorrect digit will prevent Easy CD Creator from installing.

Components dialog box pops up. As you can see in Figure 1.3, several applications can be installed, each of which is covered later in this book.

After making sure each check box for these programs is checked, click Next and the installation process will start copying files to your computer. It shouldn't take more than a minute or two to complete the remainder of the install. Assuming you're installing the 4.0 version, when all the files have been copied, you then are prompted to use the Roxio Update Disk. Basically, Roxio doesn't want to bother creating a new CD every time they make an update for their software. So, they put the changes on a floppy disk that the install program can use to bring things up to date. Simply insert the floppy disk in the correct drive and click Next.

Figure 1.3

For a custom installation, you can select the individual components to install.

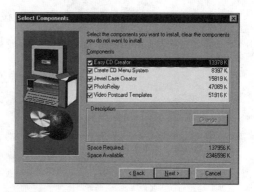

Finally, you see the Setup Complete dialog box telling you that Easy CD Creator has been installed. Click the Finish button, and you are returned to the main install menu (the Master Setup dialog box), so you can continue to install the next two products. Both are installed similarly.

Because it's a required feature, if you install DirectCD, the install program ensures that your CD recorder is capable of packet writing. If your drive can't handle it, like a cranky child, DirectCD refuses to go any further. If the test goes well then you'll see other dialog boxes similar to those used in the Easy CD Creator setup, including the prompt for the floppy update disk. You won't, however, have to enter the TSID code if you've already installed another Roxio product. At least they save you that little bit of grief!

When the DirectCD install is finished, you are again returned to the Master Setup dialog box. Select TakeTwo to finish this install. Once again, you get the same or similar dialog boxes, including the floppy disk update request. Both DirectCD and TakeTwo take only a very short time to install. When you've finished, click the Exit button on the Master Setup dialog box.

Because computer programs can never make things simple, after you exit the setup, yet another dialog box pops up telling you that you need to reboot your computer. Why? Because, it seems, computers always have to find more ways to chew up another 30–60 seconds of your day. You can choose to reboot now or later, but it's best to get it over with right away. After you've rebooted, you're just about ready to move on to the other chapters in this book and start using the features of Easy CD Creator 4 Deluxe and its companion programs.

Using Web-CheckUp to Update Roxio Software

In addition to the floppy update disk that usually comes with your software, Roxio is vigilant about posting larger updates to the software on their Web site. You can use the Web-CheckUp feature to make sure you are running the most up-to-date software. When you boot your system, you get the Roxio Create CD dialog box, prompting you to go online and see whether there are any updates for your software (see Figure 1.4).

Figure 1.4

You are prompted by Roxio to check for updates when your system boots.

Yes, that's one more thing that gets in your way of actually doing something useful. However, like rebooting, it's a pretty good idea to check for these updates so you can be sure you're working with the latest and greatest. You can fly recklessly in the face of danger by clicking No, of course, but otherwise, connect to the Internet, click that Yes button, and get it all off your plate.

If you do choose No, you can always perform the update later. Just open Easy CD Creator by clicking Start, Programs, Easy CD Creator 4. In the menu that appears, click Features and, finally, Web-Checkup.

Between Tracks

Go Away!

You can disable this update reminder by selecting the check box labeled Don't Show Me This Dialog Again at the bottom of the dialog box.

With either method, you are also prompted to register the software before you can run the Web update. Yes, yet another example of The Man making sure nothing is as simple as it should be. So, click the Register button the first time through and have that TSID number ready!

The good news is that you have to register only once and that the registration information you must type in is pretty typical: Name, address, blood type, great-great-great-grandmother's maiden name, have you ever been a member the Communist Party, and so on. After you're finished, click OK; finally, this brings up a window informing you that the program is checking for updates.

As you can see in Figure 1.5, my installation is up to date. If there had been additional patches or drivers to install, they would have been listed here.

Figure 1.5

Web-CheckUp tells you whether you need to apply any updates to the software installed on your system.

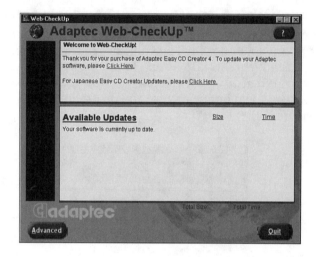

In general, after you've made this initial check for updates, you'll need to use this Web update feature only every once in a while. Besides, if your burner is working just fine and you're producing a lot of great CDs, why mess with success?

Using Music Match Jukebox Deluxe 5.0

Another interesting program that we look at in this book—though only briefly because my nasty editor tells me no one can lift a 1,000 page book without a spotter—is called MusicMatch Jukebox Deluxe 5.0. It is covered in Chapter 16. This software, while thought of mostly as a tool to be used for accessing and organizing a collection of MP3 files, has many more capabilities. Because the topic of this *Idiot's Guide* is to discuss burning CDs, that's what we'll look at when we take up MusicMatch Jukebox 5.0 later on.

Note that MusicMatch Jukebox can be used to organize your media collection, burn MP3s to CDs, and more. A lot of other programs out there will do most all of this, too, but they don't include the capability to burn a CD. You can get the most recent version of this software online by going to the Web site at www.musicmatch.com. These folks have been nice enough to lend us a version of the program, which you'll find on the CD at the back of this book. That version will allow you to do most of the fun things like playing music from all sorts of formats. However, to burn CDs, you'll need to visit their Web site, or your local computer store, and purchase the full version. Don't worry, though; it goes for a very nominal price.

Microsoft's Media Player Version 7

For less than a "nominal" price—in other words, free—this entry into the market-place is perhaps the most dramatic update to Microsoft's Media Player we've seen yet. Again, it was selected to be included in this book because it does have some capabilities to burn your music to CDs, in addition to its many other functions. Another good reason to include this application is because it's free. You can download it from Microsoft and run it on most versions of the Windows operating system.

To download Media Player 7—and it will take a while because it's pretty big—go to www.microsoft.com, click Download, and then click Windows Update. On the update Web page that follows, look for Download Windows Media Player 7.

After you download the new player, the installation is simple, using prompts to make sure you read the license and then choose an installation directory.

Are You In or Out?

Windows Media Player 7 is available for download from Microsoft for Windows 98, Windows 2000, and Windows Me. If you're still running Windows 95, you're outta luck! You can download version 6.4 for Windows 95, but not version 7. The same goes for Solaris and Mac users—hopefully, Microsoft is working on newer versions for these platforms and will release them soon.

Other Software Choices

A lot of other software applications are out there in the marketplace that can be used to acquire and organize your music files, or to burn CDs, or both. As discussed earlier, I chose Roxio's software for this book because it seemed the most comprehensive to me in its capabilities, and because it is very widely available. And, of course, you might already own a copy of an older version of the software if you already own, or if you buy, a CD burner! When learning something new it's always best to start with what you know, and then go on to more complex programs!

That doesn't mean, however, that there might not be a better package for you. The best way to find out is to look for information about new software on the Internet after you've seen the package in the store. You can go to a company's Web site and find technical information that might be of some help in making a purchasing decision. For example, what kind of audio or video file formats does the software support? You can also stay tuned to various products by subscribing to several email mailing lists, described in Chapter 15.

Where Do You Go From Here?

In the next chapter, we're going to take a very quick look at how CDs work. That is, how ordinary CDs you buy in the store are manufactured, and how they differ from the recordable CDs you buy and record using a CD burner. Heck, we'll even talk about how that CD recorder of yours burns that darn CD!

Cross Reference

You can also find a lot of tips for troubleshooting common problems in Chapter 15, "We're Gonna Need a Bigger Boat: Troubleshooting CD Recording," page 219.

The obvious question then becomes, if the process works, why worry about the how? Well, as easy as it should be, burning a CD can be a frustrating process if and when you run into problems. If you understand how a recordable CD works, you will be better empowered to troubleshoot any problems that do come up. After all, not all recorders or playback devices work the same. Although they're all round and shiny on one side, minor differences do exist in the recordable CDs you buy. There are also factors, such as the recording speed and the way you decide to write to the CD, that need to be considered.

Or, if you're like me and just want to get right to it, just skip the next chapter and go on to some fun in Chapter 3 where you can start using your CD Recorder! You can always come back to the "boring" chapter 2 later if you find yourself scratching your head trying to figure out what went wrong!

Make sure, of course, that the first CDs you back up are the ones that come with your CD software, and the CD that comes with this book!

The Least You Need to Know

➤ Yes, you really can make copies of those darned expensive audio CDs you've been buying—for backup purposes, of course.

➤ Yes, you can become your own DJ and mix and match CD and audio files on your hard drive to create your own CDs.

➤ Yes, you can preserve your family memories, both photos and videos (and of course, sound), on CDs to pass on to future generations—in a digital format!

➤ Yes, this book uses Roxio's Easy CD Creator 4.0 Deluxe, because it has lots and lots of features, and is the most widely used option because the basic 3.0 version comes with most CD-RW drives.

➤ Yes, there are other software packages that might be better suited for you. Read this book and find out!

Chapter 2

The Machine Behind the Curtain: How CDs and Recordable CDs Work

OOOH...

In This Chapter

➤ How commercial CDs are similar to phonographic records in many ways.

➤ The tracks on a CD are different from the ones on a computer hard disk.

➤ Why CDs shouldn't cost so much!

In this chapter, we take a quick look at how ordinary CDs are made and how recordable CDs that you can burn using your home computer differ. The kind of CD you buy in the store is not the same as the kind of CD that you record to. They work in a similar manner, which is why most CD readers can read most of the CDs you will write. However, some of them won't work. Some will work in one drive, but not another, and some will not work at all. It can be a big confusing mess that this chapter, and this book in general, will make much clearer.

Understanding how a regular compact disc is made, and how that compares to recordable discs, can help you figure out whether you are doing something wrong or if your CD reader is just the type that won't work with the disc you just created.

In addition, there isn't just one kind of compact disc. The typical audio CD you purchase at the mall is usually referred to as a *CD*, or more properly, *CD-DA*. The *DA* stands for digital audio. Those last two letters must now be tacked on much more often than in previous years because of all the other kinds of compact discs that are available, each of which is intended for a particular kind of use. For example, a CD-ROM is a compact disc that is used to store computer data and cannot be written to. Other formats also are available—for audio, video, photos, and combinations of all these kinds of data.

Snakes, Snails, and Puppy Dog Tails; What Are CDs Composed Of?

CDs and CD-ROM discs have something in common: They are manufactured products, much like the now old-fashioned phonograph record. As a matter of fact, although phonographic records use analog recording methods and CDs (and CD-ROMs) use digital recording methods, they have a whole lot in common.

For example, one important aspect that phonographic records and CDs share is the way the actual tracks of data are laid out on the media. In a typical magnetic hard disk (or floppy disk, for that matter), the data is laid out in a set of concentric rings. That is, circles within circles, as you can see in Figure 2.1.

Figure 2.1

Ordinary computer hard disks store data on separate tracks that are not connected. The closer to the middle of the disk, the shorter the track.

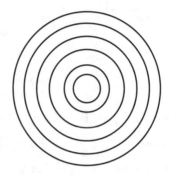

Each of these circular tracks is divided into sectors, which means the closer you get to the outside of the hard disk, the more sectors of data you can place on a track because a greater surface area exists to hold more sectors.

CDs do not use this method. Instead, similar to a phonographic record, a continuous, spiral track is used, as shown in Figure 2.2.

Figure 2.2

CDs, like phonographic records, use one long, continuous, spiral track to record data, unlike a computer's hard disk.

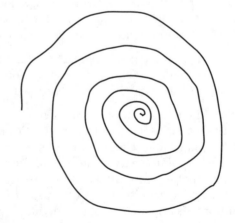

However, even though both use this spiral method for tracking, phonographic records are played by starting at the outer portion of the spiral and then following the spiral inward to the center of the record. CDs are played in just the opposite manner, by starting where the spiral begins in the center of the CD and continuing to the outermost portion of the CD.

For those who are interested in the technical details, along this spiral track is a series of *pits* and *lands*. Each pit is about 0.6 micrometers wide, and the distance between each track on the disc is about 1.6 micrometers. So basically, they're very small. But so what, right? What are they? Well, a land is just a continuous smooth section between pits that reflects the CD player's laser back to a detector.

If you were to take the spiral track and stretch it out into one long line, it would go on for about three miles. Now that's a lot of room to record data! In most cases, however, the entire disc is not used. If the CD holds the maximum amount of data possible, it will be recorded up to about 3 millimeters from the outer edge of the disc.

Between Tracks

Leaving Room for Errors

The last few millimeters at the edge of the CD are generally not used. In addition, many CD manufacturers deliberately do not use the entire 74 (or 80) minutes that are available on a compact disc. By leaving a few minutes unused, a small area exists at the outer edge of the disc that contains no audio data. This is done for two reasons. First, this makes it easier to control the quality of the CD. Second, it gives the end user a little leeway when handling the CD. This means that for some CDs, you don't have to worry too much about getting fingerprints or very small scratches on them, so long as these occur at the very outer portion of the CDs, which is where you are most likely to handle them.

Both phonograph records and compact discs are created from masters and then made into mass-produced copies by a stamping or molding method. However, before we go into describing the process by which a CD is manufactured, let's first look at what the darn thing is actually made up of and how data (including music) is stored digitally on the disc.

What About Pits and Lands?

Computers, no matter how complex they appear to be, are really just complex electronic adding machines. While I sit here and type this chapter on my computer, the actual background processes going on inside the computer involve moving around a bunch of 0s and 1s. At first glance, there doesn't seem to be much you can do when using just 0s and 1s, does there? The truth, however, is that you can digitize music and create a CD using 0s and 1s. You can compute the trajectory and flight path to send a rocket to the moon and back. In fact, 0s and 1s, or the binary numerical system, can actually be used to do a whole lot of things.

So, to put music—or data, or whatever—on a CD or CD-ROM, a method of recording 0s and 1s and reading them back again must exist. When your favorite CD is playing, what is really going on behind the scenes is that a laser beam (very tightly focused) is pointed at the CD and, depending on the amount of light that is reflected back, 0s and 1s are detected.

When the CD is played, a laser is directed from the bottom of the CD—the opposite side from the label—to the reflective surface that is encased in a protective, plastic layer. The reflective coating that lies beneath the surface of the disc reflects light back to the laser pickup device differently, depending on whether the light strikes a pit or a land. The reflective layer can be made up of gold, silver, or another reflective material, such as aluminum.

Between Tracks

The Same, But Different

With a CD, you can get away with a lot more than you can with a phonograph record! Because the audio CD employs an error correction and detection coding scheme, it also can recover more easily from minor defects or errors. With a phonograph record, one scratch becomes part of the music!

The laser simply follows this spiral of data and passes on to other electronic components the data it gathers from the light reflected. Because the laser beam must first pass through the protective plastic coating on the bottom of the CD, you might think that fingerprints, dust, and other contaminants would cause the disc to be unreadable. In the extreme case, this is true. However, because the laser beam is focused to a point past the surface of the CD to the reflective layer (about a millimeter past the bottom surface of the CD), it usually doesn't detect these minor imperfections. Major defects, yes, but not the minor ones. To understand how this works, try this the next time it rains. Look out the window. If it's a light rain, you don't see it, or at least you don't see it very clearly. If you take a minute to focus your eyes past the window to try to see the rain, you'll find you don't see the window as well as you did before, if at all.

How Are the 0s and 1s Encoded on the Disc?

Although it might seem that the most logical way to record 0s and 1s on a CD is to have a pit represent a 1 and a land represent 0, that is not the case. As a matter of fact, even magnetic media such as your computer's hard drive doesn't use such a simple method. Instead, 0s and 1s are encoded by detecting the *change* from a pit to a land, and vice versa. While the surface of the CD remains constant, the reader records a stream of 0s; however, when the CD reader detects a change from a pit to a land, it interprets this as a 1 bit. The same is true when a change is detected from a land to a pit. It doesn't matter which direction the state change takes. It just matters that a change occurs at all. Figure 2.3 shows this a little more clearly.

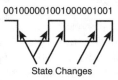

Figure 2.3

The encoding scheme encodes 1s as a state transition, no matter which direction.

As you can see from Figure 2.3, every time the laser detects a change from one to the other (pit/land), it assumes that a binary bit with a value of 1 has been detected. Everything else is interpreted as a 0 bit. It should become quickly obvious that, for this scheme to work, *the laser must read the spiral track at a constant speed*—timing is very important when reading CDs. If a constant speed is not maintained, the CD reader has no way to interpret how many 0 bits existed between state changes.

Now, as any phonograph audiophile knows, on a phonograph record, the closer to the center of the record that the stylus gets, the faster it travels in the groove of the record. Or, better put, the more surface area of the record passes beneath the needle during a particular amount of time. If this *were* the case with a compact disc, this state change from pit to land would not work. No method would exist to detect the number of 0s if the area being covered by the laser was continuously becoming slower as the CD was read from the center to the edge. To remedy the situation, the CD reader actually speeds up the rotation speed as it approaches the outer edge of the disc. Thus, a constant speed is always being maintained so the state changes that the laser experiences can be accurate.

Mastering the Mastering Process

To mass-produce CDs, like the ones you buy in music stores, you first must create a *master*, which contains the data image you want to *impress* onto a number of blanks. Several methods are available for producing a master and its family of discs, which are eventually used to mold the conventional CD.

One of the most frequently used processes starts with a glass disc that has been specially treated and examined (using a laser) to ensure that no imperfections exist which might cause problems with recording. Most of this mastering process is done in a *clean room*, so that particles of dust cannot interfere with the microscopic pits that get burned into the disc.

After the glass master has passed all tests, it can be prepared for recording. It is first coated with an adhesive material and then a photoresist material. The photoresist coating is the part of the master, which will be subjected to a burning laser that is much more powerful than the type used in the CD-RW recorders we have in our PCs. The laser etches away portions of the photoresist material to create the pits and lands of the CD. To finish the process, the glass master is cured in a special oven. It can then either be used immediately or stored for a few weeks.

After the glass master has been developed, the photoresist side of the glass is covered with a metal to further strengthen it and prepare it for the next step in the process. In many cases, silver is used for the master disc.

The master disc is then put through a plating process that, in most cases, plates the recorded surface with nickel. After this has successfully been done, *the nickel surface is separated from the glass disc* and the metal portion is called a *father*. This father is then itself subjected to an arcane process called electroplating, the results of which are separated from it. This can be done several times, creating a host of *mothers*. And then it's done yet again to create *sons*, which are the actual media used to produce the CDs you purchase at the store.

Note that because the actual CD you buy is created by a simple injection molding technique, the actual cost of the CD is minimal. I can remember when CDs were first produced, it was promised that the "high cost" would eventually come down as more were sold. That doesn't seem to be the case. As it is, manufacturing the recordable CD blanks probably costs more than mass-producing the commercial CD! Yet you can buy a set of blank CD-R discs for a buck a piece, while a new music CD can cost you upwards of $17 (as expensive today as they were in the '80s)!

Drawing the Property Lines: How Information Is Arranged on a CD

The compact disc is not simply a continuous stream of bits that contain audio or data. Instead, certain areas are set aside for such things as storing a table of contents. Other areas are used for certain control aspects of the disc as it is played. In this discussion, we are talking about only simple audio CDs. More complicated formats use these same techniques, but variances are made depending on the use of the CD and the kind of data stored.

Who Leads in This Dance: Lead In and Lead Out Areas

For most ordinary audio compact discs, a lead in and a lead out area exist. These special areas on the disc are usually situated on the innermost and outermost areas of the disc, respectively. The *lead in* area is made up of all 0s and is used to indicate the start of music data. Directly after the lead in area, there is a field called a start flag, which takes up two or three seconds of time before the actual audio tracks begin.

You can probably guess by now that the *lead out* area comes after the last audio track. However, directly before the lead out area there is another start flag of two or three seconds. This flag is used to indicate to the player that the lead out section is about to follow.

You Mean CDs Have a Table of Contents?

The table of contents on the CD works much like a table of contents in a book. This area contains information that can be used to locate other tracks on the CD. For example, the table of contents contains such things as

➤ The number of audio tracks on the CD (up to 99 total tracks)

➤ The starting time of each track. This timing information is used to locate specific tracks on the disc. This is what makes it possible for you to just push the skip button on a CD player to get past a song you don't want to hear.

➤ The specific track number of a selection (usually one song) on a CD

The table of contents is one of the first things a CD player reads when you insert the disc. This is why most modern players can show you the number of tracks, using an LED display, before the CD has actually been played. You also can use this information on most modern CD players to program a sequence in which the tracks will be played—or repeated, if you have a track you particularly like.

The Maximum Amount of Recording Time on a Disc

The maximum time on a standard compact disc is only 74 minutes. This was chosen at the beginning because these early discs were intended for audio use only. Record albums at that time did not need a longer amount of time, so it was thought that 74 minutes was a good number to choose.

As it has happened, CDs are now used for computer data (to store up to 650MB of data), photographic data, and video data. For these kinds of uses, which were not anticipated when the CD was first developed, the size of the disc and amount of data it can hold seem to be rather small.

DVDs are the current answer to this problem. Whereas a DVD can hold a 2+ hour movie on one side of a single disc, two video CDs would be required to hold that much information. In some Asian markets, such as China, VCDs are used extensively, and the players for them can be found at many stores. This is because it was cheaper to keep using an existing technology than convert to a dramatically new one. Owners of phonograph records (or those who have a large collection of 8-track tapes) can probably sympathize with this approach.

Recordable CDs Are a Burning Issue!

Now that we've spent most of this chapter telling you how CDs, in general, are manufactured and how they work, it's time to talk about a burning issue—recordable CDs, or CD-R and CD-RW discs. Because most of us can't afford to spend millions creating the clean-room environment necessary to create CD masters the hard way, we instead use CD recordable technology to make our own CDs at home, using an inexpensive laser burner.

If you'll remember back at the start of the process, the master CD is a glass disc coated with a material that is later subjected to the laser treatment. This burns through the material to create pits in the surface, which is later coated with a metallic layer and used to create molds.

CD recordable technology isn't nearly so complicated. It's a rather dyed-in-the-wool simple process.

So How Is a CD-R Different?

Instead of using a powerful laser to blast away at a hard surface, as is done when making a master CD, the laser in your CD recorder drive has a much easier task. It needs only to poke holes in a very thin layer of dye that makes up part of the CD-R disc. Underneath this layer of dye is the reflective metal layer of the blank disc. When the laser needs to create a pit, it burns a small hole in the dye layer. Then, when the result is played back, the light that bounces off the dye layer—or the reflective layer underneath—determines the pits and lands that make up the information stored on the disc. The laser mechanism in your PC is also less complicated in its mechanics. The blank CD you record, unlike a manufactured CD, has grooves impressed into the plastic that make it easier for the laser to track the spiral track, so to speak. There is no need for complicated circuitry to calculate coordinates or complicated mechanics to position the laser.

Although various dyes are used and manufacturers might use different metals for the reflective surface, that's the only thing about a CD-R that differs from a manufactured CD.

Between Tracks

Which Dye Is Which?

For those who care to know, several kinds of chemicals are used for the dye layer on recordable CDs. The most commonly used are cyanine and phthalocyanine, but I'm sure that more are already in use which we don't know about. When you look at the bottom of the CD-R blank, if it's a greenish color then most likely there's a gold metallic layer underneath. If it is more of a bluish color, silver is probably being used instead for the metallic reflective layer. This isn't a guarantee, but I just mention it to let you know different kinds of recordable CD blanks are exist.

What About Re-Writable CDs?

Another kind of recordable CD is also avaiable. It's called *CD-RW*, which, as you can guess, stands for CD rewritable. These discs are more expensive than ordinary CD-R blank discs, but they can be erased and reused. This can be done because, unlike CD-R discs that use a layer of dye to burn-in a recording, CD-RW discs use a layer of metal alloy. Instead of burning a hole through this layer, the laser changes the state of the metal from amorphous to crystalline (each of which reflects the laser light differently). When read back by the laser, the changes made to this layer cause the light reflected back to the detector to change, once again creating the illusion of the pits and lands that a manufactured CD uses.

Know Your Drive

Although most new recordable drives on the market today are CD-RW—capable of reading both CD-R and CD-RW discs—that doesn't mean your drive will. If you have an older drive, make sure that it is not just a CD-R drive that can only write—one time—to a blank CD-R disc. These drives won't recognize a CD-RW disc no matter how much your beg, plead, or bribe.

A caveat of CD-RW discs is that they will most likely not be playable in other, older CD-ROM drives and most audio CD players. However, because their use is generally to back up data that frequently changes, this should generally not be a problem.

The Size Does Matter: What About 80-Minute Discs?

A rather "new" recordable disc has been available for about two years now that claims to enable you to store up to 80 minutes on a recordable CD. These 80-minute discs, however, suffer from significant limitations that affect whether you can actually use them. Some hardware (and burning software) is programmed to stop at 74 minutes. *If this is the case with your hardware or software, these CDs won't work for you when you try to burn them.*

Because some publishers are using 80-minute discs, you might find that, when running Roxio's CD Copier program to copy a CD, you get a prompt telling you the 74-minute blank you've inserted for copying can't hold the all the data the disc you want to copy contains. In this type of situation, you have no choice but to either buy the 80-minute CD blanks or use Easy CD Creator to select a number of tracks from the original that will fit on a 74-minute CD without exceeding the time limit.

Either way, it always pays to keep up with the technology. If you are going to use 80-minute blanks, be sure your CD recorder hardware will work with them. You also might want to test your CD player(s) to ensure that it can also read these discs.

Which Is the Best CD-R Disc to Use?

There is an easy answer to that question: Use the discs that work best in your recorder! Because several combinations of dyes and metallic reflecting materials are used, what works well in one recorder or player might not work well in another! Furthermore, because several brands exist on the market—even though there is only a handful of manufacturers—you can not even be sure many times that when you continue to buy the same brand, you're getting the same disc. The brand-name distributor might be buying batches of discs from other manufacturers based on whomever has the lowest price at the moment!

Now that makes for a confusing situation! So, buy first in small quantities, find a brand that works, and stick with it until it doesn't! Also, be sure you use a recording speed for which the media is rated. You'll usually see them rated for various speeds, such as 1x, 2x, and 4x. If higher speeds don't produce good results, try the standard 1x. If that fails then try a different brand of discs.

The Least You Need to Know

➤ CDs are complex discs that have information digitally recorded on them at microscopic levels.

➤ CDs manufactured using a simple molding process are, in my opinion, highly overpriced. After all, how many of those AOL CDs did you get either in the mail or bundled free with a magazine lately? You can bet that AOL didn't spend $16 (or the wholesale equivalent) in producing those.

➤ Even though a CD is much more tolerant of fingerprints and scratches than a phonographic record, you should still treat them carefully. Error correction and detection codes can only do so much to preserve the original data. CD-ROMs, which are used to store computer data, employ additional methods to ensure that the data can be read and delivered to the program with no errors.

➤ Try 80-minute recordable blanks at your own risk. Even if your software can record to them, your CD burner might not be able to.

Part 2

Creating an Audio or a Data CD

This section is where the fun begins. Drag out those CDs, or even those old vinyl records, and get ready to start making your own. Because you can go about this in several ways, I suggest you start with Chapter 3, "Using Easy CD Creator to Make Audio CDs." Here, you find out how to use Roxio's software to make a new CD that is composed of tracks from other CDs. You can make your own best hits CD, for example. In the next chapter, we walk through a similar process, but this time we use the CD recorder to save files from the computer's hard disk to make a data CD.

As if that isn't enough fun, we follow that up with a look at the Spin Doctor. It works much like a wizard program to step you through recording audio CDs not just from other CDs, but also from records, cassette tapes, a microphone, or just about anything else you can plug in to your sound card's input jack. Want to put your favorite radio program on CD? You can. Want to record your voice or musical talents for posterity? You can!

Finally, we look at two technologies that are much simpler to use. The DirectCD program enables you to use a CD-RW disc much like any other drive attached to your computer. The last chapter in this section is one you'll probably use frequently. It discusses how to quickly use Easy CD Copier to make an exact copy of a CD. This is great for making backup copies of either audio or data CDs.

Chapter 3

Using Easy CD Creator to Make Audio CDs

In This Chapter

➤ How to create and edit an audio CD layout

➤ Creating an audio CD with Easy CD Creator

➤ Creating an image file so you can record CDs later

There is more than one way to skin a cat—so I'm told. I'd never do that because I have nosy neighbors and no desire to explain myself to the Humane Society. There is, however, also more than one way to create an audio or a data CD using Roxio's software. The Spin Doctor method, which we will talk about in Chapter 5, enables you to create audio CDs from a variety of sources—such as cassettes or phonograph records. In other chapters, I'll also show you how to create a variety of CDs, including CDs that have both data and audio recorded on them.

However, because it's always best to keep things simple to start, in this chapter you will learn how to use the Easy CD Creator program to make an audio CD.

For your music listening pleasure, you can use Easy CD Creator to create audio CDs, selecting your favorite songs from various CDs. You can also select all the songs from the same CD and change the order in which they are stored. This great program will even allow you to include MP3 or WAV files located on your hard drive on the same CD.

If all you want to do is make a copy of an entire CD, use Roxio's Easy CD Copier, see Chapter 8, "The Easiest Way to Pillage—Copying CDs Using Easy CD Copier."

MP3 Versus WAV

While several audio file formats can be used on a PC, Easy CD Creator supports the two most important ones: WAV and MP3. MP3 files are all the rage on the Internet (and in the court system), but if you really care about the quality of the sound on the finished CD, WAV files are a better format.

Because they need to be so portable, MP3 files get so compressed that they lose a little quality in the process. Not a lot, but a little. Even if you convert the MP3 file to a WAV file (which Easy CD Creator does when it burns the MP3 file to a CD), you don't get back what you've lost! The WAV format, however, is almost identical to the CD-DA format used on the CD itself.

Easy CD Creator also can be used to copy important data and program files from your hard drive to a CD for long-term storage. Yet another good reason to start with Easy CD Creator is the fact that version 3.x of the program is usually distributed with new CD recorders, so most of you will have this program. If this program does all you need to do, you won't have to purchase the more advanced Easy CD Creator 4 Deluxe, unless you need to use its advance features. You see, I'm trying to save you money!

Making Your First Audio CD

Remember from Chapter 1, "The Digital Revolution!" that you can crank up most of the Easy CD Creator features by either clicking the Desktop icon or finding the program in the Start menu. If you are running an earlier version of the program, such as Easy CD Creator 3.x, you should do the following:

1. Click Start.
2. Click Programs.
3. Click Roxio Easy CD Creator.
4. Click Easy CD Creator.

If you are using the more advanced version, Easy CD Creator 4 Deluxe, the Start menu path is nearly identical. However, after you're inside the Easy CD Creator folder, you must click Create CD. In this case, the menu shown in Figure 3.1 pops up.

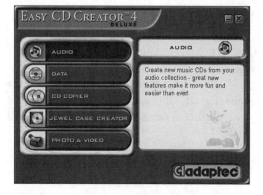

Figure 3.1

Use the Audio option on the menu to start the CD Audio Program.

You next get to choose from another menu. You have to decide whether you want to use the Audio CD program or the Spin Doctor program. Because we're not digging into Spin Doctor until Chapter 5, select Audio CD from this menu. After you make this selection, you will finally find yourself in the Easy CD Creator program (see Figure 3.2).

Shortcut!

Unless you specifically disabled it, Roxio puts an icon on your computer's taskbar (near the clock on the bottom of the screen) that you can use to access most of CD Creator's programs. Just right-click it and select the program you want from the list.

Figure 3.2

It's an easy task to get the Easy CD Creator up and running.

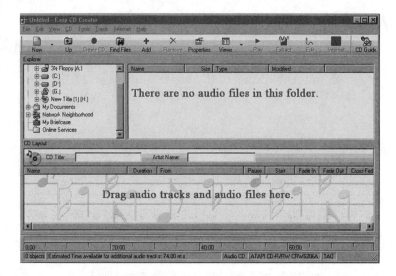

Selecting Audio Mode

Depending on how you opened Easy CD Creator, the program can come up in either audio or data mode, depending on how it was last used. You can tell which mode it's in by looking at the information bar at the *very bottom of the program window*. Here, you can see information about various aspects of creating a CD. The field we're concerned with here is in the middle and should say Audio CD. The kinds of CDs that you can create include the following:

➤ Audio CD

➤ Data CD/JOLIET

➤ Mixed Mode CD/JOLIET

➤ CD Extra/ISO9660

➤ Data CD/ISO9660

For now, you don't need to understand these different modes. You just need to ensure that Audio CD appears at the bottom of the window. If it doesn't, you will need to change to that mode. To do this, look for the New button on the toolbar at the top of the program window. You will see a very small arrow on this button pointing down. Click it and a menu appears. From this menu, select Audio CD. You should then see the words "Audio CD" at the bottom of the window.

Creating the Audio CD Layout

The most important part of creating an audio CD is building a layout. To do this, you must tell the program exactly which files or tracks you want to record, and in what order. The program then uses this information to burn the CD, rather like creating a building from a set of blueprints. You can also save the layout so that you can recall it for use at a later time.

There are two good reasons for saving the layout after it's created. First, you might want to change the order, or maybe add or delete some tracks, in the future. For example, if you are an aspiring musician with a band, you might be using your CD burner to create demo CDs. The songs appropriate for one industry contact might not be suitable for another.

Second, even though copying digital media does not produce significant errors from one generation to the next, errors do occur. With an audio CD, you might not notice any problems right away, but if you make a copy, then a copy of a copy, and so on, eventually you will most likely notice some degradation in the quality of the sound. If you want to make a large number of copies of a particular CD, using a single source CD is a good idea. Using a disk image on your hard drive, explained later, is an even better idea!

If you glance ahead to Figure 3.3 you can see the actual program. The two panes at the top comprise the Explorer pane. Use the left side to navigate the disks and folders on your PC in search of music files and tracks. You can click the drive—either the CD drive or disk drive—from which you want to select audio tracks to include in the CD layout.

Between Tracks

Keep Your Music Files Organized!

If you are going to be doing a lot of audio CD recording, and are using WAV or MP3 files, you can locate these files more easily if you keep them all in one folder, or set of folders. Windows has a My Documents folder built in for this purpose. If you own Windows Me, you will find My Documents also contains a My Music folder!

You'll know you're in the right place for audio when the pane on the right side shows audio tracks—either CD audio, MP3, or WAV files. In the example shown in Figure 3.2, the program practically shouts out to you that no audio files are in the selected folder. This is because, in this example, I've selected just the C: drive, and I don't have any audio files stored there at this time. However, I have inserted an audio CD in my CD-ROM drive, so selecting that drive in the Explorer pane changes the display to show each track on that CD (Figure 3.3).

Figure 3.3

Here the CD drive is selected in the Explorer Pane, so audio tracks appear on the right.

Explorer Pane

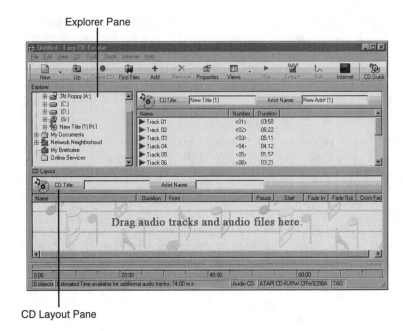

CD Layout Pane

Adding Audio Tracks to the Layout

Now you are ready to start adding audio tracks to the layout. The easiest method is to use your mouse to drag a track from the Explorer pane to the Layout pane. Just place your cursor over the track you want to add, click and hold down the left mouse button, and then move the mouse until it is over the CD Layout pane at the bottom of the window. Release the mouse button and the track will show up as part of the layout, as you can see in Figure 3.4.

Figure 3.4

After you drag a track to the bottom pane, it becomes part of the new CD layout.

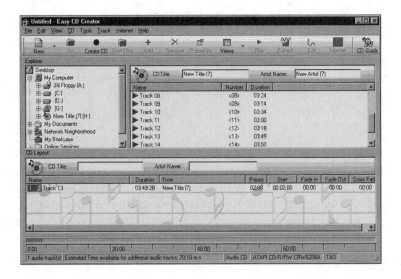

As you can see I have added track 13 to this lay-out. Notice that on the right side of the Explorer pane, a scrollbar appears. If the selection you want to add to the layout doesn't appear onscreen, click either the up or down arrow on the scrollbar to move through all the tracks on the CD.

You can use another method to add tracks to the layout. Notice that the toolbar near the top of the window has an Add button, with a plus sign (+) on it. You can probably guess that all you need to do is click a track once and then click the Add button to add it to the layout. Use whichever method is easiest for you.

Get More Real Estate

To ensure you can see as many tracks as possible, be sure to maximize the program window so that it fills the entire computer screen. To do so, click the middle button on the very top-right corner of the window.

So far we've just selected one audio track for the new CD we are going to create. Notice, again in Figure 3.4, that at the bottom of the screen a timeline shows how much of the CD's available time you've used up. Underneath this timeline, the program tells you how many audio tracks you've added and gives you an estimate of how much time you have left on the CD. Anyone who has ever tried to make audio cassettes from several sources will appreciate knowing exactly how much time they have to deal with. Here there's no running out of tape with just 30 seconds left on the last song. With Easy CD Creator (or virtually any other CD burning software), if you use up more space than exists on the CD, the program tells you how much *overtime* you've run before the first track is ever recorded. This way, you can determine how many and which tracks you will have to remove from the layout to create the CD layout.

Grab Them All at Once!

You can select multiple tracks or audio files to add to the layout all at once rather than clicking them one at a time. To do so, click the first one, hold down the Shift key, and click the last file. All the files in between, including the ones you clicked, will be selected. Then, click the Add button.

You can select multiple tracks or files that aren't all in a row by using Ctrl-click. That is, click the first file you want to select; then, hold down the control button (Ctrl) and click each of the other files you want selected just once. They do not have to be contiguous in the listing. Click Add and they all appear in the audio layout.

Adding MP3 and WAV Files to the Layout

Aside from the source, no real difference exists between selecting tracks from an audio CD and selecting MP3 or WAV files. You can mix all three kinds together in the same layout, and Easy CD Creator takes care of the rest.

To add an MP3 or WAV file, use the Explorer pane to locate the directory that contains the files. After you've selected the directory, any files found there will show up in the upper-right pane, just like tracks from an audio CD. Add them the same way, by dragging or using the Add button.

Which Track Is Which?

Although an MP3 or WAV file is generally named after the song it plays, songs copied from another CD aren't quite so descriptive. It can be a real pain to have to look on the CD cover to find out which track is which when you are deciding what tracks to add to the layout because CD Creator can only name songs by their track number. After all, "Track 13" is not very descriptive.

But you don't have to worry if you have an active Internet connection. A Web site is available that Easy CD Creator can access to download information about the CD. This includes the CD title, the name of the artist, and the names of the audio tracks.

To enable this service so that it works automatically, click Tools at the top of the Easy CD Creator and then Options. As you can see in Figure 3.5, you can use several options to configure the program. However, for now we are interested only in the Internet service called CDDB Internet.

Figure 3.5

Use the Options properties page from the Tools menu to enable automatic downloading of CD information from the Internet.

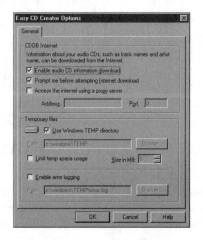

Three check boxes are available here. The first is all you need to enable the CD information downloading capability. However, if you are connecting to the Internet through a modem it's a good idea to check the second check box too so that the program asks before performing the download, giving you a chance to make your Internet connection if you haven't already.

If you are using Easy CD Creator in a work environment, or perhaps in a small office at home, where a proxy server is used to access the Internet, you'll have to select the third check box, too. If you do, be sure to fill in its name or address and the port to use after you select that check box. You must get this information from your network administrator at your place of business.

Huh? Proxy?

A proxy server is a component of a *firewall*, which is used to protect the network from evildoers on the Internet. For home users, don't worry about it!

Taking Control

If you don't want Easy CD Creator looking to the Internet every time you put in a music CD, you can disable the automatic download of CD information. Instead, use the Internet button located on the far right of the toolbar to tell the program when you want the information downloaded. This way you can download only when you really have a need to.

If you tell Easy CD Creator to notify you before downloading CD information, it tosses the dialog box in Figure 3.6 onto the screen when you insert a music CD.

One-Shot Download

Each time you download the information for a particular CD, Easy CD Creator stores the information in a database file on your hard disk so that it will not have to look up the information again.

Figure 3.6

Easy CD Creator prompts you before downloading CD information if you select that option.

Click OK to begin the download. A few seconds later, the information you see about the current CD dramatically changes. In Figure 3.7, you can see that we are selecting songs from a Beatles album. Each audio track is identified by the name of the song, which makes creating the layout for the new CD much easier.

Figure 3.7

After the download finishes, the display makes a lot more sense!

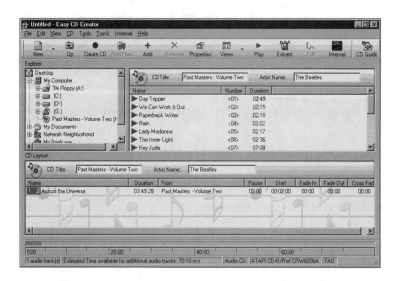

Rare is the CD that Easy CD Creator can't find information about on the Internet (unless it's a custom compilation). If this happens, you can enter track information manually, which we'll discuss in "Adding Artist, CD Title, and Song Title Information," later in this chapter.

Using Multiple CDs

Because you have a full 74 minutes of recording time, you can keep adding tracks until you've designed the CD you want or until you run out of space (time) on the CD. Sure, you can select all the tracks from the same CD, but that's only useful if you want to duplicate a single disc.

What does make sense, though, is to create a CD of songs using tracks from several CDs—a best hits CD, so to speak. To do this, just insert one CD at a time, selecting and adding the songs you want to the layout for each disc until you run out of space.

This is where it becomes important to download CD information from the Internet. Without that download, Easy CD Creator uses its own generic naming system—Disk 1, Disk 2, and so on—instead of the actual CD and artist name. This can get really hard to keep track of if you're using a lot of CDs. Again, if the CD information is not available online, never fear, you can put the information in yourself.

Adding Artist, CD Title, and Song Title Information

In the right side of Explorer section of Easy CD Creator, the first thing you see is CD Title and Artist Name. As explained in the last section, if you haven't taken advantage of the Internet download service to get this information (or can't), you can enter this information manually. Just click these fields and type away.

Changing the name of the track is a little trickier, but certainly no challenge. Just highlight the track by clicking it once and then click the Properties button on the toolbar. You can use this method to manually rename each track in the layout, either as you select the tracks or after you've finished the layout—whichever is easier.

Changing the Order of Audio Tracks

When you use the Add button to add an audio track to the layout, it is automatically added to the end of the layout. When you drag a track, you can place it directly over a track already in the layout and the new track will be inserted directly before that one. But what if, right before recording, you realize in a spark of divine inspiration that Van Halen's "Top of the World" should come right after Eric Clapton's "Wonderful Tonight," instead of before it?

No worries! Use the drag method described previously to move tracks around as they exist in the layout pane. At any time, whether you're halfway through creating the layout or if you're finished adding songs, you can click a track in the layout pane and drag it to a new position. When you move a track around like this, the program takes care of renumbering all the other tracks.

Removing an Audio Track from the Layout

Just as adding a track to the layout is easy, removing one is also easy. So, when you decide that "Purple Rain" doesn't work on the same CD as "Imagine," you can use two methods to cut one of them:

➤ Right-click the track in the layout pane and, on the menu that appears, click Remove.

➤ Click the song once in the layout pane and click the Remove button on the toolbar at the top of the program window. The Remove button is easy to find because it has a big "X" right above it.

Changing the order of songs in a layout and removing songs from a layout are not only convenient when you are first creating the layout, but also when you decide to use a layout that was saved from a previous session.

Saving the Layout for Later Use

After creating the layout, you can then go right ahead and create the CD. However, if you think you might want to use this layout again or if you don't have time to create the CD right away, you can save it to your hard disk for later use. To save the layout simply perform these steps:

Cross Reference

In addition to saving a song layout, you can actually copy CD songs to your hard drive. See "Creating WAV Files from CDs" later in this chapter to learn how.

1. Click File at the top of the Easy CD Creator program.

2. Select Save As. A dialog box appears that you can use to select the location on your hard disk to which to save the layout. Just give it a name, using the File Name field and click Save.

3. Click the Save button.

Note that *saving the layout doesn't save any of the songs*—it just saves the information that Easy CD Creator uses to create a new CD. If you use a saved layout at a later time, you still must have the CDs or other files that were used to select songs to create the layout.

Starting the Copying Process

Having come this far, let's make a CD from the layout we've created. As you might guess, several ways are available to do this. You can use either of the following methods:

➤ Use the CD layout to create the CD directly.

➤ Use the CD layout to create an image of the CD on your hard disk and then use that image to create one or more CDs.

Image?

When you create a CD image, you are essentially creating a file on your hard disk that has all the audio information necessary to create the CD. You can't play this huge file, but you can use it at a later time to burn as many copies of the CD as you like. For more about using CD images, see "Creating a Disc Image for Later Copying," later in this chapter.

We'll dig into each of these two methods in the following sections. However, in either case, the first thing you need to do is make sure a blank, recordable CD is in your CD-RW drive. Don't worry; if you forget this, you'll get prompted when it comes time to start recording.

Using the Layout to Create the CD Directly

After you have created a layout, or if you have used the File menu to open a previously saved layout, you can start the recording process. The Easy CD Creator program prompts you to insert each CD. To start recording, you can click the Create CD button at the top of the program window, or you can select Create CD from the File menu. In Figure 3.8, you can see the CD Creation Setup dialog box that pops up and allows you to make some decisions about the recording process. To see all the options, be sure to click the Advanced button.

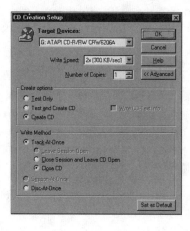

Figure 3.8

The CD Creation Setup dialog box first prompts you about how the CD will be recorded.

Arcane CD Speak

Underrun = Death!

A *buffer underrun* is a real drag. It's an error that can occur when your computer can't keep up with your CD-RW drive causing it to not have data to write when it needs it. For more information about this kind of error, and things you can do to avoid it, see Chapter 15, "We're Gonna Need a Bigger Boat: Troubleshooting CD Recording."

We'll get into each of these options over the course of this section. For now, let's focus on the first three:

➤ **Target Devices**—This is the drive letter of the CD-RW drive that holds the blank recordable CD. If you have more than one CD-RW device in your computer, which is not likely, you can choose between the devices.

➤ **Write Speed**—The values available in this field depend on the type of CD-RW disc drive you have. Some drives are capable of writing at a faster rate than others. However, don't go out and buy a CD-RW drive based solely on its maximum speed. Even though a higher speed if preferable, you might end up lowering it anyway to prevent errors such as *buffer underruns*.

➤ **Number of Copies**—What can I say? This is the number of CDs you want to create, obviously!

With the Advanced button clicked, you can see the other advanced options available for you to choose from. These fall into two categories. The first is Create Options, where you can decide whether you want to perform a test or just create the CD. The second set of options, called Write Method, get a little more complicated, but we'll steer you through those murky waters.

Arcane CD Speak

Coaster?

You'll often hear the term *coaster* applied to a CD that didn't make it all the way through the burning process. Because you can't rewrite a CD-R disc, a failed burn leaves you with a disc that's only good for setting drinks on.

From the Create Options, you can choose one of the following options:

➤ **Test Only**—This option test writes the entire CD burning process and is a good idea if you're having problems burning discs, using a new computer, or have just installed a new CD-RW drive. If you're not having any problems, you don't need to go through this lengthy process.

➤ **Test and Create CD**—Similar to the last option, except that if the test is successful, Easy CD Creator automatically starts to burn your CD.

➤ **Create CD**—This option enables you to skip the testing process altogether. If you've been using the drive for a while and are confident in its capabilities, choose this option. If you run into a problem and find you are making coasters instead of CDs, go back and select one of the test options first.

➤ **Write CD-Text Info**—Off to the side, you will notice this button. Not all CD-RW drives have this capability, but if yours does, you can select this option and the information about the artist, CD title, and song titles are saved on the CD you create. If played in a CD player that recognizes this kind of data, you will see this information displayed when the CD is played.

CDs work in tracks and sessions, and regardless of whether they are open or closed. Tracks are individual chunks of information—for example, in this case, a song. A group of tracks burned in one process is called a *session*. Finally, a disc remains open and able to store more sessions until it is closed. You can choose how to write a disc from the Write Method options list:

➤ **Track-At-Once**—This means that each track is written individually, with a two-second gap between each track. Under this option you can choose to

➤ **Leave Session Open**—This leaves both the session and disc open so you can add more tracks later on. However, you won't be able to play the disc in a CD player.

➤ **Close Session and Leave the CD Open**—This completes the session, but leaves the disc open so more sessions can be added later. It's important to remember that most audio CD players cannot read beyond the first session of a disc, so this option isn't very useful for music CDs. Also, because the disc is left open, you'll be able to use it only in your CD-RW drive.

➤ **Close CD**—This option, naturally, closes the CD. After this is done, you can no longer add any tracks or sessions to the disc. You can, however, play it in a regular audio player.

➤ **Session-At-Once**—This option causes the program to write the entire session in one pass. If you are creating a CD with the first session containing audio tracks and plan to add a second session with data, this is a good choice. It also eliminates the two-second gap the track-at-once method places between each track. The CD remains open after the session is written.

➤ **Disc-At-Once**—This causes the entire disc to be written, as you have designed it in the layout, and then the CD to be closed. Because multiple sessions aren't of much use with a music CD, this is usually the best choice. This method also prevents the two-second gap from being created between tracks on the disc.

Between Tracks

When in Doubt, Use Disc-at-Once

Using the disc-at-once method has a few other advantages over the track- or session-at-once methods. With the other methods, you don't switch between source discs until each disc has written the track according to the order of the layout. This means you must sit through the entire burning process so you can switch discs when called upon to do so. Disc-at-once prompts you to enter each CD right away so it can extract the audio tracks you have placed in the layout. So instead of writing each track out, and making you wait while it does so, it extracts each track and creates a temporary file on your hard disk. When all the tracks have been read, it then writes the entire CD, and you can go off and tend to other matters.

Arcane CD Speak

Digital Audio What?

Digital audio extraction (DAE) refers to the process of taking the data straight from the CD, still in digital format, and sending it to the program (Easy CD Creator in this case) that is "ripping" the data from the CD.

Finally, if you find that the preset options Easy CD Creator uses for this dialog box don't suit your needs, you can use the Set as Default button after making the necessary changes to make the program remember the current settings.

When you are ready, click the OK button to start recording. When Easy CD Creator is first installed and used to create a CD, it tests the source CD-ROM drive to ensure that it supports digital audio extraction. It also makes sure that the drive can keep up with the speed at which the CD-RW drive will be writing the new CD.

It is important to understand that if you selected the disc-at-once method, after the laser starts to burn the CD, it can't stop or pause for even a second until the entire CD is written. The burning of a track, session, or entire disc is a continuous process that cannot be interrupted from beginning to end. If the buffer becomes empty in the middle of writing a track, which can happen for various reasons, a buffer underrun occurs and your disc becomes a coaster.

After testing your drive's capabilities (which should happen only once unless you re-install the program or install a new CD-RW drive), the CD creation process begins. If you are using the track-at-once method, the program writes the table of contents first. Then, it prompts you for a CD, writing the necessary tracks to the recordable disc, before requesting the next CD it needs (see Figure 3.9).

Don't Get Burned

Hands off!

When you are using your computer to record a CD, *don't use it for anything else,* unless you have a very fast CPU and don't plan on making heavy use of other resources, such as memory. As a rule of thumb, leave the computer alone while it's burning the CD!

Between Tracks

Making Multiple Copies

Because disc-at-once writes the audio tracks to your hard drive first, it is much easier and faster to use this method when making multiple copies of CDs that use the same layout. After those tracks are on your hard drive, it can write as many copies as you desire without requiring you to insert any more CDs.

If you are using the disc-at-once method, the program prompts you for each CD first, reading the tracks it needs, and then storing them in a temporary file on your local hard drive. After all the necessary CDs have been read, the program then writes the table of contents and, finally, begins writing the disc.

Figure 3.9

Easy CD Creator prompts you to insert each CD you have used for the layout.

After the program reads the last CD, one of two things happens. For track-at-once, the program writes the final track, closing the session or disc as you instructed. In contrast, for disc-at-once, the next step is to write the table of contents and then begin writing each track. In Figure 3.10, you can see the dialog box named CD Creation Process. This display shows you where the program is in the CD burning process.

Figure 3.10

The CD Creation Process dialog box shows the progress Easy CD Creator is making.

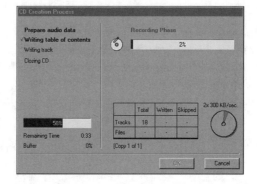

In the upper-left corner are four lines of text. The order of these lines depends on the method with which you're burning the disc. While it is creating the CD, the program places a check mark next to the line that describes what is happening at that moment. The four phases of the process are:

➤ **Prepare Audio Data**—This means the program is reading the track from your CD or hard disk and converting it to the format that will be used to write the disc.

➤ **Writing Table of Contents**—This works just like the table of contents for this book, which tells you where you can find specific chapters. In this case, it tells your CD player where each track is on the disc.

➤ **Writing Track**—When this selection is checked, the program is writing a track to your CD-RW drive.

➤ **Closing CD**—This line of text gets the check mark when the program is finishing things up and marking the CD as closed.

At the bottom-left part of this window is an indicator that shows the progress for writing each individual track. In the upper-right of the display is another indicator you can use to judge the total progress of writing the CD.

Watch that Buffer

The Buffer field, beneath the progress bar for the current track, is an important one to watch when the CD–RW drive is writing. Ideally, it will always say 100%. If this figure drops too much, usually below about 75%, you are likely to have a buffer underrun on your hands, reducing your CD to a coaster. For ways to avoid this kind of error, see Chapter 15.

If percentages aren't enough for you, at the bottom-right you can see a small chart showing the number of tracks contained in the layout, and the number that have been written so far. If you are having a bad day, you might also see something under the Skipped column, which means that the program could not write that particular track and moved on to the next one. If you're making more than one CD, the text beneath the chart lets you know how many copies have been completed and how many are left to go.

If you get bored with the process, or decide you've made a big mistake, click the Cancel button at the bottom. This aborts the process, and, regardless of what has been written to the CD, you'll have another coaster to put your drinks on.

After everything is finished, Easy CD Creator informs you by placing a big check mark over the CD symbol next to the progress indicator at the top-right of the screen (see Figure 3.11).

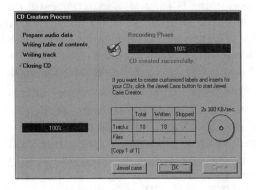

Figure 3.11

Easy CD Creator tells you when it has finished successfully.

Another One Bites the Dust

If problems occur during the creation process, or if the program terminates prematurely, you will see a big red "X" over the CD symbol instead of a check mark. This means something has gone terribly wrong and the CD will most likely not be playable.

Image Files Are BIG

It's important to remember, especially when creating music CDs, that image files can eat up a lot of your hard drive's real estate (up to 650MB). With hard disk capacity getting larger and larger with each passing year, this has become less of a concern than it used to be. However, if you create a lot of these image files and don't delete them when they're no longer needed, the amount of space they use will add up very quickly.

Notice that a new button, Jewel Case, has been added to this dialog box. Click that button if you want to create the jewel case inserts for you new disc. Of course, you can always do that later, as you will find out in Chapters 11, "Using Jewel Case Creator to Create Labels and Inserts," and 12, "You've Got the Look: Using Graphics and Other Advanced Stuff with Jewel Case Creator."

Assuming all went well, click the OK button to close the program. Take the CD out of the recorder and enjoy! If you did experience problems, see Chapter 15 for some help in identifying what went wrong and how to fix it.

Creating a Disc Image for Copying Later

Instead of burning straight to a CD you can use Easy CD Creator to make an image of the CD on your hard drive. I can hear the question now. Why do this? Well, if you want to create multiple CDs, creating a CD image on your hard disk and using the image to create new CDs as you need them is faster. Because they read and write information so much more quickly, copying from your hard drive can also be more reliable than from a CD-ROM drive.

Just like burning straight to a recordable CD, creating a CD image requires a CD layout. However, instead of using the Create CD button, use the Create CD Image option in the File menu. Easy CD Creator prompts you to select the location for the image file (be sure you have enough space on the hard disk!) and to give it a name. When you click the Save button, it then creates the image file. This won't take nearly as long as it does to burn a CD.

When you are ready to use an image file to create a CD, go back to the File menu and select Create CD from CD Image. You will be asked to select the image file on your hard drive to use, and then prompted to insert a blank recordable CD in the CD-RW drive. From there, the process works pretty much the same as for copying from other CDs (minus all that nasty disc swapping).

More Fun Things to Do with Audio Tracks

Just when you thought we were ready to move on to Chapter 4 and learn about making data CDs, I must tell that you about a few more things you can do when making audio CDs with Easy CD Creator.

Creating WAV Files from CDs

You can save tracks from your CDs on your hard disk by using Easy CD Creator to create a WAV file. This is a good way to keep audio tracks that you might expect to use frequently in one place. Start by bringing up Easy CD Creator in Audio CD mode. Insert the CD that has the track you want to copy. Select the track you want to extract by clicking it once, and then click the Extract button on the toolbar. You can also select multiple tracks, using the Shift or Ctrl keys, as we discussed earlier in the chapter.

Where's the Problem?

In addition to allowing you to gather together a large number of audio files from various sources, extracting to WAV files can be good for troubleshooting, too. If you're having problems with sound quality on burned CDs, try extracting the audio track to a WAV file and playing it from your hard drive. If you can't play the file at all or problems with the quality exist, the culprit is probably your CD-ROM drive and not your burner.

A small dialog box pops up, enabling you to enter the location and filename for the file(s) to be created. In this dialog box, the default file type is WAV. If you want to work with smaller, but somewhat lower quality files, you can change this option to MP3. The default format is PCM 44,100Hz, 16 Bit, Stereo, which is basically equivalent to the format used on an audio CD. Believe me, you won't be able to tell the difference.

If you're extracting just one track, you also can give the file a name. For multiple tracks, Easy CD Creator does the naming for you using the track titles (yet another good reason to download CD information from the Web). All you have to do to finish the job is click the Save button; the track is written to your hard disk in just a few seconds.

In addition to this simple save job, you also can be a little more choosy in how the file gets saved. If you click the Advanced button, you can see some new options that give you even more control (see Figure 3.12).

Figure 3.12

The Advanced features enable you to merge tracks into a single file, among other things.

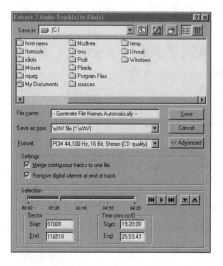

In the Settings area, there are two check boxes that might prove useful based on your needs:

Splitting Tracks

If you've merged two tracks into a single WAV file, you can split them apart again easily. After you've saved the file, just find it using the Explorer pane and highlight it by clicking it once. Then, click the Tracks menu and select Split Tracks.

➤ **Merge Contiguous Tracks to One File**—This feature enables you to save two audio tracks together in one file. If you have one or more songs you want to keep together, this can save time later because you'll only have to select the one WAV file when it's time to make a CD.

➤ **Remove Digital Silence at End of Track**—This editing feature can get rid of the dead air time at the end of a track. This might be useful if you are going to use the file in an editing program and just want the WAV file to contain the audible portion of the track.

In the Selection portion at the bottom of the window, you can use the Play button to play the track(s) with which you are working. You can use the sliding time bar to move to different points in the file. If you've selected multiple tracks, use the forward and back buttons to choose the one you want to hear.

When you're finished playing around, just click the Save button!

Fade Out, Fade In!

When you created the audio CD layout, you might have noticed that in addition to showing you the tracks (or the song titles if you used the Internet service to download them), other information appeared on each line in the layout. After each track or title are some fields you can manipulate easily. These are

➤ **Pause**—You can insert a pause before a song gets played. You can indicate how many seconds and frames (there are about 75 frames per second) to use for the length of the pause.

➤ **Fade In**—Use this to fade in slowly when the song starts. The song will start out in dead silence and gradually fade in up to the track's normal volume, all in the amount of time you select.

➤ **Fade Out**—This works the same way as the Fade In option, but is applied at the end of a song, starting with full volume for the track and gradually fading out to silence, over the time period you specify.

➤ **Cross Fade**—This one's a really great feature! With this option, you can have one song fade out while another fades in. Of course, you must select two tracks to use this function.

To use the Fade In/Fade Out feature, first select the track (or tracks) to which you want to apply it. You select them in the layout pane. After you've made your selection, click the Track menu at the top of the program window and select Edit audio effects. A small dialog box will pop up to enable you to specify the seconds/frames for the pause, fade in, and fade out values. If you've selected two tracks, you can select the amount of time to use for the cross fade.

The Least You Need to Know

➤ Easy CD Creator is the simplest method to create a CD using other CDs, WAV files, or MP3 files.

➤ Don't use Easy CD Creator if you want to make an exact copy of a CD—*use Easy CD Copier instead.*

➤ For making audio CDs, it's usually best to use the disc-at-once method.

➤ If you might need to periodically burn new copies of a CD layout, create an image file on your hard drive instead of burning right to the disc. This enables you to create CDs from the image whenever you want, without having to find the original source CDs.

➤ If you regularly get buffer underrun errors, be sure to leave your PC alone while it's burning a CD! If that doesn't help, check out Chapter 15 to find out other ways to avoid this error.

Chapter 4

EASY AS PIE.

Using Easy CD Creator to Make Data CDs

In This Chapter

➤ How to create and edit a data CD layout

➤ Burning a data CD with Easy CD Creator

➤ Creating a bootable CD

➤ Creating an image file so you can record CDs later

If you're still feeling the burn from your audio CD creating workout, the good news is that it's not much different using Easy CD Creator to burn your own data CDs. You audiophiles may be wondering why you'd want to take time out to make a data CD when there's a new top ten music CD you want to burn. Well, remember that your computer isn't infallible and accidents do happen. If you value what's on your computer, burning a good data CD to back up your important files, programs, or even your operating system (Windows for most of you) is some of the best protection you can have. No power surge is going to affect a small disc sitting on a CD rack.

Creating Data CDs the Easy Way

In the last chapter, "Using Easy CD Creator to Make Audio CDs," you learned about the many ways to start the Easy CD Creator program. In most of those methods, you chose Audio CD from a menu. If you want to copy some of your computer files to CD and create a data CD, the process isn't much different. However, instead of choosing Audio CD, you choose Data CD, using the same methods.

Cross Reference

This chapter shows you how to use Easy CD Creator to create a CD that contains just files that you select. If you want to simply make a copy of a data CD, check out Chapter 8, "The Easiest Way to Pillage—Copying CDs Using Easy CD Copier."

Between Tracks

Just the Data, Ma'am

In this chapter, we are just creating an ordinary data CD—like the ones you get when you buy computer software. In other chapters, we'll walk through making other types of data CDs, such as photo and video CDs.

If you launch Easy CD Creator from the Features menu, remember that the program comes up in whatever mode—audio or data—for which it was last used. So, if you look at the bottom of the program window, you should see Data CD/Joliet if you want to make an ordinary data CD. If you don't see this then you can change modes by clicking the down-arrow directly to the right of the New button on the toolbar. A short menu pops up from which you can select Data CD.

In Figure 4.1, you can see that the Easy CD Creator program looks similar to what it does when it is used to create an audio CD. However, no fields are available for you to use to enter the artist name or CD title. Another difference is that although the Explorer pane is still intact, the upper-right part of the display now shows files on the computer instead of audio files or tracks.

Selecting Files and Directories to Add

Even though you're working with data rather than music, adding that information to the CD Layout is done in the same way. You can select individual or groups of files or even entire folders when creating the layout you want to use to create the CD. To select files, navigate the disks on your computer by using the Explorer pane. If you refer back to Figure 4.1 you can see that this computer has two hard drives, a connection to another hard drive over a network, and two CD drives.

You can use all the same methods to select files or directories, from any of the drives shown, that you use for making audio CDs. You can drag the file (or the folder) to the layout, and you can highlight the file or folder (or groups of them) by clicking it once and then clicking the Add button on the toolbar. Like the audio files from the previous section, it will appear in the CD layout pane near the bottom of the window.

Notice also that at the bottom of the application window you can see indicators of how much space you've used so far when you are creating the layout. Whereas with audio CDs you needed to worry about keeping less than 74 minutes of audio in your layout, data CDs work in megabytes (MB). So what looks like a ruler running across the bottom of the Easy CD Creator window measures megabytes instead of minutes!

Also, directly under this indicator you can see the field labeled "Estimated Free CD Space." Use this as a guide when adding files or folders to the data layout. After the number hits or goes below 0, you need to scale back your layout a bit.

Explorer Pane

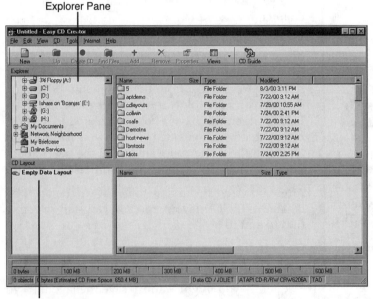

Figure 4.1

When creating a data CD, the program shows files instead of tracks.

CD Layout Pane

Deleting or Renaming Files

If you change your mind about the files included in your layout, you can remove entries from the layout by highlighting them and then clicking the Remove button. You might think you could also drag something from the layout back to the top pane, but this program apparently didn't think that far ahead so that doesn't work! However, another neat trick can be used for removing something from the layout. Similar to most Windows functions, you can right-click a file or folder and then, from the submenu that appears, select Remove.

Another interesting trick you can perform from this menu is renaming a file so that it takes on

Don't Get Burned

Look But Don't Touch

If you insert an audio CD in one of the CD drives, the program shows you the tracks on the CD. However, because you are making a data CD, it won't let you drag them down to the CD layout pane at the bottom.

a different name on the CD from the one it currently uses on your computer's hard disk. This feature might be useful when, for example, you archive files on a monthly

Between Tracks

MP3s on CD

Even though we're creating a data CD in this chapter, it's worth mentioning that you can use your MP3 files with a data CD. When you select MP3 files using Easy CD Creator to create an audio CD, it converts the MP3 files to CD-DA format before it writes it to the disc. With data CDs, they remain MP3 files. Because MP3 files are dramatically smaller than CD-DA, you can fit a lot more of them on a CD. The catch is that your audio CD player may or may not recognize MP3 files. Some newer players can, but this is something you'll want to check on before you spend time burning a CD of MP3 tracks that you can't play in your car or home stereo.

basis. While the original filename stays the same, you can rename the backup copy you're making on a CD to reflect the date or some other criteria that makes it easy to understand the contents of the file. Or, if you happen to be a writer, you might want to change a filename to reflect a different version of a chapter, for example.

You can even create a new folder on the new CD that doesn't exist on your hard drive, and then add files from your hard drive to this new folder. Do this by selecting New Folder from the Edit menu. When you do this, you see a folder in the CD layout called New Folder, which will have a box drawn around it. This means that it's in rename mode, so you can just start typing in the name you want to call the new folder. The text you enter replaces the "New Folder" text.

After you've created a new folder, it will be open by default in the CD layout and you can start selecting files to add to it.

Saving the Layout for Later Use

Frequently you might want to save the layout so you can use it again later. For example, you could create a layout that would copy all your important folders and use it to make a CD backup of your important stuff. To save the layout, just click File and then click Save As. When the Save As dialog box pops up, enter the name you want to give the layout and select the folder you want to save it in. Click the Save button, and you're done.

When you want to use a layout again, start the Easy CD Creator program and then select Open CD Layout from the File menu. If you then input the folder name and layout name, the layout is restored. Because the layout in this example involves folder names rather than specific files, Easy CD Creator doesn't know and doesn't care how the content inside the folders may have changed. It just copies everything that's in there, leaving no stone unturned. For repetitive jobs, such as backing up the contents of your My Documents folder, this can save a lot of time. Another benefit is that you don't have to worry about forgetting to include a folder or file. If you create the layout right the first time, it won't forget when you use it again. Of course, should your needs change, you can always modify the layout as you see fit.

Between Tracks

Changing Filenames

If you accidentally click away from the New Folder before you can rename it, you're not stuck with a folder you can't use. Similar to changing filenames in Windows Explorer, you can single-click the folder, wait for a second, and click it again, allowing you to change the name.

Starting the Copying Process

In Figure 4.2 you can see a CD layout that is ready for burning.

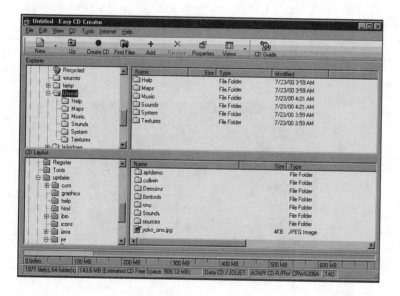

Figure 4.2

After you have created the layout, it's time to burn the CD.

To start the copying process—you guessed it—click the Create CD button on the toolbar. You also can select Create CD from the File menu, if you prefer. Either way, you will once again see the CD Creation Setup dialog box that allows you to select the target CD-RW drive and the same options you could select for audio CDs, such as Track-At-Once or Disc-At-Once.

This kind of CD is one you might want to consider making a multisession CD. This would be handy if you have data you want to write to the CD, but not its full capacity of 650 megabytes. You can select the option Close Session and Leave CD Open.

This enables you to add another session later. Roxio's software has a session selector that can be used to switch between sessions, so you can use this method to fill up a CD over time.

Cross Reference

In Chapter 9, "Understanding and Using Multisession CDs," you will find more information about using sessions. For more information about using Roxio's Session Selector to change the active session, see Chapter 13, "Other Roxio Utilities."

Figure 4.3 shows the CD Creation Process display used for data CDs. Here you can see that it is a little different from that used for the audio CD. The steps that will be performed to create a data CD are as follows:

➤ File system generation

➤ Copying files

➤ Writing track

➤ Closing session (or closing CD)

After the program finishes creating the necessary data structures on the CD to create a JOLIET file system, it then starts copying files from your hard disk to a temporary location. Next, it writes a single track out to the CD-RW drive. If you chose to close the session, but leave the CD open, you'll see Closing session as a step in the CD creation process. If you selected to close the CD, you'll see Closing CD in the CD Creation Process dialog box.

Figure 4.3

Easy CD Creator displays its progress as it writes the data CD.

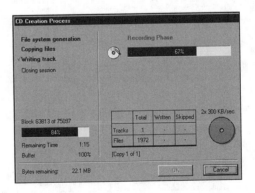

You can keep adding sessions to the CD until you run out of space on the disc. Even if you leave the CD open, you can use the disc in the CD recorder or in most CD-ROM drives—just as long as the *session* itself is closed. If you want to prevent any additional sessions from being added to the CD (fino, absoluto, it's all over now), you can choose to close it.

When you're ready to close a CD, just select Close CD instead of Close session when you add the last session to the CD.

Creating Disc Images for Data CDs

In the last chapter, you learned that you can burn CDs more quickly if you first create a CD image file on your hard disk. You can do the same for data CDs. This feature is most useful when you are creating more than one copy of the CD. For example, you might want to send out a CD containing family photos to your friends during the holiday season. You could burn the CDs straight from the CD layout. For this to work, however, all the files you selected for the layout will need to still be available on your computer. If you create the disc image file (click File, Create Disc Image), you simply must tell Easy CD Creator to burn the CD using that image (click File, Create CD from Disc Image). For more information about using this feature, see "Creating a Disc Image for Copying Later" in Chapter 3.

Arcane CD Speak

File System Generation?

The first thing the program does, file system generation, might sound weird. So if you're wondering what that means, it's the "JOLIET" part of the "Data CD/JOLIET" text the program displays in the layout window when you are creating the layout. This is just the file system used to organize data files on a CD. Other formats also exist, but your CD burning pastime will be simpler if you let Easy CD Creator worry about that.

How to Make a Bootable CD—And Why You Might Want One

Wait, there's more! Just when you thought we had exhausted all the possibilities of using Easy CD Creator, there's one more we will look at in this chapter. It's a little more complicated to create, and becomes a lot more complicated to use because it requires that you understand a few MS-DOS commands.

A bootable floppy disk can be a lifesaver when your computer goes south and you can't get it back up. If you installed Windows yourself, odds are it had you create one during the installation process. Why are they handy (and necessary)? Maybe you accidentally changed some critical file on your hard disk before you rebooted, or maybe a file has become corrupted. With a bootable floppy disk, you can always boot into the MS-DOS environment and poke around to try to determine what has happened.

A bootable CD can be used for the same purpose. Because you can always use the floppy disk, why might you want to use a bootable CD instead? Here are just a few of the reasons:

DOS?

Microsoft DOS (Disk Operating System) was the Operating System used in the original IBM home PCs that began bringing computers into the home as well as the workplace. It lasted for many years, until Microsoft phased it out in favor of Windows. DOS's legacy still exists in Windows, though, and making a bootable CD with Easy CD Creator requires some of its tools. If that's not your cup of tea, turn the page and go on to the next chapter because learning to use DOS is another book in and of itself!

Your PC Must Help, Too

Before you start to create a bootable CD, you might want to check the documentation that came with your computer to make sure it supports this feature. Many pre–Pentium computers cannot do this, whereas most newer Pentium class PCs are well equipped for the process.

➤ Your floppy drive stops working. Bet you saw that one coming.

➤ It's more convenient and durable. CDs hold up better to wear and tear than a floppy. And you won't have to worry about magnets, the bane of a floppy disk, screwing things up.

➤ Because a CD can hold hundreds of times more information than a standard floppy disk, you can fit more useful tools and troubleshooting utilities on the disc to help set your computer straight.

➤ It's a neat, fun thing to do.

To make a bootable CD, you must have a bootable floppy disk. If you don't have one, you can have Windows create one.

For Windows 9x/Me users, the easiest thing to do is to create the bootable floppy using the startup disk method:

1. Double-click the My Computer desktop icon.
2. Double-click the Control Panel icon.
3. Double-click the Add/Remove Programs icon.
4. Click the Startup Disk tab; a dialog box appears prompting you to create the startup disk. Make sure you have a blank floppy disk inserted in the floppy drive.
5. Click the Create Disk button.

The first thing to do when you finish creating the startup disk is to make sure it works. Try restarting your computer using the disk you just created. If it works then it will most likely work when used to make the bootable CD.

When Windows creates the startup disk, it contains several files the DOS-savvy user can use to help troubleshoot problems. Using these tools can get complicated, though. Therefore, if you're not familiar with them, it's best not to use them until you can get the help of a DOS-geek friend or a good DOS book.

After you have created the bootable floppy, it's time to create the bootable CD. Open Easy CD Creator, use the down-arrow button (next to the New button on the toolbar), and select Bootable CD from the list presented. It's important to note that at the bottom of your Easy Creator CD program window you will not see this same text, but instead you'll see Data/ISO9660. As Figure 4.4 shows, after you choose this method, you get a dialog box, which prompts you to insert the bootable floppy in the floppy drive.

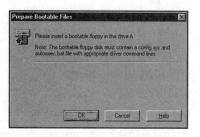

Figure 4.4

The first thing Easy CD Creator asks you to do is to load the bootable floppy disk so it can read the information.

After you click the OK button, the program reads in the contents of the floppy disk, and from there on out it's pretty much the same as making an ordinary data CD. The same dialog boxes that Easy CD Creator uses for burning a CD are used here. The CD Creation Setup dialog box enables you to make choices about how to create the CD, including the speed to use and whether to leave the CD open or closed when finished. For this bootable CD, simply select the disk-at-once method so that it closes the CD when it's finished. When you are ready to continue, click the OK button.

Next, the CD Creation Process dialog box keeps you company and lets you know what is happening as the CD is burned. The whole process, even at 1X writing speed, won't take but a few minutes. When finished, a large green check mark appears next to the CD icon in the CD Creation Process dialog box. Click OK; you can then remove the CD and test it by trying to boot your computer.

The Least You Need to Know

➤ Easy CD Creator is the simplest method to create a data CD so you can store valuable files offline.

➤ Some CD-ROM drives read MP3 files from a data disc, which enables you to put much more music on a disc than you could using regular CD digital audio.

➤ Don't use Easy CD Creator if you want to make an exact copy of a CD—*use Easy CD Copier instead.*

➤ You can use Easy CD Creator to create bootable CDs that can pull you back from oblivion if your computer goes south.

Chapter 5

OKAY PEOPLE!
LET'S GET
ANOTHER TAKE!

Your Very Own Record Studio: Using the CD Spin Doctor

In This Chapterzz

➤ It's as easy as 1, 2, 3!

➤ Copy old LPs and cassettes to your hard disk or to a CD.

➤ Clean up pops and scratches and those other annoying sound problems found on older recording mediums.

If the audio features of Easy CD Creator don't get you everything you need, Roxio's CD burning software suite has something else that probably will: the CD Spin Doctor. You can do a lot using the Spin Doctor application that goes even beyond the capabilities of Easy CD Creator. In this chapter, we'll walk through making a simple copy of a song using the Spin Doctor. We'll also discuss some of the options you can use, such as cleaning up the sound, and even take a look at recording files on your hard disk so that you can further play with and modify the sound to get it just how you like it.

What Is the Spin Doctor?

The Spin Doctor might sound like someone who treats people suffering from vertigo, but in this case we're talking about a great program that comes with Easy CD Creator 4 Deluxe. In the previous two chapters, we looked at using the Easy CD Creator application to create CDs from other CDs, WAV and MP3 files, and plain old computer data and applications. In Chapter 8 we'll talk about using Easy CD Copier to make simple copies of CDs. The Spin Doctor application expands your recording abilities by letting you choose as the input source for your music almost anything you can plug into the soundcard in the back your computer. For example, you can use Spin Doctor to create CDs from records (45s, 78s, EPs, and LPs), cassette tapes, radio signals, microphones, and even your TV or VCR.

After you've recorded the audio tracks you want, you can apply options that allow you to clean up some of the background noise inherent with older recordings such as records. Other options enable you to add special effects to the sounds you record. When you are ready to burn a CD, you can do it directly from the source, or you can create WAV files on your hard disk that you can experiment with, using the clean up and morphing effect tools, before sending them to a shiny new CD.

A Word About Phonographs

Stop With the Needling!

Playing vinyl records on a banged up phonograph, particularly one with a badly worn needle, can further degrade the only copy you own of a particular record.

One thing that I particularly like about the Spin Doctor is that it allows me to continue to listen to the many records I bought either as I was growing up or from yard sales and flea markets over the past few years. This way, I can make a CD copy of these fragile LPs so that they don't have to be subjected to an eventual slow death when I play them over and over again.

To transfer the audio from old phonograph records you have lying around, you, obviously, must have a phonograph player. Although that might seem redundant, keep in mind that finding a good phonograph player in the new millennium might require the assistance of an archaeologist on par with Indiana Jones. You can look around in yard sales and such, but I caution you to beware of that source. You're likely to get a unit that either doesn't work, or that has a needle in such bad condition that the end results won't be worth the effort or cost.

Although you aren't likely to find phonograph players at the local discount retailers or even some of the supposedly totally-audio/video concept stores, you will find them here and there. While the few totally new players that can be found might not be cheap, believe me when I say that it is worth the cost. Shelling out a little over a $100 dollars is a worthy expense if you are going to use the device to transfer music from vinyl to CDs that might never be re-mastered by their masters.

And, if you like the results you get using Spin Doctor, you might start frequenting yard sales a little more often to look for some long out of print titles and discover music you once thought lost.

When purchasing a phonograph player, however, there is one important factor to consider. In the "olden" days of component stereo systems, you bought a receiver/amplifier, speakers, tape deck, and phonograph as separate items. The phonograph plugged into the receiver using a special port that directed its sound through a pre-amplifier. If you use this kind of phonograph with your sound card, there's no pre-amp, so you'll either have to buy one—check Radio Shack, they'll know what you're talking about—or buy a new phonograph that has audio/video outputs, which means that it has its own pre-amp built into its guts.

Between Tracks

Pre-amp Workaround

If you're stuck trying to plug a pre-ampless phonograph player into your sound-card, there's another way to get around the problem than buying a new "amp'd" phonograph player. If you can connect your current player to a component stereo system that has a headphone jack, you can connect your sound card to the receiver using a headphone cable that has the appropriate plugs at both ends. You might lose a touch of sound quality, but it's cheaper than buying a new phonograph player!

Creating a CD as Easy as 1, 2, 3

Because using Spin Doctor to create CDs from other music CDs or MP3 files is not much different from doing so in Easy CD Creator, this section focuses on using Spin Doctor to burn a CD directly from an LP album. After that, we look at creating WAV files on your hard disk that can be further modified before recording them to a CD.

Starting up the Spin Doctor application is simple. Just double-click the Create CD Desktop icon, select Audio, and then select Spin Doctor from the menu that pops up. You can also get the Spin Doctor working for you by using the Start menu. Click Start, Programs, Roxio Easy CD Creator 4, Features, and then, finally, CD Spin Doctor.

This starts the Spin Doctor, bringing up an application window that looks very different from Easy CD Creator. In Figure 5.1, you see the 123 window, which functions much like a wizard or menu. You can select from the first two icons to tell Spin Doctor where the music is coming from and where it is going to. Button number three enables you to start the recording process.

Figure 5.1

Creating a CD is as easy as clicking 1, 2, and 3.

Where Are My Numbers?

If you don't see the 123 window when Spin Doctor pops up, or if you are already deep in the program and just want to go back to the beginning, click the View menu and select 123 Window from there.

We'll dissect each of the 1, 2, and 3 buttons in the following section. If you look near the bottom of Figure 5.1, you can also see that an Options button lets you use several helpful tools for getting more from your audio. Keep this button in the back of your mind for now; we'll come back to it soon.

Selecting the Source and Destination for the Recording

For this example, we are going to extract an entire LP album and write it directly to the CD-R disc. This means we won't be able to do any editing to the sound; but then, the pops, hisses, and scratches are what make vinyl great. For an LP that is in pretty good condition, this is the easy way to do it. However, if you want to change the order of songs, or make other edits to the audio tracks, you must record them to files instead of directly to the CD-RW drive. We cover how to do that in the next example.

To select the source and destination for this simple copy, use the following steps:

1. In the left pane of Spin Doctor, click the 1 button to select a source for the audio information.

2. In the Select Music Source dialog box, you are given the choice of audio inputs (see Figure 5.2). Notice that you can choose from any of your CD-ROM drives, audio tape, and even files on your hard disk. For this example, we will use LP and click Select.

Figure 5.2

You can select from a variety of sources for audio input with the Spin Doctor.

3. In the first pane of the Spin Doctor, the number 1 button now looks like an LP album. If you aren't going to stick around to turn the LP over after the first side has been recorded select the check box that says Automatically Stop Recording When Silent! Otherwise, the Doctor acts like a dunce and just keeps recording the silence.

4. In the right pane, click the number 2 button to select the destination for the recording. A dialog box similar to the one used to select the source appears. Because we're recording directly to the CD, click CD Recorder and then the Select button.

5. The second pane in the Spin Doctor now has the number 2 button replaced with an icon that looks like a CD.

You might be assuming at this point that the next step is to click the 3 button in the top-right corner of the Spin Doctor window. Reign those horses in, cowboy! Before you continue on to the next button, number 3, you can elect to use some options that will change how your recorded output will sound or how it will be organized. These options can be used when recording from the audio source directly to the CD, or you can use them on WAV files you've recorded from the original source. What methods to use depend on your circumstances, the condition of the source, and your expectations of the output.

Choose Your Options

There are a host of options you can choose from that can be used to modify the quality of the sound to be recorded. Right under the first pane in the Spin Doctor is, amazingly, a button labeled Options. So, before we get started with this recording, let's look at the available options. Click that button and you'll see a dialog box called Recording Options, as shown in Figure 5.3.

This Recording Options dialog box gives you a lot of control over how this CD is going to sound. A few other options not related to the audio output are also available, such as the test and close CD options. When you click a button for a particular option, another dialog box pops up to allow you to fine-tune the control by selecting a tab for each one.

Figure 5.3

You can use the Recording Options dialog box to clean up or change the audio before it is recorded.

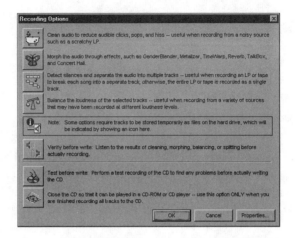

You also can click the Options button in the toolbar to turn on or off these options, and to get to the Properties page.

For the first four options, you can also use the Properties button at the bottom of the Recording Options dialog box to bring up property pages for each of these tools.

Clean Up That Audio!

For some, a record that has scratches on it and other noise such as background hiss is part of reliving the nostalgic experience of a long-since-gone era. The rest of us find them more annoying than listening to political talk radio. The first button on the Options page can help make the sound on an older LP a little better. There is no guarantee, however, that you'll like the output any better. Experience with this option has shown that it shouldn't be selected every time you create a CD from an LP. As a matter of fact, if the LP is in excellent condition, and has few if any defects, using this option can make the output sound worse than the input, dulling it quite a bit.

To use this control, click the button and then click the Properties button at the bottom of this dialog box. In Figure 5.4, you can see the Properties page for controlling the cleaning tool allows you to select the degree of cleanup, categorized into Noise Filtering and Pop Removal.

If you click the check box labeled Adjust for Source Type, the Noise Filtering and Pop Removal values will be set to a default value for you automatically. Or, you can use the slider bars to customize the degree for either of these to your tastes and experience. It is best to use the Preview button to listen to the end result, rather than to burn the CD and find you don't like the sound. Experiment first! The Preview button enables you to do this by extracting the audio to a temporary file. It doesn't change the actual audio data; that's done when you start to burn the CD.

Keep Your Area Clean

Don't forget to clean up your source before you use the cleanup options of Spin Doctor. Use a good record cleaning kit to make sure the LP is in tiptop condition before you record. If you haven't used the phonograph in a while, make sure the needle is clean and take appropriate action. For tape decks, you can usually use isopropyl alcohol and a cotton swab to clean the tape heads. Doing all this sort of work up front can only help to improve the sound you get recorded to CD.

Although Spin Doctor can perform some cleanup of the sound outputted from your LP, this is done based strictly on the audio signal it gets. For some of its work, Spin Doctor looks for specific patterns in the signal, based on the degree you tell Spin Doctor to look for (thus the sliding bars in the options menu). When it sees these patterns, it either eliminates them (as in pops and clicks from scratches) or tones them down (as when it performs a general sound cleanup). Sometimes a particular frequency is toned down or removed—whether it is background noise or part of the intended song, Spin Doctor cannot tell. You should record your audio to a file and experiment with Spin Doctor to find out which settings work best—for each LP you record from!

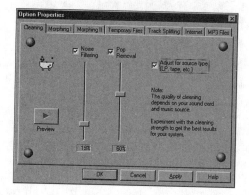

Figure 5.4

You can control the degree to which the cleanup process attempts to alter the input audio.

Morphing Effects

The second button on the Recording Options dialog box gives you the ability to substantially alter the audio input. Unlike the previous option, this one won't clean up the sound, but it does enable you to apply special effects to really change it. If you're looking to join that DJ wannabe crowd and want to be creative, the following effects are available:

➤ **Concert Hall**—This is supposed to add "depth" to the audio sound.

➤ **Reverb**—This adds an echo effect or makes the audio sound like it was recorded on a sound stage.

➤ **GenderBlender**—This effect allows you to shift the pitch of the output.

➤ **Metalizer**—This is a weird effect that gives the output a robotic sound.

➤ **TimeWarp**—This is another weird effect that no description will give justice to. You'll just have to try it yourself!

➤ **TalkBox**—You can make your guitar talk with this one.

Again, use the Properties button on the Recording Options dialog box to bring up the properties pages for these effects. In Figure 5.5, you can see that there are actually two separate tabs for using morphing effects. The first three effects are available via the Morphing I tab. For Concert Hall, you just select the effect using the check box. For Reverb and GenderBlender, you can use the sliding bar. For experimentation, there's a Preview button here, as well.

Figure 5.5

The Morphing I tab shows the first three special audio effects you can use.

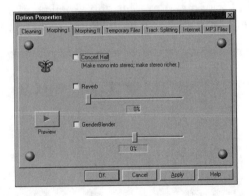

The second special effects tab, Morphing II, works nearly the same as the previous tab. Here, you can use a sliding bar to apply the TimeWarp effect, or click the Metalizer check box for a robotic sound effect. To use the TalkBox function, you need to click the Browse button and select an audio file that will be used to modulate the sound. Don't forget to use the Preview button to test your modifications before you settle on them!

Relocating Temporary Files

Although it doesn't have a button on the Recording Options window, you can click Properties and gain access to a Temporary Files tab, shown in Figure 5.6. When Spin Doctor records tracks from your CD, tape, phonograph, and so on, it actually stores the audio in temporary files before writing them to the CD. After it writes the tracks, Spin Doctor deletes these files. The Temporary Files tab lets you specify where Spin Doctor stores those temporary files.

For most people, I recommend letting Spin Doctor make that determination by checking the box labeled Put Temporary Files Where There Is the Most Room. If, however, you have multiple disk drives on your system, or if space is a problem, it might be a better idea to use the second radio button on this page to change the path used for temporary files. This radio button defaults to using the Temp folder in your Windows directory, which is a folder that every Windows user has. You can, however, use the Browse button to choose a new location.

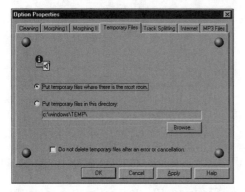

Figure 5.6

You can control where temporary files are created during the recording process.

If you're having problems recording your audio, you might want to use the check box at the bottom of this dialog box because it causes Spin Doctor to keep files that are ended because of an error or a cancellation. This can be useful for troubleshooting purposes, a subject tackled in Chapter 15. Remember, though, that keeping these files on your drive can use up disk space quickly if you don't monitor it and remove them yourself when they're no longer needed.

Splitting Audio into Tracks

In addition to superior sound quality, CDs had another big advantage over LPs and cassettes when they first found their way into the hands of consumers. Finally, we could just skip directly to any track on the disc without guessing where to put a needle or how much tape to fast-forward or rewind.

Breaks between songs on a CD are defined very carefully, which is not the case on a cassette or LP recording. Instead, on CDs, tracks are separated by a short duration of silence. By detecting this silence between portions of the sampled audio, Spin Doctor can break your audio input into separate tracks. The only other options you have is to record an LP or cassette as one long track or create a huge WAV file and use the Sound Editor (explained in chapter 13) for hours trying to cut out each track and store it as a separate file. Needless to say, neither of these is a particularly ideal option when the good Doctor can do it for you.

The Recording Options dialog box has a button for splitting audio tracks. But, to set the details, you once again must open up the Properties dialog box; this time using the Track Splitting tab shown in Figure 5.7.

Figure 5.7

Use the Track Splitting tab to divide LP or cassette audio input into separate tracks for each song.

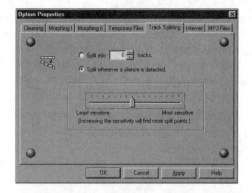

Here, you can use the Split into Tracks radio button to specify how many tracks you want the audio input divided into. The number 6 is shown by default because that's about the average number of songs that will fit on one side of an LP. If you choose to specify the number of tracks to split the recording into, then Spin Doctor attempts to do this for you. Of course, all you have to do is look on the LP (or other source) and find out how many songs it has. Spin Doctor will, after recording from the source, attempt to split the recorded audio into the number of tracks you have specified. This is not a perfect method, however, because some songs actually have silences in them. The problem with this is that, if you specify a certain number of tracks, you might find that Spin Doctor finds more splits than you specify! If this happens, you might find one song overwritten by part of another one.

The second button, Split Wherever a Silence Is Detected, can also be used, and you can use the slide bar to increase the sensitivity of this control. If you have a lot of background static or noise on the input source, you should move this control toward the Most Sensitive side. Otherwise, the default might be adequate.

Whichever method you use, Spin Doctor names the files by concatenating the name you chose for the output file and appending the text - `Split 1.wav` and so on, thus numbering the output files for you. You can always rename the files later to match them up to the song titles they represent.

Balancing the Volume From Multiple Sources

The next button on the Recording Options properties sheet is the Balance Loudness button. This is useful when you are going to create a CD that has songs you've extracted from a variety of sources. You might not know it, but there isn't a standard volume level for recording vinyl LPs, for example. Some play back at a louder volume than others. Using this option causes Spin Doctor to examine each file you've decided to commit to CD recording and adjust the volume for each track so that the resulting CD sounds as if it were created at the same volume level.

As with every option here, pitfalls do exist, however. If you have tracks that contain a wide variety of volume levels, expect to see them all be adjusted **down**. This means you might have to pump up the volume a bit more than usual when playing the music.

Stop the Music!

For track splitting to work when detecting silence, you need to click the check box labeled Automatically Stop Recording, which can be found in the Source Selection dialog box by using button number 1.

The Internet Tab

The second to last tab on the Option Properties dialog box enables you to specify that your computer use a proxy server to access the Internet. Most work environments that have more than a few PCs will probably be using a proxy server, so if Spin Doctor needs Internet access to get CD track titles, you must see your network administrator to get the information necessary to get around the proxy server.

If you're dialing in from home and using an Internet service provider, you don't need to worry about this tab.

Proxy What?

A *proxy server* is basically a device that sits between a computer network and the Internet and attempts to regulate which kind of traffic is allowed in and which kind is allowed out.

Setting Up MP3 Files

The final tab on the Options Properties dialog box is the MP3 Files tab. This tab allows you to specify the kind of MP3 format used to write MP3 files. If you decide to create an MP3 file, rather than record directly to the CD, it will be created according to the format selected here. One important note, however, is that Easy CD Creator doesn't come with an MP3 encoder. If you already have installed another software application that comes with one, you'll see information on this tab about the kind of MP3 files you can write. If you don't feel like spending a lot of money on another application, you might try downloading a demo copy of a program that does produce MP3 files. When the demo time period expires, you will most likely find that the MP3 encoder doesn't get removed from the system, and Easy CD Creator will be able to use it.

Remember also that MP3 is a compression algorithm that actually "loses" some of the data from the actual recording. That is, if you were to record a CD track to an MP3 file, and then reverse the process, the result would not be the high quality you normally expect from a CD track. However, unless you have a $10,000 stereo system at home, you might find that MP3s are an adequate method for storing music.

Closing Discs

After you close a disc, you can't reopen it. Make certain that you are finished burning tracks to a disc before closing it!

A Few Final Details

After you've finished deciding whether or not to clean up the audio or use any of the other effects, you must decide on a few final details before finally recording to your disc. Clicking the Verify Before Write button enables you to listen to your audio tracks with all the morphing and filtering options applied, so you can be sure you're getting what you want before wasting a CD. This works in the same way as the Preview buttons on some of the tabs described previously, except that it includes all selected options.

You can click the Test Before Write button to check out the recording process to see that your CD-RW drive is up to it. This isn't always a foolproof test in that a test write can work just fine, but fail when the burner gets to the real deal. If you do have trouble, see Chapter 15 for some troubleshooting help.

Finally, you can use the Close the CD button to close the CD so that it can be played on an ordinary audio CD player. If you forget to choose this option, the tracks will still be playable in the CD-RW recorder drive, but not in other audio CD players. Fortunately, you can close a CD whenever you want. Just insert the CD in the CD-RW drive and start up Spin Doctor. Click button number 2 for the music destination and select your CD-RW drive. Back in the main Spin Doctor program, you'll note that at the bottom of the pane that holds button number 2 is now a button labeled Close CD. Click it, and Spin Doctor closes the disc. This can take a few minutes, so be patient!

Start Recording!

After you've chosen all the options you want to use and have gone through the process of verifying the sound, it is time to burn the results to the CD-R disc. If you still have it open, click the OK button to get out of the Recording Options dialog box.

Spin Doctor records a disc in three stages: First, assuming you are using a phonograph or an audio cassette as in this example, it records the information it receives from the sound card. Second, it writes that information out to a temporary file, applying any filtering or morphing schemes you set in the Recording Options dialog box. Finally, the CD is burned.

To get the process started, look to the Record to CD-R button located in the top-right of the application window. When recording from an analog source, another dialog box pops up as a last minute reminder that recording begins immediately, so you need to have the source audio ready to play. After you give it the go ahead to record, get your record or tape playing ASAP!

Between Tracks

Differences in Recording

If you are using a digital source, such as a CD as the input source, then Spin Doctor doesn't have to prompt you before it starts to record. Unlike a vinyl LP or cassette tape, Spin Doctor can simply grab the data from the when it wants it.

You also won't hear the audio during the recording process if you use a digital input. This is because Spin Doctor can simply extract the digital audio tracks at higher speeds (depending on the CD drive's capabilities) and doesn't want to waste your time doing all this in 1x real time speed if you have a 12x drive!

Because the recording is performed in real-time when using an analog source (to a temporary file), the Recording Progress dialog box pops up and keeps you company while your computer's speakers play the audio that is input (see Figure 5.8). On the Recording Progress dialog box display, you can see the amount of time available on your hard disk to continue recording.

If you get tired of those weird musical characters walking across the dialog box that are supposed to entertain you, click the Freeze the Animation check box. If you have limited system resources, this is a good idea anyway because it's one less thing that requires your computer's attention.

When it is time to pause the recording so that you can flip the album over, click the Pause button. Notice that after you click it, the Pause button then turns into a Record button. Get the other side of the record ready for playing, click the Record button, and the recording will continue.

Figure 5.8

The Recording Progress dialog box shows you the progress made during the recording.

When the Record's Over

After the last track on the LP has been played, click the Stop button on the Recording Progress dialog box. Now that Spin Doctor knows you're ready to record, it finishes writing the sampled audio data to a temporary file on your hard disk and then starts burning the CD. In Figure 5.9, you can see that the progress of the burn is shown as a percentage. The amount of time it takes to finish the CD depends on the amount of music you recorded, of course, and the speed to which your CD-RW drive has been set.

Figure 5.9

You can watch the progress of the actual CD burn after the audio has been sampled and recorded to a temporary file.

After the recording is complete, you have a new CD! If you hadn't selected to close the CD after the recording, you can click that button at the bottom of the Spin Doctor window now. You'll get prompted with a box telling you that after the CD is closed you won't be able to add any more tracks to it. Click the Close CD button and the Recording Progress dialog box reappears with text telling you it is closing the CD. This process will take a minute or two, depending on the speed of the drive.

When the CD has been closed, you'll notice a change in the main application window at the bottom of the right pane. While this was used during the recording process to show how much space was available on your CD-R (assuming your CD-RW drive was the destination for your audio), the text "The destination CD is not record-able" now appears.

Instead of a blank layout, the destination window pane of Spin Doctor now shows what was recorded to the disc. If you set up Spin Doctor to split your source into multiple tracks, you see a listing for each track and its length. If you recorded it as a single track, even if it was composed of several songs, you see just one track listed with the total length of the recording.

Use Your Hard Disk First

If you are going to use the option to split an LP or cassette tape into separate tracks—which is a good idea from a playback standpoint—then it is best to do so by directing the output to a set of files on your hard disk that you can further work with. You might find two songs run together that didn't get detected and split apart. You can fix this kind of problem using the Sound Editor (see Chapter 13, "Other Roxio Utilities") and then record the CD from the collection of WAV files you've modified.

Even though, when everything clicks, recording directly from source to CD (while Spin Doctor uses temporary files) is the fastest and easiest way to copy your music, it's not always the best. The next thing we'll look at is how to record your audio tracks to a file(s) on your hard disk.

Recording to a WAV File

Whether you're recording from a CD, LP, or cassette, recording to a WAV file on your hard disk is probably the best option, especially if that audio requires some editing and cleanup work. By recording to a sound file, you can use both Spin Doctor (to clean up the sound and add effects) and the Sound Editor to remove dead space and other problems.

Recording to WAV files doesn't require any knowledge that wasn't already presented in the previous section. You have to change the process only a little from recording directly to a CD:

➤ In the first pane (with the number 1 button), you can give the file a name by entering it in the field labeled Record under the name.

➤ In the second pane, click the Destination button (with the number 2 or the icon for whichever device you most recently used for output) and choose to store your files to your hard disk from the list that appears. From here, you can change the location for the WAV file by using the Change Directory button.

After this, the rest is pretty much the same. You can choose your options using the Options button, and after you click the Record to Disk button, be ready to start the audio source!

When you are finished recording to a disk file, you see the recorded track(s) listed in the destination pane, as shown in Figure 5.10. In this case, a single side from an album is recorded as one file. I'll worry about breaking the tracks out later.

Figure 5.10

As you can see, the file glenn1.wav *was created by the Sound Doctor.*

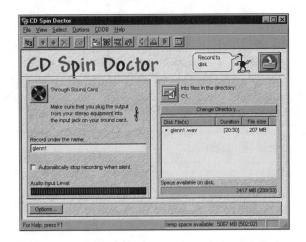

Re-Recording from WAV to WAV

Even if you want to apply morphing or filters, you don't have to use the Options button when you create a WAV file. Instead, you can choose to record the audio raw, in its original format. Then, you can apply various settings to the WAV file, even going so far as to use effects found in the Sound Editor. After you've decided on the mix you like, you can re-record the WAV file to yet another file and then use that result to create the CD. All that's required is a little more finagling of Spin Doctor.

To use a WAV or MP3 file on your hard disk as the source, just click the number 1 button to select the file as source for the audio input.

After you click the 1 button, the Select Music Source dialog box appears. Click Files(s) on Hard Drive and then click Select. A typical Windows Open dialog box appears, enabling you to find and select the file or files you are going to re-record (see Figure

5.11). When you return to the Spin Doctor main window, you can always click the Add Files button that now appears to add more files if you want.

Figure 5.11

You can select a previously recorded WAV file to use for audio input.

Notice in this example, our `glenn1.wav` file is hiding off to the right side of the Open dialog box.

Making sure that you still have your hard disk selected as the destination location of choice on the number 2 button, select a new directory for the re-recorded WAV file to go to. If you originally recorded an entire LP or cassette to one file, this is a good time to break it into tracks and clean up the noise a little using the Options button.

When you are ready to start, click the Record to Disk button, just as you did when recording to CD.

The Recording Progress dialog box keeps you company as the file is first read in. After this is complete, you see the text at the top of this box change, telling you that it is applying the track-splitting and morphing effects that were chosen and then that it is writing the output file(s). When the Spin Doctor has to split files, you might wonder how it names them. Well, that's simple! It takes your original filename and adds text to differentiate the filename. For example, if you were recording from Yoko Ono's LP *Approximately Infinite Universe* (which I highly recommend), and you gave the output filename as something such as AIU, each track would be named in a fashion that tells you where the splits were made. You'd end up with filenames for each track named `AIU - Split 1.wav`, `AIU - Split 2.wav`, and so on.

Between Tracks

Keep It Organized

I am the world's lousiest housekeeper. In my apartment you'll find books, CDs, and tons of other junk strewn throughout the place willy-nilly. In other words, I'm not a freak about organization. However, if you're going to be doing a lot of Spin Doctoring, you might want to create a special folder to hold the files you produce. This way, you won't have to go looking for that particular song you recorded weeks ago and now need in a hurry!

No Saving Allowed

One advantage that Easy CD Creator has over Spin Doctor when recording files from your hard disk to a CD is that you can create a layout (list of songs), and save it to your hard disk for later use. With Spin Doctor, you can't save a layout. So, it's burn now or redo the list later!

Finally! Recording from WAV or MP3 Files to CD

After you've finished working with each track to get the sound how you want it, you can use Spin Doctor to record the files to the CD-R disc. When recording WAV or MP3 files to disc, you could also use the Easy CD Creator application, but because you're already in Spin Doctor, you might as well go ahead and use it!

Once again, you must ensure that you have selected your hard disk as a source. Then, use the Add File(s) button in the first pane to select the files you want to burn to the CD. Although it's easier if your audio files are all in one location on your hard disk, you can collect them from any folder on your disk. Remember, if you change your mind before you choose to actually record the CD, you can always come back to this pane and change your selections.

Note that as you add files, you can see an approximation of the amount of time these files will take up on the recordable disc. This information is displayed in the Total field at the bottom of this pane (see Figure 5.12). Pay close attention to this number because, depending on whether you are using a 74- or 80-minute recordable disc, you might find that you need to cut a track to fit everything in or you might have enough room left over to add another track or two.

Figure 5.12

You can determine how much time you've used up while adding audio files by looking at the bottom of the first pane.

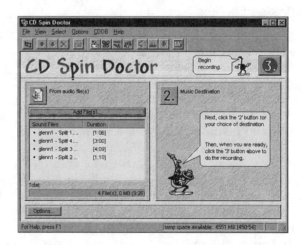

If you want to use any final options, such as the one to close the CD, use the Options button and make your choices now. When you are finally ready to record, make sure your destination pane points to the CD-RW disc and then click the Record to CD-R button in the top right of the application window. A Recording Progress dialog box pops up and displays information about each track as it is read in and written to the CD.

If you chose to leave the CD open in the Recording Options window, after the CD has been burned, you can select the Close CD Now button in pane number 2 to finish the job. Or, if you want to add more to the CD at a later time, leave it open. Remember, if you leave the disc open, you can play it in only a CD-RW drive, or a CD-ROM that can read open discs. You must close the CD before you can listen to it in a normal audio CD player.

If you choose to close the CD, the Close CD Now button gives you a last-chance dialog box warning that you cannot add more tracks if you close the CD. Click Close CD and wait a few minutes as the process completes. Because this can take three or four minutes, now is a good time to refill your glass or stretch your legs.

When the Closing CD dialog box disappears, your CD has been burned and is now ready for use.

The Least You Need to Know

➤ Start with a clean source when using analog recordings as input to Spin Doctor.

➤ Use Spin Doctor's cleaning options to do some cleanup work on audio that doesn't play as clearly as it used to.

➤ You can add special audio effects using Spin Doctor. If you are creating your own music, this can be a great benefit of the program.

➤ You can record from almost any kind of analog source—phonograph, cassette player, and microphone—directly to the CD recorder, by way of a temporary file. Or, you can record WAV files and edit them first.

➤ If you only want to copy a CD, use Easy CD Copier instead of Spin Doctor.

➤ If you want to select audio tracks from CDs and no analog input will be used, use Easy CD Creator. Even if you want to use some of the special audio effects in Spin Doctor, you can still use Easy CD Creator to record to the hard drive first, and then re-record the WAV files using Spin Doctor.

Chapter 6

Toss Your VCR: Using Video CD Creator to Create Video CDs

In This Chapter

➤ What is the MPEG standard?

➤ Creating simple sequence video CDs

➤ Creating video CDs with menus

➤ Using the VCD Creator

Ever notice how your older videotapes don't look quite as good as the day they were purchased (or first recorded)? I've been using VHS tape for more than 20 years to store videos I like. One of the problems with videotape, however, is that it suffers from wear and tear and, of course, the ravages of time. The analog format in which the video and audio are recorded on a tape doesn't provide for the complex error correction that can be accomplished when recording digitally.

In this chapter we will look not at digital videotape, but at the process of putting audio and video onto a recordable CD so that you can view it on your computer or most DVD players. Like many of the other chapters in this book, we're using Roxio's Easy CD Creator as the application of choice—it is important to remember that other options are available and that the overall process remains quite similar.

Although your VHS tape might last a few decades, the expected lifetime for recordable CDs is at least 100 years. Barring some major medical breakthroughs, that's long enough for most people! When you use the VCD Creator program of the Easy CD Creator software to make a video CD, there are a few tradeoffs, however. The first is in time, and the second is in quality. A DVD disc can hold an entire movie, along with alternate camera angles and subtitles and so on, but a CD can't provide that kind of capacity. So, if you are planning to put more than about an hour of video on a CD, plan on using two instead.

Secondly, a DVD movie is encoded using an MPEG-2 video standard. Video CDs, however, use MPEG-1 instead. While many differences exist between the two standards, the most important one is in quality. For those wondering what these formats mean, stay tuned as MPEG gets explained in the following sections.

Record Video Too!

Even though you can use MPEG-1 video clips only to create a video CD, don't forget that you can still record video in MPEG-2 format and use Easy CD Creator to copy the files to a recordable CD. That enables you to still recall the MPEG-2 files and use a suitable program to display them. They won't be usable in a DVD player, but on your computer, you should have no problems.

Until DVD recorders become available at a reasonable price, and a means is found to legally make copies of DVDs, given their copy protection schemes, I guess you'll have to settle for second best: using CD-R technology.

White Book?

The White book describes the standard format for making a video CD. By creating a standard CD format, various manufacturers can produce players that can use the CDs.

How Do You Play Video CDs?

The video CD—let's start calling this a VCD to save space—that you can create using Roxio's Video CD Creator follows the standards set forth in the White book of standards for CDs. For a quick overview of the White book, take a look at Appendix A, "A Quick Overview of the Book Standards."

Your VCD should play in any DVD player installed in your computer or on an ordinary DVD player connected to your TV set. Note that your mileage might vary, so it's good practice to perform a test before you spend a lot of time and money creating VCDs that might not work. Particularly, if you have an older DVD player, you might not be able to play a VCD using it.

You can run into the same kind of problem when trying to play CD-R audio discs on older CD players. Sometimes they just don't work.

The VCD should also work in a CD-I player, if you have one. These are usually used for commercial purposes, so if that's your business, you can use Video CD Creator to make discs.

What Is MPEG and Who Are These Motion Picture Experts, Anyway?

The term *MPEG* comes from the standards body that created the MPEG standards: the Motion Picture Experts Group. This body has released several versions of MPEG standards, proving that even the "experts" can't get it right on the first try. For creating a true White book–compliant VCD, you will need to use MPEG-1. This is an important thing to remember when you decide to buy a video capture card to transfer videotapes or other recorded material to your computer for the purposes of creating a VCD.

Buying a Video Capture Card

Before you can worry about recording video using your CD burner, you need to worry about putting video on your PC. Unless you're downloading video from the Internet or recording from a camera attached to your PC, you need a video capture card. Most video cards that I've seen in the stores lately can save a captured video in several formats. If you have a card that doesn't support saving the video file in MPEG-1 format, you're not out of luck yet. If you have a video editing program, you might be able to read in a video file in one format and then save it as MPEG-1. Although these boards generally do include an editing program of some kind, they're not always the best, and buying a quality capture board or editing program isn't always cheap!

You have several options when it comes to purchasing a video capture device. You can get an internal card to put inside your computer, or you can buy an external device that hooks up to the back of your computer via a cable, usually of the USB (Universal Serial Bus) variety. If you're comfortable working with the hardware in your computer, making a purchase and getting it all set up should be no problem. But for those who prefer to just let the magic happen, you'll need the help of that techno-geek friend of yours or the store where you buy the capture board.

Converting File Formats

As I said just a few paragraphs ago, you'll have to get your video clip files into MPEG-1 format. To make matters a little more complicated, variations on the MPEG-1 format exist, specified in levels. The one you'll need to worry about is the one used for a

White book VCD. When you save a file using an editor, look for a "file type" option that specifies a VCD format. For example, one popular program gives me the choice of NTSC VCD 352x240 NTSC (29.97 f/s), which is suitable for a VCD.

Bizarre Codes?

For the previous example, the key letters to look for are *VCD*. But, for the curious, *NTSC* refers to the type of video signal used to display the image. Ever watched a TV in North America? That signal is NTSC. Many other countries use different signals. The 29.97 is the number of frames per second for the video clip. A video image is really just a series of still frames shown very quickly to create the illusion of motion. North American television shows 30 of these frames each second. So why does my software say 29.97 instead of 30? Well, if I ever meet the programmers, I'll have to ask.

Several editors are available on the market, and I don't want to make any recommendations. However, keep in mind that most video capture cards come with additional bonus software. Sometimes you'll find a game CD, and sometimes you'll find video editing software. If you want one more than the other then it pays to read the whole package!

Creating a Video CD

The VCD Creator program gives you a quick and easy way to create VCDs using your CD-RW drive. As with the other Roxio programs that are part of the 4.0 Deluxe version (unfortunately this does not come with the 3.0 version), you can start up Video CD Creator by using the Desktop icon or the Start menu. To get the program up and running using the Start menu, use the following steps:

1. Click Start, Roxio Easy CD Creator 4, Features.

2. Near the bottom of the Features submenu you should see Video CD Creator. Click it.

3. Finally, the VCD Creator window appears, with the Video CD Creator Wizard sitting on top of it.

Using the Desktop icon (Create CD), you simply select Photo & Video from the first menu that pops up; then, from the second menu, you click Video CD. After you make this selection, the VCD Creator window pops up, and, just as in the Start menu method, the Video CD Creator Wizard appears on the screen (see Figure 6.1).

Figure 6.1

The Video CD Creator Wizard can help simplify the process of creating a VCD.

Two ways are available to create Video CDs. You can use the program itself, or you can use this wizard. Although easier, the wizard does limit what you can do with the program, so go ahead and dismiss this wizard dialog box using the Cancel button. This way we can get straight into the VCD Creator program itself, which really isn't that difficult to use in the first place.

Using the VCD Creator

Even though the Wizard might be an easy method for creating simple VCDs, you might find using the program directly saves time if you are familiar with it and have a specific goal in mind.

Between Tracks

Go Away, Mr. Wizard!

To keep the wizard from popping up every time you use Video CD Creator, you can select the check box named Do Not Run Wizard at Startup from the wizard's first dialog box. You can re-enable the Wizard at startup by using the Preferences option in the File menu of the main program.

Figure 6.2 shows the VCD Creator program. Here you can see the recognizable File, Edit, and View menus. In addition, menus are available for Video CD and Playback. Help, as always, is there if you need it. So long as you have this book around, hopefully you won't ever need to use the Help option.

Figure 6.2

Use the VCD Creator program to create the VCD layout and burn the VCD.

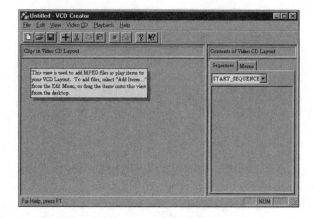

The pane on the left side of the program window is titled Clips in Video CD Layout. After you start adding segments of video (clips) to the layout, they show up in this pane. On the right side of the program window, you can see the Contents of Video CD Layout pane, which has two tabs. The first, Sequences, is where the order in which the video clips will play is determined. The second tab, called Menus, enables you to add menus to the CD so the viewer can switch between clips just like song tracks on an audio CD.

Setting Program Preferences

As with many applications, you can set certain options for the program to customize it for your needs. The Preferences option on the File menu brings up the dialog box shown in Figure 6.3. This enables you to make decisions that affect some aspects of how the program works.

Figure 6.3

The VCD Creator Preferences dialog box gives you control over the program.

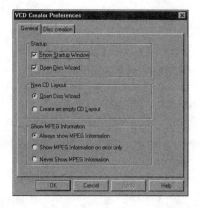

This dialog box has two tabs. In Figure 6.3, you can see the General tab and the preferences it enables you to set. These preferences fall under the groupings Startup, New CD Layout, and Show MPEG Information.

You can control the following program Startup options:

➤ **Show Startup Window**—If selected, this just means that the program's logo will be shown when the application is first started up. I know, big yeah! Feel free to disable this one.

➤ **Open Disc Wizard**—This is the check box you select or deselect, depending on whether you want the Wizard to be your main interface when you launch the program. If you're more comfortable with the Wizard, keep this box enabled.

Preferences you can set to control what happens when you select New CD Layout from the File menu are

➤ **Open Disc Wizard**—If this option is selected, every time you want to create a new CD layout, the Wizard pops up to walk you through it. You won't have to restart the program to get the Wizard running. For this to work, however, you also must select Open Disc Wizard in the Startup selections just discussed.

➤ **Create an Empty CD Layout**—If you select this, instead of the Wizard, the main VCD Creator program becomes the standard method you use to create the video CD.

Under the Show MPEG Information section, you can control when the MPEG information sheet is displayed.

➤ **Always Show MPEG Information**—If you select this, you'll see the MPEG information sheet for all files you choose to add. This includes files that meet the White book VCD specifications as well as those that contain errors.

➤ **Show MPEG Information on Error Only**—If you get tired of clicking a lot of MPEG information sheets that show good files, selecting this preference causes the program to show the MPEG information sheet only when a bad file crops up.

Similar to Easy CD Creator, when VCD burns a disc, it places temporary files on your hard disk to make the process run smoothly. Under the second tab on the VCD Creator Preferences dialog box, you can control the temporary files created by the program. The default, as you can see in Figure 6.4, is to use the Windows TEMP directory, which already exists on Windows systems. However, you can deselect this check box and add other locations.

Figure 6.4

You can control the disk locations used for temporary storage.

If you do elect to create other directories instead of using the default, another dialog box will pop up and enable you to enter the path and filename for the temporary file. If you want, you can also set a limit as to the amount of space that can be used. You can add more temporary locations as needed.

Generally, unless you really understand how to navigate your hard drive, create and move folders, and so on, you are better off leaving these options alone.

Creating the Video CD Layout and Adding Items

Starting with a clean layout—that is, you've just opened the program or you've selected New VCD Layout from the File menu—you can add video clips to the layout you want to create. To add a clip, click the Edit menu and then select Add Item. This brings up the Add Play Items dialog box shown in Figure 6.5, from which you can select the files that contain your MPEG data.

Figure 6.5

Use the Add New Play Items dialog box to add video clips to your layout.

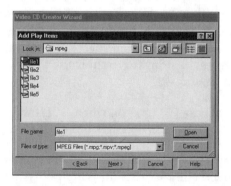

To select a file for inclusion in the layout, double-click it in this dialog box or highlight it by clicking it once and then clicking the Open button. Continue using the Add Play Items dialog box until you have added all the video clips you want on the VCD.

Each time you add a file using this method, an MPEG Information dialog box appears, telling you whether the clip to be added to the layout meets the MPEG-1 specifications laid out in that pesky White book for making VCDs. If VCD Creator has no complaints, this dialog box has a nice, friendly, green check mark at the top. If it gets finicky and doesn't like your files, however, a red X will appear. From there, you need to look to the file information beneath it to find out what it doesn't like. A yellow exclamation point next to an item indicates that it will probably be okay, but is a little off the standard. A big, red X character next to an item indicates that it most likely will not be playable in a DVD player (or a CDI player) if you include it in the layout.

You'd think these standards guys could make the whole process a bit more reliable... but you'd be wrong. After all, if they got it right the first time, who would pay them to fix it?

Click the Add button if the clip is okay and VCD Creator adds it to your layout. If you want to use a clip that does not meet the standards, click the Add Anyway button that takes the place of the Add button. Just don't say we didn't warn you! After you've added the clip, it appears in the Video CD Layout pane as a small box with the clip's file name on it.

Editing or Removing Items from the Layout

Removing an item from the layout is as easy as either highlighting it (clicking it once) and then selecting the scissors icon from the toolbar or selecting Delete from the Edit menu. Either way, the program prompts you before it actually deletes the item from the layout. If you change your mind later, you can always put it back in again. Other options under the Edit menu enable you to cut, copy, and paste items. Sometimes you might want to use the same clip more than once in the layout. One way of doing so is to add it more than once. But, you can save a little time and effort if you use Copy from the Edit menu and then use Paste to insert another copy of the particular clip in the layout. Remember that at this point, we're working with only the layout itself, not the actual files. Thus, editing a layout doesn't have to take a lot of time.

The Playback Menu

If, at the last minute of your production, you want to look at either a single clip or the entire layout (if you have created a sequence for it), you can do so by using the Playback menu found at the top of the VCD Creator application window. The menu gives you two options. First, you can choose VCD Layout to play the entire video production you've created with your layout. Or, you can take the second option, Selected Clip. This enables you to view any single video clip in the layout. Simply click the clip once to highlight it and then select the second option from the Playback menu.

When you've made your selection, a small window opens to play the clip. Additionally, a set of standard VCR-like controls appear that you can use to control the playback, as you can see in Figure 6.6. If you select to play just one clip, the Play, Pause, and Stop buttons are available. If you choose to play the entire VCD layout, buttons are added so you can skip to the next track or go back to the previous track. If you have defined a menu for the VCD (to be covered soon), the number keys on the controls enable you to jump to the clip for each of the menu's numbered entries.

Figure 6.6

The MPEG Playback dialog box provides the controls you can use to playback a sequence or an entire VCD layout.

Note that until you create a playback sequence (as covered in the next section), you won't be able to use the VCD Layout option from this menu.

Set the Order of Play for the Images—Creating a Playback Sequence

For VCD Creator to make a VCD, you must create a sequence in which the items in the layout will be played. You do this by selecting each clip in the Clips pane (on the left) and adding it to the Contents pane (on the right). You can create two kinds of sequences for your VCD. The first is a simple sequence, in which all video clips are played in the order they are found in the particular sequence, from start to finish. The second method involves creating a menu that enables the viewer to select the clip to watch.

Creating a Simple Sequence

The Simple Sequence method plays all video clips in the layout sequence from start to end. For many home-made videos that have been captured and made ready for a VCD, this is an appropriate choice.

To start the process of creating a sequence, click the Sequences tab in the Contents pane and then ensure that START_SEQUENCE—the default here—is visible in the drop-down menu that shows up on the tab. First, we'll add a clip that will serve as the start sequence that plays when the VCD first runs. When you create menu sequences, this drop-down menu will allow you to switch between them.

Now, to add a clip, simply drag it from the Clips pane back to Contents, in the area underneath START_SEQUENCE. The item should now appear in this pane.

Continue dragging each clip, being sure to place them in the order you want them in the final playback of the VCD. Use the vertical scrollbar in either pane to get to clips that don't fit in the current view. Figure 6.7 shows the VCD Creator window with clips added to the simple sequence. If you change your mind about the order of the clips, simply use your mouse to drag them around in the Contents pane until you get the order you want.

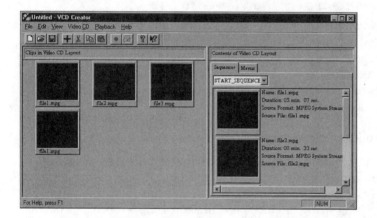

Figure 6.7

The VCD Creator enables you to specify the order of video clips in a simple sequence.

Notice that information about the clips changes when moved between the left and right panes. In the Clips pane, VCD Creator attaches the filename to the clip's icon. In the Contents pane, however, the clip icon is not directly labeled. The filename and additional information about the clip's size, format, and source file (the file on your hard drive that the clip comes from) are listed to the right of the icon. Because filenames don't always match the subject matter of a particular clip, you might want to change its name to something more recognizable using its Properties page.

To get to the Properties page for a clip, simply right-click it and select Properties from the menu that pops up. The first field on the page is called Item Name. Simply type over the existing name in this field and then click the OK button. The clip is now displayed in the Sequences pane with the new name. In the Clips pane, however, notice that the clip is still identified by its filename.

Saving the CD Layout to a File

Now that you've gotten this far, you can create the disc, gear up for creating a menu sequence for the VCD, or save the layout for future use. To save the layout you have created, use the Save or Save As option from the File menu. Using Save As enables you to specify the path and filename for the layout file. Use Save if you have previously saved this layout and are simply updating it.

When you want open a saved layout, use the Open VCD Layout option from the File menu. You'll have to know where you saved the file, so keeping them all in one place is a good idea. When you open a saved layout, you can make changes to it and save it under the same name or a new name (using Save As).

If you are ready to create a VCD using this simple sequence, jump ahead to the section called "Starting the Recording Process." If you want to learn about creating simple menus for your VCD, stay where you are and we'll talk about that in the next section.

Creating a Menu Sequence for the Viewer to Use

The VCD Creator program enables you to create simple, one-level menus the viewer can use to navigate between the clips on the VCD. The best way to think of these menus is like a chapter list on a DVD movie. On a DVD, this list enables you to advance to various sections of the movie by choosing which part (clip) of the movie you want to watch. Usually, these chapters won't all fit on the same page, so you can use your remote to scroll through to more screens that contain more chapters. Although the method of control might vary based on the type of player you are using, a VCD menu works in much the same way.

To some, it might seem like adding a menu is more trouble than it's worth, but adding a simple menu can be a good idea if you have a lot of video clips on the VCD and want them to be easily accessed. After all, you don't want to torture the viewer by making her watch a long string of video clips that she has seen before when a menu can jump right to the important stuff—then again, if it's your in-laws watching, maybe you do.

Don't Get Burned

Important Differences Between a DVD Chapter List and a VCD Menu

Although the comparison to a DVD chapter list makes it easier to understand a VCD menu, they don't work exactly the same. If you select a chapter on a DVD, the movie picks up from that point and plays through to the end. With a VCD, using the menu to play a clip will play only that individual clip. You can, however, group a set of clips under one menu selection if you want.

To create a VCD with a simple menu you first create a START_SEQUENCE sequence that will play each time the VCD is first played. Click the Menus tab in the Contents pane (see Figure 6.8).

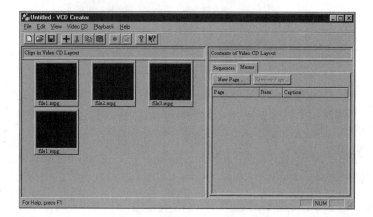

Figure 6.8

The Menus tab enables you to create a one-level menu structure for your viewers.

Arcane CD Speak

What's a Page?

A page is where you put the menu items a user needs to advance to specific clips on the VCD. If necessary, you can use more than one page to apply to different groups of clips. After you've created a menu page, it appears on the Menus tab. You can right-click and select Properties to get to the Properties page for this menu page. Here, you can select how many times the background menu clip is played and the number of seconds between each play, if any.

As you can see in Figure 6.8, two basic selections can be used: New Page or Remove Page. To start the first page of a menu, click the New Page button. Figure 6.9 shows the first dialog box you can use to select a background for the page. You can choose one of the video clips from your layout or click the Add From File button if you want to choose another MPEG file. This allows you to choose from a file that wasn't added to the Layout pane. Note that choosing a file here will not put it into the Layout pane; it will just include it in the menu you are creating. This clip, video, or still image should show the menu selections to the user, so you need to use a video or photo editing program to create the file used here.

Figure 6.9

The first dialog box asks you to select a file to be used for the menu background.

When you've made your selection, click the Next button. In Figure 6.10, you can see that the next step for creating a menu page is to enter the number of items that will be in the menu. In this figure we have entered the number 3. This means that we will now have to create three play sequences, one for each selection. When the viewer is using this VCD, he will be able to enter a number (usually using a remote control) to select each menu choice. You can enter up to 99 menu selections, if needed!

Figure 6.10

Enter the number of choices you want on the menu page.

Turn the Page

If you create more than one menu page, the viewer can use the left and right arrow keys on the controls of the VCD player to move through menu pages.

After selecting the number of menu items you want, click the Next button.

A dialog box now appears that enables you to see and edit which menu number is attached to which play sequence. If you'll remember, we started out creating the START_SEQUENCE, which plays when the CD is first started. After you've decided on the number of menu choices you want, you must create a *play sequence* of clips for each menu choice.

The names of these play sequences are set by default according to sequential order, so menu item 1 defaults to PLAY_SEQUENCE1, item two to PLAY_SEQUENCE2, and so on (see Figure 6.11). In addition to not being particularly descriptive, this will probably bore the reader of the menu. Fortunately, you can change them by clicking the Edit button.

Figure 6.11

*You can use the Edit but-
ton to change the text
associated with a menu
selection.*

When you are done, click the Finish button. You'll find yourself back in the VCD
Creator window. Now, however, you will see your menu page on screen.

Starting the Recording Process

When you're ready to create the VCD using the layout you have compiled, all that's
left to do to kick off the recording process is click the button on the toolbar that has a
large red dot on it.

However, before you start recording, you can use an option to check the contents of the
CD layout to ensure that all the files can still be found. This is a good idea if you are
using a saved layout, or one you have made a lot of changes to. Select Validate Layout
from the Video CD menu, and the program will perform this quick examination.

If everything checks out okay, you are ready to record. You can either click the red
button or select (from the Video CD menu) the option titled Create CD from Layout.
Note that in this same menu you can create a disk image of the VCD on your hard
disk. This option can be useful when making multiple copies of the same layout.

After you start the recording process, the CD Creation Setup dialog box appears. This
dialog box is used by most of the Roxio programs to enable you to make some decisions about how the disc is to be recorded. You should take the default for a VCD for
most of the items in this box. You can, however, select to make more than one copy
of the VCD. If you are just starting to use a CD-RW drive to create a VCD, you might
want to use one of the Test options. You can tell the program to test write to the
recording drive, or you can tell the program to perform the test and then automatically create the CD if the test is okay. Remember that it takes just as long to test a CD
as it does to write to it, so this can add a lot of time to the creation process. On the
other hand, it can also save you from turning a disc into a coaster. If you're pretty
sure your recorder won't have any problems writing the disc, just leave the radio button labeled Create CD selected. Finally, you should make sure the program closes the
VCD when it's finished.

Click the OK button to start burning the VCD.

If you haven't already inserted a blank recordable CD, VCD Creator prompts you to
insert one. When you do, you see the standard CD Creation Process dialog box that

shows the progress of the recording session. As you can see in Figure 6.12, this dialog box looks and works the same as the one you get when recording CDs using Easy CD Creator.

Figure 6.12

The familiar CD Creation Process dialog box shows the progress when burning a VCD.

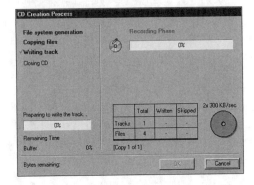

The recording process runs through the usual recording phases. If you want more details on this process, see Chapter 4, "Using Easy CD Creator to Make Data CDs." However, the only important thing is for the recording to succeed. You'll know this is complete when the CD Created Successfully text appears, along with the big green check mark, in the Creation Process dialog box.

The Least You Need to Know

➤ If you want to create a video CD, you must have MPEG-1 files. These aren't the best quality video files available today, but they can fit a lot more video onto a lot less space.

➤ VCD Creator has a Clips pane where you choose which video clips to include in your layout and a Contents pane that lets you choose in what order you want to burn those clips to a VCD.

➤ The VCD Creator program enables you to create menus to make playback easier for your viewers.

➤ A VCD will play in your computer's DVD, on most set-top DVD players, or on specialized VCD players such as the CD-I.

Chapter 7

Using Your CD Recorder Like a Hard Disk

In This Chapter

➤ What is packet writing?

➤ Using read/write discs (CD-RW) or write-once discs (CD-R)

➤ Formatting the disc

➤ Erasing files and reformatting a disc

➤ Making a CD-R disc usable by ordinary CD-ROM drives

In earlier chapters, we talked about writing tracks and sessions, and the limitations on what you can write to a recordable CD. Using packet-writing software, the rules can be bent a little. Instead of having to write an entire track at once, you can use the recordable disc much like an ordinary hard disk. The DirectCD program from Roxio takes advantage of this feature and can be very useful.

Packet writing enables small amounts of data to be written to the CD simultaneously. Instead of a whole track of data, small chunks can be written. This takes up a little more space on the disc, but the convenience it provides to the user makes up for this. Using a CD-RW or CD-R disc as if it were a hard disk means you can use your everyday Windows applications and utilities to write to the disc. So, when using Microsoft Word, for example, you can use the Save or Save As option to save your latest masterpiece directly to a CD.

CD-R, CD-RW, DirectCD, and You

As you probably already know, two main types of recordable CDs exist: CD-R discs, which are write-once, and CD-RW discs, which allow you to write, erase, and write again. You can use both of these kinds of recordable CDs with DirectCD. The difference between them is cost: CD-RW discs are much more expensive than write-once technology. Their cost is justified, however, if you need a disc that can be updated frequently.

RW = No Coasters

Another advantage of using the RW discs is that if a problem occurs during recording to the disc, you can always erase it and start over. With a CD-R disc, if the write fails for any reason, the disc is toast.

Both types of discs enable you to update or modify data on the disc. However, the CD-RW drive can erase RW data that's no longer needed. The CD-R disc simply marks as deleted the blocks of data that are changed and writes new blocks of data instead. Of course, because the "deleted" material is technically still on the disc, if you use CD-R discs with DirectCD, you'll eventually run out of space if you modify the information too much.

Using DirectCD from Roxio

To bring up DirectCD, click on Start, Programs, Roxio Easy CD Creator 4 and then Create CD. Select Data from the menu presented. The next menu allows you to select which program in Easy CD Creator you want to use. Click DirectCD.

For DirectCD to work properly, it must prep the recordable disc in your RW drive. If the disc in your drive has not been set up when you launch DirectCD, a wizard pops up. This wizard will configure the disc it finds so that it can be used with the program. Therefore, if you insert a disc that has already been through this process before, the wizard won't pop up. Instead, you can simply start using your disc just as if it were a floppy or hard disk installed in your computer.

Figure 7.1 shows the wizard's opening dialog box. Click Next after you've inserted a CD-RW or CD-R disc in your computer's CD-RW drive.

Figure 7.1

The Roxio DirectCD Wizard pops up if this is the first time the CD-RW or CD-R has been used with DirectCD.

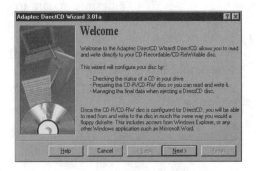

After examining the disc inserted in your CD recorder, DirectCD then shows you information about all the CD-RW drives installed in your computer and the type of disc inserted. In Figure 7.2, you can see that only one CD-RW drive exists on this computer and that a read/write disc is in the drive.

Figure 7.2

This display shows that a read/write disc is inserted in the CD-RW drive.

Under the Media Status section of this display, you can see that, although the CD-RW disc is blank, it has not yet been formatted by the DirectCD program. Until formatting has occurred, you cannot give the disc a label name or use it to store any data. The Properties button on this screen shows you information about the disc and brings up a Properties sheet that contains three tabs: General, Settings, and DirectCD Wizard.

The General Properties Tab

There's not a whole lot for you to worry about under this tab. Here, you can see the volume label (essentially the disc's name), which is blank before a disc has been formatted (see Figure 7.3). Also, a display shows the amount of free and used space on the disc, which is probably the only useful information you'll need from the screen. Finally, a field shows what the disc's file system is. Let DirectCD worry about this one.

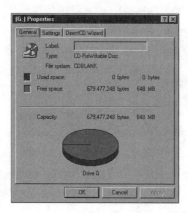

Figure 7.3

The General tab on the Properties sheet is useful for showing the amount of free space on the disc.

107

The Settings Tab

This tab, shown in Figure 7.4, first shows you information about the CD-RW drive. The first set of fields grouped under Device show the drive type and name (model), along with information about the drive's firmware. You can safely ignore this information.

Figure 7.4

The Settings tab enables you to select the read/ write speed used for this disc.

Next, comes a brief description of the media inserted in the drive. If for any reason DirectCD can't use the disc you have inserted, it will say so here.

Finally, at the bottom of this dialog box is something you can actually have control over. As you can see, this section lets you select the read and write speeds for this disc. The values available in these drop-down menus depend on the capabilities of your CD-RW drive, so you cannot actually choose an incorrect setting. However, you will probably do best to take whatever the default values are for these and adjust them later, based on your experience. For example, most likely you will be able to set the read speed much higher than the write speed. This is because reading data is a much simpler process for the drive than writing or erasing it is.

Between Tracks

Lowering the Write Speed

If you have problems writing to the disc, try selecting a slower write speed of 1x and increasing incrementally until you get up to a speed you can reliably use. If you don't get a good disc write at 1x, something is probably wrong with your disc or the drive you are using.

The DirectCD Wizard Tab

This tab starts out with two options that are useful only if a CD-R disc is being used (see Figure 7.5). The first is to make the disc compatible with a standard CD-ROM player. Thus, after you've finished writing the disc, you can use it in any CD-ROM drive, and not just in the CD-RW drive you used to record it. The second option you can set for a CD-R disc is to have the Eject Disc wizard prompt you before you ejecting a DirectCD disc.

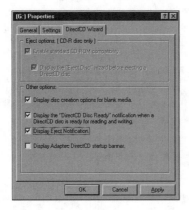

Figure 7.5

You can set options for CD-R media, along with other options for the wizard.

Other options in this tab apply to general wizard functions. The options you can select include

➤ **Display disc creation options for blank media**—If this is selected, when you insert a blank CD in the CD recorder drive, the Easy CD Creator menu will automatically pop up so you can get started quickly. If it's not selected, after you insert a blank CD, you'll have to start the program yourself, using either the Start menu or the Desktop icon.

➤ **Display the "DirectCD Disc Ready" notification...**—Selecting this check box causes a prompt to inform you when a DirectCD disc (a disc that DirectCD has already formatted) has been inserted in the drive. This is similar to the first option, but involves detection of a recordable CD that has been formatted for use by DirectCD.

➤ **Display Eject Notification**—Selecting this causes a message to be displayed when you eject a disc.

➤ **Display Roxio DirectCD startup banner**—Selecting this option causes a banner announcing the DirectCD program to be displayed when you boot your computer.

The first option is a sensible one. By selecting this, you don't have to click the desktop icon to start up the Roxio menu sequence. Instead, as soon as the blank CD is detected, the menu pops up by itself. Imagine the hundreds of left-clicks you can save each year by using this option! You'll have to find another exercise program.

109

Even though it doesn't actually affect how the disc gets used, the second option is a good one to use also. After you've inserted a disc in the drive, a short time might elapse before the system recognizes the disc. Using this option lets you know when DirectCD has recognized the disc so you can begin using it.

The last two options might or might not prove useful to you. If you are going to eject a disc, why do you need to have a message pop up telling you so? Why would you want the Roxio DirectCD banner displayed during the system boot? Well, if you are using DirectCD in an office environment and move from PC to PC, this might be useful. You'll know quickly whether the PC you are about to use is set up to use DirectCD discs. If you're using DirectCD at home, however, just disable these two options to get them out of your way.

After you've finished reviewing these property pages, click the Apply button if you've made any changes, or just click the OK button to continue. This will put you back in the Drive Information dialog box. From here you can just click Next to continue the process of setting up the disc for use by DirectCD.

Formatting a Disc Before Its First Use

The next dialog box, called Format Disc, simply prompts you to click Next to start the formatting process. After you click the Next button, the Name Your Disc dialog box appears (see Figure 7.6). Here, you can give the disc a label (name) that makes it easy to distinguish from others you create.

Figure 7.6

Give the disc a label here. When you use Windows Explorer, you'll see this name to help you identify the disc.

Use up to 11 characters in the label, but make it something meaningful that you'll recognize later. You also can use the only check box found on this dialog box to enable compression on the disc. Compressing information makes it take up less space on a disc, but it also requires you to be running DirectCD to read the disc. Don't use this option if you plan to read the disc on another computer that doesn't have DirectCD installed.

Notice in this figure that the Next button is not available—it's grayed-out. Instead, use the Finish button to start the format. One final confirmation dialog appears to give you a final opportunity to change your mind. If this is the first time DirectCD has formatted this disc, this prompt tells you that it will most likely take an hour or more to format this disc. If you have the time to spare, click the OK button and we're off!

During the progress of the format a dialog box enables you to see the elapsed time, as well as an estimate of how much longer you'll have to wait until the disc has been formatted.

When the formatting process has completed successfully, you'll get a dialog box telling you that the disc is now ready for read/write operations using ordinary Windows applications. This is shown in Figure 7.7.

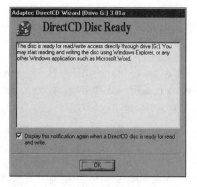

Figure 7.7

The DirectCD Disc Ready dialog box tells you the formatting process is complete.

Click OK to start using the disc.

If you bring up the Windows Explorer and examine the properties of the disc you've just formatted, you'll see that you lost a little real estate during the process. Because DirectCD program has to use up some of the space on your disc to so that it can use it like a hard drive, your CD doesn't have as much free space as it did before the format. In my case, a 650MB CD (the normal 74-minute disc) was left with 558MB of space after the format. While that is a fairly large chunk of space, it's the price you pay for the convenience of not needing Easy CD Creator and all that data layout stuff to write to your CDs!

Using the DirectCD Disc

Once formatted, you can treat the DirectCD disc just like it is a hard drive on your system. You can save files to it, copy files to it, or use other commands from application programs. In Figure 7.8, you can see that a disc I formatted and named "storage1" is in my CD-RW CD drive.

Figure 7.8

The G: drive contains a disc labeled "storage1", which is accessible through most Windows applications, such as Windows Explorer.

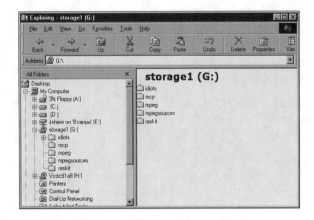

As you can see, I've already written some files and folders to this disc. If you are using CD-R media, remember that, even though you can mark a file or folder as deleted, that doesn't free up any disc space because as the data is not actually removed from the disc. So, if you are going to use CD-R discs under DirectCD, it's better to use them to copy only data that you do not need to modify or delete. A good example for this is copying report files to the CD-R disc for long-term storage.

Given that I devoted a lot of pages in Chapter 4, "Using Easy CD Creator to Make Data CDs," to showing you how to make a data CD, you might wonder why you would want to use DirectCD and have to go through all that formatting mumbo-jumbo. The truth is that, depending on your needs, you might not want to. However, don't underestimate the convenience of having the ability to add data to a disc from ordinary Windows programs.

Ejecting a DirectCD Disc

When you use the eject button on the CD drive a dialog box pops up after the disc has been physically ejected. The information displayed tells you that you can now use the disc on other CD-RW drives, and on CD-ROM drives if they have the Roxio UDF Reader software installed. Click the OK button to dismiss this dialog box.

If you have selected to use the Eject Disc wizard—from the Properties page—*and* if you are using CD-R media, when ejecting the disc you have the option of closing the CD so that information is written to it that makes it compatible with most ordinary CD-ROM drives without the need for UDF software (see Figure 7.9). This can be done for only CD-R media, not for CD-RW.

When you eject the disc, the Eject Wizard pops up and reminds you that you can either keep adding data to the disc or go ahead and close it and make it available for use on ordinary CD-ROM drives. This dialog box is shown in Figure 7.9.

Getting a UDF Reader

The Roxio UDF Reader is a program that enables you to make use of DirectCD discs on other computers that don't have DirectCD installed on them. You can download it for free from www.roxio.com.

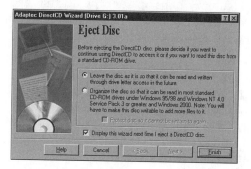

Figure 7.9

You can elect to close the disc and make it available to other CD-ROM drives.

Come Back, Mr. Wizard!

If you forget to make these selections on the DirectCD Wizard tab, you can always do so later. Just right-click the CD's icon in your system tray (next to the clock on your taskbar). Select Properties and then click the DirectCD Wizard tab and make the changes before you eject the disc.

If you choose the second option in Figure 7.9—to make the disc usable by most CD-ROM drives—you can also select the check box under that selection that will mark the disc so that it cannot be written to in the future. If you don't select this option, it is still possible to reopen the disc for writing. See "Reopening a CD-R Disc After Closing" later in this chapter.

After you make your choice, click the Finish button to let the program write the necessary data to make the disc readable and close the disc. Another dialog box shows you the program's progress as it writes these files to the CD-R. Because of the size of the files necessary to close the disc (about 22MB), be sure that you leave adequate space on the CD-R disc before you eject it using this method.

After this process has finished, a final dialog box tells you that the disc is now ready to be used on other CD-ROM drives. Click OK and start using your disc!

Re-Inserting a DirectCD-Formatted Disc

When you are ready to start using a disc that has already been formatted by DirectCD, all you have to do is re-insert it in the CD-RW drive. The same DirectCD Disc Ready dialog box you saw in Figure 7.7 pops up after the disc has been recognized. The information here tells you the drive letter—in case you've forgotten. You can click the OK button and then once again start using the disc just like you could before.

Don't Get Burned

Exception to the Rule

This process applies only if you are using an RW disc or an R disc that you have not closed (using the steps in the previous section).

Note, however, that this dialog box will not pop up if you insert the DirectCD formatted disc in an ordinary CD-ROM drive on the computer. Because it is available only for reading on such a drive, it appears just like any other CD when you use Windows applications or utilities. You just can't write to it.

Erasing a CD-RW Disc

Sometimes when dealing with CD media, wiping the slate clean is just easier than cleaning up a mess. You obviously cannot erase a CD-R disc because it is write-once media. However, you can erase the data on a CD-RW disc and start using it again from scratch.

Of course, you can erase files the usual way—just delete them as you would any file or folder on your hard drive. However, an easier method is available that you can use to erase a disc that has a lot of data on it without having to select all the files to delete. Just right-click the CD's icon in the system tray. The three menu choices here are always Eject, Format, and Properties if you're using a CD-RW disc. Just select Format to start the long formatting process again.

In Figure 7.10 you can see that you have more choices when formatting a disc that has been previously formatted.

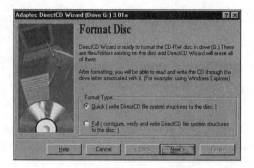

Figure 7.10

You can reformat a CD-RW disc to erase all the data.

Fortunately, reformatting a used RW disc is not the hour-long process that formatting a new one is. Here you can select a Quick format, which just writes a small amount of data to the disc that controls the file system. Or, if you want, you can select the Full option. This option takes a lot longer, but that is because it writes the entire file system to the disc from scratch, and wipes out data as it goes.

Both options also prompt you to enter a label for the disc, just as you did when you formatted it for the first time.

Reopening a CD-R Disc After Closing

If you have a CD-R disc that you closed in order to make it readable by ordinary CD-ROM drives, you can—provided space is available on the disc—still open it again and write more data to it. That is, unless you chose to close it using the check box that prevents DirectCD from ever writing to the disc again.

Insert the CD-R disc in the CD recorder drive and start the DirectCD program again. You'll see the Welcome message that is the first dialog box that the DirectCD Wizard shows; click Next (refer to Figure 7.1). The Drive Information dialog box tells you that the status of the CD-R media is read-only (see Figure 7.11). However, it also tells you that you can continue to reopen the CD to make it writable again by DirectCD.

Figure 7.11

You can reopen a disc you've made ready for ordinary CD-ROMs.

Click the Next button to continue. The Make Disc Writable dialog box appears, informing you that it will reopen the disc for reading/writing by DirectCD. To do so, click Next. If you've changed your mind, click Cancel.

Short Cut

To get to this Make Disc Writable dialog box more quickly, simply right-click the taskbar icon for the CD drive and select *Make Writable* from the options presented! Because DirectCD can't close RW discs to begin with, this option won't appear if you have one of these in your drive.

If you decide to go ahead, you are given the chance to give a new label to the disc, or keep the old one. In this Name Your Disc dialog box, click Finish when you've made your choice. The DirectCD program then makes the disc available by writing some additional data structures on the disc. You'll see one more dialog box letting you know the disc is ready to go.

The Least You Need to Know

➤ You can use DirectCD with CD-R or CD-RW discs.

➤ DirectCD has to format a disc before it can use it.

➤ Once formatted, the CD acts just like a hard disk when used in the RW drive.

➤ You can continue to add, modify, and delete files on a CD-RW disc, but you cannot delete (or at least recover space) from an R disc.

➤ You can close CD-R discs so normal CD-ROM drives can read them, but you must also reopen them using DirectCD if you want to add more data to the disc.

Chapter 8

The Easiest Way to Pillage— Copying CDs Using Easy CD Copier

In This Chapter

➤ Copying disc to disc!

➤ Using only your CD-RW drive for copying CDs.

➤ Advanced options can help fine-tune the copying process.

In Chapters 3, "Using Easy CD Creator to Make Audio CDs," 4, "Using Easy CD Creator to Make Data CDs," and 5, "Your Very Own Record Studio: Using the CD Spin Doctor," I showed you how to create your own audio and data CDs by using Easy CD Creator. The Spin Doctor and Easy CD Creators programs make it an easy task to select audio tracks or data files, create a CD layout, and then use the layout to burn a CD using your CD-RW drive.

If all you want to do is make a straight copy of a CD, though, you don't have to go through all that trouble. You don't have to create a CD layout, and you don't have to worry about editing tracks or using special effects such as fade in, fade out, or cross-fade. Indeed, making a copy is much simpler. To sum it up in just a few words, launch Easy CD Copier, insert the CD you want to copy and the blank recordable disc into the correct drives, and click OK—then you're on your way.

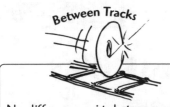

Between Tracks

No difference exists between copying an audio CD or a data CD. In both cases, you simply use Easy CD Creator's CD Copier.

So, why devote a chapter to such a simple process? Well, there are a few twists to this process, and there are some tips I will show you that can make the job easier. However, it really is a simply matter to make a copy of almost any CD, unless it has some sort of copy protection scheme encoded into the data, or unless your particular CD-RW drive has some problems with the CD-R blank media you have purchased.

What Kinds of CDs Can You Copy?

CD Copier allows you to make copies of most kinds of CDs. This includes not only audio and data CDs, but also mixed-mode and CD Extra CDs and other kinds of CDs that are discussed in this book. Some game CDs, however, might prove to be a problem, because of copy protection schemes that are employed by many of the game publishers.

Don't Get Burned

No Get of Jail Free Cards Here

Unless you're already reading this book from your jail cell, you might want to check the "terms and conditions" or other such text that comes with any CD you buy. Although the copyright laws do allow "fair use" copying for audio CDs, the licensing terms for game or software application CDs might prohibit you from doing so. I'd hate to tell you how to create CD copies and then have you send me email from the pokey.

You will know that you have a CD that cannot easily be copied when one of the following things occurs. First, you make a copy, and the copy process appears to succeed. However, when you try to use the copied CD, it doesn't work. This type of problem is particularly frustrating for those of us with slower CD-RW drives (2x or less) because the process usually takes more than an hour. Second, you try to make a copy of a CD and find that CD Copier is incapable of reading the CD, or perhaps just a track on the CD.

A third kind of problem you might run into when trying to copy a CD has nothing to do with copy protection schemes. Some commercial CDs have also been recorded past the 74-minute limit that is the standard. When CD Copier detects that more data is on the source CD than will fit on the blank CD you've installed in the CD recorder, it will eject the blank and tell you to insert a blank disc with a higher capacity.

To solve this problem, you can find 80-minute CD-R blanks at most computer stores. Whether or not they will work in your CD burner depends on your drive, as well as the software you are using. Roxio's CD Copier that is included with the 4.0 Deluxe version will gladly make copies to 80-minute blanks. However, just because CD Copier will work past the 74-minute limit, *that doesn't mean your CD recorder will!* This is a hardware and software issue! Some CD recorder vendors simply assumed that 74 minutes was always going to be the maximum amount of time on a CD and built their drives to operate in that manner.

CD Copier enables you to copy many kinds of CDs. In later chapters, we'll talk about photo CDs and video CDs. These kinds of CDs use a CD format called CD-ROM XA. Some CD-ROM drives don't read these types of discs, so you might run into a problem there.

Another feature, which is covered in Chapter 7, "Using Your CD Recorder Like a Hard Disk," is DirectCD. This is a packet-mode program that enables you to write to CD-R and CD-RW (rewritable CD) blanks a little at a time. However, when you make a copy of a CD that was written this way, it might or might not work. Roxio recommends you look for a CD-ROM drive that has multiread capabilities if you want to copy these sorts of discs.

Copy Protection Schemes Making Life Difficult?

Many kinds of copy protection schemes publishers are now using on audio and software CDs make them difficult or impossible to copy. Some involve formatting the disc a little differently from the standards, whereas others embed data that is easy to detect—if you know where to look for it. This latter kind of problem can be easily implemented by simply screwing up the table of contents. If the program or application knows that the table of contents isn't necessarily correct, but knows how to read it, the original CD works just fine. When copying the CD, however, this kind of thing can make the copy unusable.

Whatever method is employed, just remember that you will simply not be able to copy some CDs due to these protection schemes. We could argue about the pros and cons regarding the need for these schemes, but that won't change anything. If you feel a moral obligation to pull out your soapbox against copy protection, the obvious solution is to write to companies that employ these methods and tell them what you think. Or, just don't buy their software or audio CDs.

For audio CDs, one thing you might try, however, is to extract each audio track to a separate WAV file and then use Easy CD Creator to re-create the CD. Using Easy CD Creator instead of CD Copier enables the program to create its own table of contents and other formatting information on the blank CD.

Making Copies

To start up the CD Copier, you use just about the same methods that you do for starting up Easy CD Creator. If you like using the Start menu, the following steps should get you started using the program:

1. Click Start.
2. Click Programs.
3. Click Roxio Easy CD Creator.
4. Click Create CD.

In Figure 8.1 you can see the menu that Easy CD Creator pops up for you. From this menu, select CD Copier.

Figure 8.1

Select CD Copier from the menu that Easy CD Creator displays.

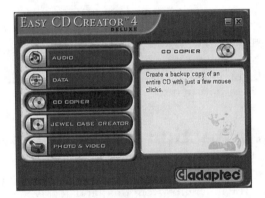

Copying from CD-ROM Drive to a CD-RW Drive

The CD Copier program is much simpler than the Easy CD Creator program. You don't have to select audio tracks, files, or folders. You also don't have to insert more than one CD so that the program can read tracks from each CD. Instead, you only have to place the CD to be copied into the regular CD-ROM drive that's in your computer and insert a CD-R blank into the CD-RW recorder drive. As you can see in Figure 8.2, few options exist for a simple copy.

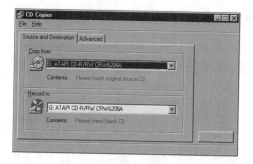

Figure 8.2

The CD Copier program is much simpler than other programs in this suite.

In Figure 8.2 you can see that neither drive has a CD (or a CD-R blank) inserted. If you have just started up the program, this is normal. It will take a few seconds or perhaps a minute, depending on how powerful your computer is, before the CDs are detected. If, however, you have yet to put the CDs in the appropriate drives, now is a good time to do it!

Also note in Figure 8.2 that both the source and the destination drives use the same drive letter: G. This is incorrect for most operations. After you have inserted the CDs in the right drives, use the down arrow located on the right of each device display to select the correct drive. Note that the Copy button is grayed out because the program knows it is not possible to make a copy given the current situation.

When you do have the CDs inserted in the correct drives, and have ensured that the Copy From and Copy To drives have been selected correctly, the program tests the drive that holds the CD-ROM to be copied (see Figure 8.3). It performs this test only once to be sure that the drive can support audio extraction and data copying at the rate necessary to write the CD-R disc. This happens whenever you use one of the Easy CD Creator 4.0 Deluxe programs for the first time, or after you add new CD hardware. After the initial test, the program stores the results so it won't happen again.

Figure 8.3

The program tests the CD-ROM drive to ensure it can keep up with the rate at which audio or data files will be read.

Finally, in Figure 8.4 you can see that we are set up now to make a copy of a CD. Both source and destination drives are now properly selected and both have the correct CD media inserted. In this figure, note that the first disc we will make a copy of is, of course, Easy CD Creator itself! This is one of the most basic functions of the copy program. That is, to make backup copies of all your important software CDs, so that, if the original becomes corrupted or otherwise unusable, you will still have a copy from which to work. Because most software costs so much these days, keeping an extra copy around is not only a good idea, it's almost a necessity. When you spend several hundred dollars on an office suite of applications, wouldn't you rather have a copy laying around in case of an emergency? Sure, you can register the software and then wait for a few days for the vendor to mail you a new CD (which they will probably charge a handling fee for). Making copies of all your important software CDs is a very good idea from a time and economic standpoint.

Figure 8.4

The first CD we will copy is the Easy CD Creator disc itself.

Another way to think of your copy is not as a backup copy, but as the original instead. Why? Because the original is a precious commodity. You can always make one or more copies of it, but the best copies always come from the original, not from another copy. I would suggest that whether you are copying audio or data CDs, you use the copy as your original and stick the original itself away for safekeeping.

After all, if you're using the copy, you really don't have to be as careful as you would with the original—you can always make another copy. And, because the fair use clause in the newest copyright act allows you to make copies for your own personal use, you can make copies of audio CDs for both your home CD player and your car. Going to the beach this summer? Why take a CD along that cost $16 when you can take a copy that cost less than $1 to make?

Start Copying

After all the media is ready to go, CD Copier will know it and enable the Copy button. Give that button a click when you're ready to take the plunge! After you do, another program window appears, called the CD Creation Process.

If you've read chapters 4 or 6, this window should look familiar. However, if you've skipped ahead, it has several features that show you what is going on during the copy process. These include the following:

➤ **Prepare Data**—Because this is a data CD, during this phase, the program examines the CD that will be copied.

➤ **Writing Table of Contents**—Because the CD starts at the center of the disc and is written from there toward the outer portion of the disc, the table of contents is the first thing that must be written after the CD Copier prepares the data.

➤ **Writing Track**—In Figure 8.5, this option has a check mark next to it because that is the phase the program is currently in. In this phase CD Copier begins copying the actual data of the CD to the CD-RW recorder. Because this is a data CD, only one large track will be written, which will contain several files and folders.

➤ **Closing CD**—When you see the check mark next to this item, it means that the program is closing the CD so that it can be read in CD players of any kind (mainly so music CDs can play in normal audio CD players).

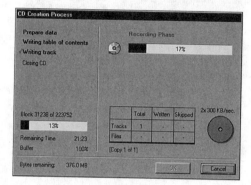

Figure 8.5

You can follow the progress as the CD is written.

You can gather some more information from the display shown in Figure 8.5. For example, just like when using Easy CD Creator, at the bottom is a Remaining Time indicator and a Buffer indicator. The Buffer indicator is a very important one in ensuring you don't experience a buffer underrun.

It doesn't matter whether the buffer is at 0% when the program is preparing the data. When the actual tracks are written, however, you want this field, ideally, to be at 100%, or close to that. If this Buffer indicator ever goes down to 0%, your burn will almost definitely fail.

If you refer back to Figure 8.5 you can see the track being written. Notice the all-important Buffer indicator is staying at 100%.

Crossing the Finish Line

As you can see, making a copy is not nearly as complicated or time-consuming as creating a layout for a CD. Figure 8.6 shows the CD Creation dialog box when it has finished copying a CD. This display is similar to the one you saw when you used Easy CD Creator to make CDs. Near the center of the display, toward the top, you can see the CD symbol with a large

Cross Reference

You can do certain things to help ensure that buffer underruns do not occur. For more information, see Chapter 15, "We're Gonna Need a Bigger Boat: Troubleshooting CD Recording," for troubleshooting tips.

check mark placed over it, indicating success. The text next to it tells you the CD was created successfully. If anything has gone awry, then you'll find a big red "X" on top of the CD symbol instead of the green checkmark! There are many reasons a copy can go bad. If you do get the horrid red X, look to see how many files were copied and start your troubleshooting efforts with that track on the original source CD (and then consult Chapter 15)!

Figure 8.6

CD Copier tells you when the CD has been success-fully copied.

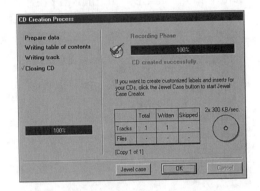

From here you can select the Jewel Case button at the bottom if you want to make a label for the CD and create inserts for the jewel case. Or, if you want to do that at a later time, just click the OK button.

Using Advanced Copying Features

Now that we've made a simple copy, let's look at the advanced features you can use to control the copying process a little more precisely. For the most part, you can use the procedures we've just discussed to make all your copies. However, if you plan to make several copies and want to speed up the process, you might want to use the advanced features of CD Copier to change the speed at which the copying is performed.

Figure 8.7 shows the CD Copier program with the Advanced tab selected. Since this tab doesn't have a ton of features to choose from, you might want to consider trying each one, just to see what works best for you.

Figure 8.7

The Advanced tab of CD Copier enables you to more precisely control the copying process.

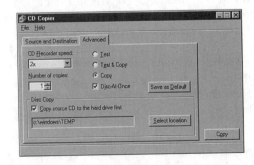

The advanced features include

➤ **CD-Recorder Speed**—If your CD-RW drive can write at a faster rate, you can select it here. CD Copier will display only speeds at which your drive is capable of performing. Thus, you might see higher speeds on one computer than on another.

➤ **Number of Copies**—If you want to make more than one copy of the disc, select the number of copies here.

➤ **Copy Source CD to the Hard Drive First**—This option is a good one to use if you are making more than one copy of the CD. This is because the program can usually extract data from a temporary file on your hard disk much more quickly than it can from the CD-ROM drive in your computer.

➤ **Test**—Use this option if you want to test whether or not the CD can be success-fully written. When you select this option, CD Copier performs the copy process, but no data is actually copied to the CD-R blank disc. Use this option if you are having problems copying a CD or if you have just installed a new drive and want to ensure it is in working order.

➤ **Test & Copy**—Similar to the preceding option, this one enables you to perform the test first, and then, if the test is successful, automatically begin burning the CD.

➤ **Copy**—This is the default. Just go ahead and make the copy without any of that sissy testing stuff!

➤ **Disk-At-Once**—This is a good selection to make especially if you have an audio CD that has more than one track—and how many don't? It prevents the mandatory two-second gap between each track from occurring. For some CDs, where tracks just blend together, this is something you absolutely need to do if you want an exact copy of the disc.

➤ **Select Location**—This option enables you to change the default location that will be used as a temporary file by the program. You shouldn't need to do this unless you have other disks installed and don't have enough space in the default directory.

➤ **Save as Default**—If you make changes to these options and want to make your changes the new default settings for when the program is started up again, click this button.

As you can see, there aren't many options to worry about, and for the most part they are self-explanatory. However, you should consider a few things when making a copy of a CD.

The Disk-at-Once option won't work when copying a data CD that has more than one session on it. Also, your CD-RW drive must support this mode. Don't worry, however, because most of the newer drives do.

If you have more than one physical hard disk drive installed on your computer, you should probably select it as the location for the temporary file. Even though you might not be using any other applications while the copying is occurring, the operating system (Windows for most readers of this book) still uses the C: drive. Putting the temporary file on another disk can avoid any possibility of the hard disk becoming a choke point.

If you find that CD Copier is not finishing successfully, it might be that the blank CD-R media you are using doesn't work well with high recording speeds. I've had trouble recording at 4X with media that specifically said it would work at that speed. Just goes to show you that you can't always trust the manufacturer to give you all the facts. If this happens, try dropping the recording speed down to 1X and see whether that works. If it doesn't work at 1X speed then you have some other problems. If it does work at that speed, try increasing the speed a notch at a time with other copies until you find out how well that particular brand of media works with your CD-RW drive.

Why Make an Image Copy First?

Of all the advanced options we just went over, copying the source CD data to the hard disk first—before making the CD-R copy—is one of the more important ones. Why? For several reasons, one of which we have already mentioned: The hard disk in your computer is faster than the CD-ROM drive you have installed in your computer. At the rate technology is advancing, this isn't likely to change in the near future.

Another good reason is for making multiple copies. After the CD has been read the first time, and copied to the temporary file, the remaining copies should be made more quickly because the CD won't have to be read each time. Instead, the program uses the copy made on your hard disk. Then, provided you aren't using a bunch of other programs that hog memory or make a lot of use of your hard drive, the program will be able to keep the buffer full (at 100%) while it writes the remaining copies. By keeping the buffer full, and by selecting a fast write speed, you can save yourself a lot of time when making multiple copies.

Dancing Alone: Copying Using Only the CD-R Recorder

Using your hard drive as a temporary place to store the CD data brings up another interesting subject. Suppose, for some reason, you can't use your CD-ROM as a source drive. Perhaps it has stopped working or had some other, gremlin-caused, problems. You can still use CD Copier to copy discs.

Instead, just use the CD-RW drive to read the source CD, and copy it to the hard drive first. This way you can bypass using your CD-ROM drive entirely! It might take a little longer (having an extra step), but at least you can make copies. After the program has finished reading the original CD and has copied its data to the hard disk in your computer, it then prompts you to replace the source CD with a blank recordable one.

The following are a few things to think about when using your hard drive as a staging ground for the data to be written to a CD:

➤ Make sure enough space is available on the hard disk! A full CD-ROM can hold up to 650MB of data, and more if it was written on an 80-minute blank.

➤ Keep your hard disk in good shape. Windows has a variety of system tools you can use to keep things running smoothly, but you'll need a book tailored to your version of Windows (95, 98, Me, NT4, 2000) to get the most out of them. However, the main two programs to look for are Disk Defragmenter and ScanDisk, which are found by clicking Start, Programs, Accessories, System Tools and then looking for the program name.

➤ Don't use your hard disk extensively while the CD Copier is working. Oh, you can try, but don't be surprised if you end up with a coaster when all is said and done.

The Least You Need to Know

➤ Use CD Copier, not Easy CD Creator, when you want to make a copy of a single CD.

➤ You can't use CD Copier to create a CD that has tracks from multiple sources.

➤ Use the advanced options to copy the CD to your hard disk when making multiple copies. This speeds up the copying process.

➤ You don't have to have two CD drives in your computer to use CD Copier. You can use the CD-RW drive as both the source and destination.

➤ Make copies of your software and music CDs for normal everyday use. Save your originals as the precious commodities that they are. If the copy takes some abuse and becomes unusable, you can always make a new copy from the original.

➤ Some CDs simply cannot be copied. These are usually games, but some newer audio CDs also employ various protection schemes. With audio CDs, try extracting single tracks to your hard disk and re-creating the CD from there instead of using Easy CD Creator.

Part 3

Entering Murky Waters: Creating Multisession CDs

As you probably know, CDs can be used in many ways. You can use them to store music or computer data files. You can also create CDs that have more than one "session" on the disc. It's kind of like having more than one CD on the same disc. You've probably noticed new CD-extra CDs at the local CD shop that have not only an artist's latest songs, but also a video to go with them. This can be done using a single or a multisession CD. Although Easy CD Creator assists you in burning this kind of CD, you'll have to use a multimedia authoring program to get the files you need first.

For aspiring musicians or very creative people, the chapters in this section should prove intriguing.

Chapter 9

Understanding and Using Multisession CDs

In This Chapter

➤ Sessions are collections of tracks written with one pass of the laser.

➤ Multisessions enable you to add data to a CD over time.

➤ You can use multisessions for both audio and data CDs, but more practical uses exist for a data CD recorded this way.

As you've probably already found out, burning CDs isn't always a straightforward process. Many times, you might want to add more data to a CD you've already burned to once (but that still has space for more). Or, you might want to put music and data on the same disc. This is done by writing multiple sessions to a CD. A *multisession* CD is one that groups tracks together into *sessions*. Each session has its own table of contents and is essentially a mini-CD on a CD.

The Scoop on Multisession CDs

If you will remember back in Chapter 2, "The Machine Behind the Curtain: How CDs and Recordable CDs Work," we discussed how tracks are laid out on a CD. In Chapters 3 and 4, where I talked about using Easy CD Creator to make audio or data CDs, you learned that writing a disc using the *track-at-once (TAO)* method allows you to write one track at a time, pausing in between. Note, however, that using that method requires a two-second gap between each track for synchronization purposes. In one way, TAO offers more flexibility when you are putting together an audio CD because you can record a few songs and then later add a few more, closing the CD when you are ready to play it.

However, if you don't want those mandatory two-second gaps, you need another method for recording the CD, such as session-at-once (SAO) or disc-at-once (DAO). In this chapter, we discuss using the session-at-once method to write a set of tracks in one operation. Both of these methods enable you to record more than one track in a single session and then close the CD when you've finished writing to the disc.

What Is a Session, Anyway?

Sessions are basically just collections of tracks written in a single pass of the laser. The *session-at-once (SAO)* method enables you to add groups of tracks that can, on the appropriate player, be played before the CD is closed. After you've decided not add more sessions (or you just run out of space), you can close the CD so that it plays in a wider variety of players. The SAO method, like the disc-at-once (DAO) method, avoids the mandatory two-second gap between each track. This does not, however, remove any silence that might be inherent in the actual start or finish of the track itself.

The best way to think of a session is as a small CD on the disc. There is a table of contents where the session starts and, as discussed in Chapter 2, a run-out track at the end of the session. The sessions are linked as they are created, one pointing to the other. On most new CD-ROM drives, you can read each session regardless of whether or not the disc has been closed. If you aren't sure which CD-ROM drives a multisession disc will get used in, then closing the CD when you know that you've written the last session is a good idea.

Sessions Cost Real Estate

One thing you should note when using multiple sessions on a CD is that there is an overhead cost to bear. Each session is like its own CD to the reader and has a lead-in and a run-out track. This overhead is about 20MB for the first track and 13MB for the remaining sessions you add. For an audio CD, this translates into losing about nine minutes worth of space for each session.

Because each session is kind of its own disc, when inserting a multisession data CD-R in a CD-ROM drive, the drive must pick one to read first. Most drives first read the last session written to the disc, the idea being that if you use the same CD-R disc to back up the same data several times, the last session contains the most up-to-date information. In this case, reading the last session first makes the most sense. However, you might want to save space by recording some tracks now and some later and want to be able to access all sessions on the disc.

Fortunately, you can tell your CD-ROM drive which session you want to read. In Chapter 13, "Other Roxio Utilities," you can learn about the Roxio Session Selector that can change the active session for a multisession CD. Of course, this won't overcome the fact that you won't be able to play all sessions on an ordinary audio player. But, if you use the CD-R to back up important data, or if you use it for music and play it back on your computer, the Session Selector is very helpful.

Audio Sessions Come First

Although you can have multiple audio sessions on a CD-R, most home/car stereo CD players see only the first session on the disc and ignore the rest.

Which Format Should You Use?

You can create multisession CDs in two formats. The first is the one you have already been exposed to in this book—the standard *CD-ROM Mode 1* format. However, the preferred format for a multisession disc is called *CD-ROM/XA*, which is often referred to as *Mode 2*. This is because some CD drives recognize only this format for a multi-session CD. You don't really need to worry too much about the specifics of each of these formats. The multimedia authoring software you use to create the information you will burn to the CD will most likely specify the format you must use. Again, the most popular format, CD-ROM/XA, is probably what you'll end up using.

Whatever you do, be sure that the format you use is common to all the sessions you record on the CD. You shouldn't mix modes, so to speak, on a multisession CD. Some players might read a mixed-mode CD, but don't count on it! Because Easy CD Creator allows you to do it any way you want, it won't remind or caution you if you attempt to write multiple formats to the same disc.

Step into the Multisession CD Recording Studio

The good news is that creating a multisession CD is nearly as simple as creating a regular CD in that you pretty much use the same procedures. After you have a layout ready using Easy CD Creator, the program allows you to select many options when recording, including which method to use in writing the session. For a multisession CD, we're going to use the session-at-once method.

Recording the First Session

To begin, bring up the Easy CD Creator program and create a layout for the tracks or files you want to add at this time. On the CD Creator toolbar, click Tools and Properties to bring up the CD Layout Properties page shown in Figure 9.1.

Figure 9.1

The CD Layout Properties page is where you can select the CD format.

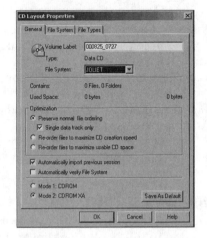

For more information about using the Easy CD Creator program to create a layout and record a CD, see Chapters 3, "Using Easy CD Creator to Make Audio CDs," and 4, "Using Easy CD Creator to Make Data CDs."

Here, you need to choose whether to use a Mode 1 or Mode 2 format for the CD using the radio buttons at the very bottom of the page. If you're not sure, remember that Mode 2 is generally the more widely accepted standard. In Figure 9.2, you can see the CD Creation dialog box (with the Advanced button selected), with the correct selections made.

Figure 9.2

Leave the CD open when you record the first session.

The dialog box in Figure 9.2 is set to record a single session all at once, close the session, *and leave the CD open*. Click OK to start recording the first session. When the session has been successfully recorded and closed, the CD Creation dialog box will tell you. From this point, you can either go ahead and add another session or remove the CD for later use.

Adding One or More Additional Sessions

Adding more sessions to an existing CD is done in the same way as recording the first session. Use Easy CD Creator and create a layout of the tracks or files/folders you want to put in this session. Then, record the session to the CD-R using the same options described in the previous section. You now have two sessions on the CD. You can keep adding sessions until you either run out of room or close the CD.

When you're finished adding sessions to a disc, you can close it so that you can be reasonably sure it will play nice with a larger variety of other CD-ROM players. To finally close out the CD, just select Close CD from the CD Creation dialog box when you record the last session.

Plan Ahead!

One annoyance in the way CD Creator closes CDs is that it can't close a disc without first burning a track or session. This means you can't use the program to just close the CD. Be sure you plan ahead so you know to close the disc when it comes time to write the last session.

Where Can You Use Multisession CDs?

Where you can play or use a multisession CD depends on the player and the composition of the CD. Older players can usually read only one session and no others. Most newer CD-ROM drives will look at the last session first. With these kinds of players, however, you can use Roxio's Session Selector, as covered in Chapter 13, to choose which session to read.

If you record audio in the first session on a CD-R multisession, your ordinary CD player will probably play this first session. Don't expect it to play any more than that, though. You can easily play any session's audio tracks back using your computer, however. Just choose the correct session from Session Selector.

There are variations on multisession CDs, though. It is possible to use programs in one session to control the playback of audio or other multimedia content located in another session. The two methods for doing this are called writing CD-extra CDs or writing mixed-mode CDs and are covered in the next chapter.

The Least You Need to Know

➤ Track-at-once, session-at-once, and disc-at-once are different methods for recording a CD, and each has its strengths.

➤ Two modes control the format of a CD. The preferred format for a multisession CD is CD-ROM/XA.

➤ You can add one session, which can contain one or more tracks, at a time to a multisession CD.

➤ Close the CD when you are finished adding sessions!

➤ An audio CD with multiple sessions will play only the first session on a regular audio CD player.

Chapter 10

Best of Both Worlds: Creating CDs with Both Audio and Data

In This Chapter

➤ Creating mixed-mode CDs

➤ Creating CD-extra CDs

Today, the term *multimedia*, when it comes to computers, generally means a presentation that includes both audio and video, under the control of computer programs. Some are interactive and some are not. To burn a multimedia presentation onto a CD—in other words, using audio and data—Easy CD Creator offers the two standard methods: mixed-mode and CD-extra. However, remember that Easy CD Creator only burns the disc in the correct format; it does not help you create any of the material you need to burn. For this, you must use one of the many multimedia-authoring programs on the market today, at a wide range of costs.

After you have that material, however, Easy CD Creator is there to help you burn a multimedia presentation to a recordable CD.

Choosing Between Mixed-Mode and the CD-Extra Method

A CD-extra disc has two sessions—one to hold data and one to hold audio files. Because the first session holds the CD-DA (digital audio) tracks, you can play this kind of CD in your ordinary CD audio player to listen to just the music. The second session is written using the CD-ROM/XA data CD format. To use the programs or other data

Cross Reference

If you don't remember what makes a multisession CD unique, be sure to visit (or revisit) Chapter 9, "Understanding and Using Multisession CDs."

stored in the second session, you need a computer with a CD-ROM drive that supports multisessions. Don't worry, though, because most new drives do.

Because this is a multisession CD, the last session is activated and used by the CD-ROM drive first. Programs and data found in this session can be used with the audio session to present a multimedia presentation to the viewer. Although you won't see the packaging say so, several CDs in your local CD shop were created using the CD-extra method. Do you have any music CDs that also include "CD-ROM" features? Odds are those are done using CD-extra.

Unlike CD-extra, a mixed-mode CD is not a multisession CD. Instead, the audio and data are put into one single session. The first track contains the data. It also instructs your CD-ROM drive on how to make read the audio (CD-DA) tracks that come next. This first track can be in either the CD-ROM format or CD-ROM/XA.

Don't Get Burned

Danger, Will Robinson!

One caveat of a mixed-mode CD is that if you put it in an older audio player (or a cheaper, new one), it might attempt to play the first track with disastrous results! Like what, you ask? How about frying your speakers with a shrill siren call that could wake up Elvis? In other words, don't try this at home.

The important thing to remember about ;recording mixed-mode versus CD Extra discs is that one method uses a single session on the CD, whereas the other method uses two sessions. Of these types of CDs, the CD-extra seems to be more popular because of its capability to be used in any ordinary CD player without incident.

Creating a Mixed-Mode CD

To create a mixed-mode CD, you must use Easy CD Creator, which is discussed in Chapters 3, "Using Easy CD Creator to Make Audio CDs," and 4, "Using Easy CD Creator to Make Data CDs." If you find yourself getting lost trying to use the program in this chapter, make sure you've read and understand these two chapters.

The first thing you need to do is make sure Easy CD Creator is in the right mode. So, after you have started the program, look for the New button on the left end of the toolbar and click the down arrow that is right next to it. A small menu appears. Click Mixed Mode CD. Alternatively, you can use the File menu, select New, and then select Mixed Mode CD. After that, the process is quite simple. In Figure 10.1, you can see the layout window used by Easy CD Creator.

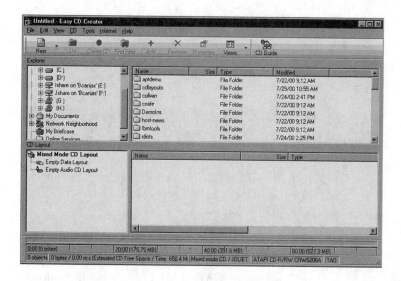

Figure 10.1

The Easy CD Creator program can be used to create mixed-mode CDs.

In the top left of this display is the Explorer pane, from which you select audio tracks or files/folders. Beneath the Explorer pane is the CD Layout pane, which you can see is now ready for you to create a mixed-mode CD layout. Remember that the process for burning a CD with Easy CD Creator is to first create a layout and then create the CD based on the layout. The process is a simple one:

1. Click the Empty Data Layout folder in the CD Layout window and then use the Explorer pane to find the programs or files you want to copy to the layout. When you select the directory in the Explorer pane on the left side of the window, you see the files and subfolders for that folder in the right side of the window.

2. Drag the programs or data from the Explorer's pane to the CD Layout pane, which is directly beneath it. Or, click the file or folder once and then click the Add button; the item then appears in the layout. The applications will appear in the layout pane, as shown in Figure 10.2.

Figure 10.2

You drag the applications from the upper Explorer pane to the lower CD Layout pane to add them to the CD.

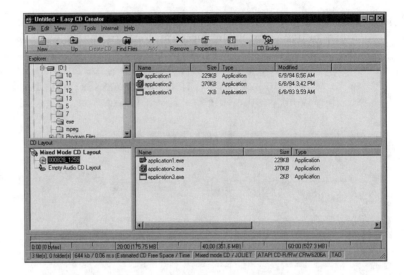

Remember the Internet

Don't forget that it's easier to tell tracks and discs apart in the audio layout if you use the Internet to identify the artist, disc, and song names (or enter them yourself).

Image Me!

If you're going to create more than one copy of this layout over time, you might want to create an image file of the layout first, as discussed in Chapter 3.

3. When you are finished selecting the data content for the CD, click the Empty Audio CD Layout in the CD Layout pane.

4. If the audio tracks are to be taken from a CD, insert the proper CD and select it in the Explorer pane when it becomes available. If the tracks are to come from WAV or MP3 files, use the Explorer pane to find them.

5. To add a track, WAV file, or MP3 file to the audio layout, drag it to the layout portion of the window just like you did for the data files and folders. Note that you can mix tracks from several CDs, along with MP3 and WAV files, to create the audio layout. The results should be similar to what is shown in Figure 10.3.

6. When you've finished creating the layout, use the Record button (the big red dot on the toolbar) or use the File menu and click Create CD.

7. The CD Creation Setup dialog box then pops up, allowing you to set some options for burning the CD (see Figure 10.4). Click the Advanced button to see all the options available in this dialog box.

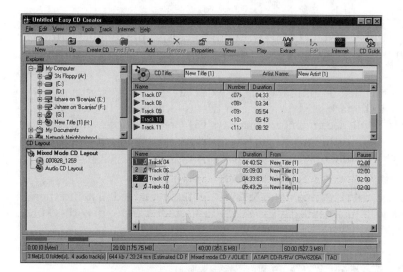

Figure 10.3

You drag audio tracks to the layout in a similar manner after first clicking Audio CD Layout.

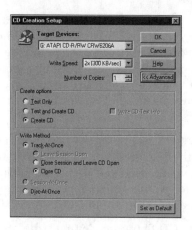

Figure 10.4

The CD Creation Setup dialog box enables you to set recording options.

8. For all practical purposes, just take the defaults shown in Figure 10.4 for the Create Options and the Write Method options. If you want more than one CD burned, use the Number of Copies field. Use the fields at the top of this dialog box to change the write speed as you deem necessary (based on the quality of your recordings) or even the CD-RW drive, if you have more than one. To start the recording, click OK.

9. The program will test the data transfer rate from your source drives to ensure that it can write the CD. After these System Test dialog boxes disappear, the CD Creation dialog box pops up to keep you informed of the progress of burning the CD. If you haven't already inserted a blank CD, you'll get told to do that, also.

Finally, the process steps through file system generation, copying the tracks for data and audio files. The number of tracks to be written, along with the number written so far, can be viewed in the CD Creation Process dialog box. Finally, when finished recording, Easy CD Creator closes the disc.

When the program is finished burning the CD, the CD Creation Process dialog box shows a large, green check mark over the CD icon that is located by the Recording Phase text. Below this, you'll see green text that says CD Created Successfully. If you get the dreaded red "X" of death, look to see which errors were reported and then, read Chapter 15, "We're Gonna Need a Bigger Boat: Troubleshooting CD Recording," to see whether you can figure out how to fix what went wrong.

Remember that, because this is a mixed-mode CD, the files get added first and then the audio tracks are added in second. This is why you shouldn't try to play this kind of disc in an ordinary CD player.

Creating a CD–Extra CD

This kind of CD is basically a multisession CD that has audio and data information, each secure in its own session. Again, you can use Easy CD Creator to make this kind of CD. In addition, this type is usually preferred over the mixed-mode CD if you are going to use a lot of audio. This is because, with the first session containing the audio tracks, most audio players can be used to listen to that session without blowing out a speaker. To activate the programs in the data session, you must use the CD-ROM on your computer.

To start the process, just bring up Easy CD Creator. Once again, you can use the little arrow that is positioned right next to the New button on the toolbar, or you can use the File menu and select New. Whichever method you use, from the menu that pops up, select CD-extra. The Easy CD Creator window then appears a little different from when it is used for a mixed-mode CD, as you can see in Figure 10.5.

Under the CD Layout pane, it now says CD Extra. Inside that pane, the first item in the tree is the CD-extra Layout. Under this, you can see the audio session (Empty Audio CD Layout). Furthermore, there's a folder called CDPLUS.

To create the CD-extra CD, follow these steps:

1. First click Empty Audio CD Layout in the left side of the CD Layout. On the right side of the layout pane, you'll see in large red letters the text "Drag audio tracks and audio files here." Guess what we're going to do next?

2. Add the audio files you want. Use the Explorer pane to select them from CD drives or from WAV or MP3 files on your hard disk. To add the audio files to the layout pane, drag them there or click the track once and then click the Add button. Similar to creating a regular audio CD, you can see that each track you add is listed in order in the CD Layout pane.

You can continue to add audio tracks from multiple CDs. The program prompts you to insert the CDs again when the recording starts.

3. In the left side of the CD Layout, right under the Audio CD Layout entry, is a numbered entry. It's the date in year, month, and day format, along with some other numbers pulled from the fifth dimension. To start adding files or data to the CD, click this entry. The right pane of the CD layout now shows only the folder CDPLUS, as you can see in Figure 10.6.

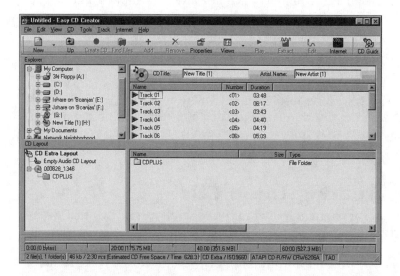

Figure 10.5

The CD-extra window looks a little different from the mixed-mode window.

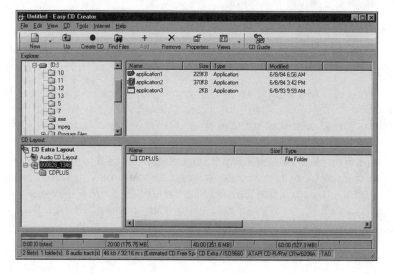

Figure 10.6

Easy CD Creator is ready for you to add files to the layout now.

143

4. Select the files you want to add by using the Explorer panes above and either drag the files to the CD Layout or use the Add button just like you did with the audio selections.

5. When you're ready to record, just click the Create CD button on the toolbar (the one with the big red dot), or select Create CD from the File menu. The CD Creation Setup dialog box shows up and looks just like it did back in Figure 10.4. Again, I recommend using the settings shown in this figure. Make any changes you want, such as the number of copies, and click the OK button to start recording.

6. If you haven't inserted a recordable CD into the CD-RW drive yet, you will be prompted to do so now. After you insert the blank CD, click the Retry button and the application continues.

From here on out, the process works just like it did for creating a mixed-mode CD earlier in this chapter. The CD Creation Process dialog box keeps you posted on what is going on, such as how many files or tracks have been written. When you get the CD Successfully Created Message, the CD is ready for testing and use.

Other Tips for Creating These CDs

Because the Easy CD Creator program is used to create both types of CDs that we've covered in this chapter, I thought it would be a good idea to remind you of some of the other features Easy CD Creator offers. You can learn more about most of these topics in Chapters 3 and 4, which deal with using Easy CD Creator to make audio and data CDs, but here are some of the key points:

➤ **Save and restore layouts**—You can save your CD layout at any time, storing it under a unique filename, and open the file at a later date to either use it or continue working on it. Use File/Save or File/Save As (the first time), and File/Open CD Layout.

➤ **Editing**—The Edit menu offers the standard cut, copy, paste, rename, and remove selections. You can also usually right-click an item in the layout to bring up this editing menu. Use the editing features to rearrange your selections if necessary.

➤ **Create a CD image file**—You can create an image file on your hard disk that can then be used to create one or more copies of the CD any time you want. Use File/Create CD Image to create the file and File/Create CD From CD Image to burn that image to a CD. If you want to make multiple copies of a CD, especially if you plan to do so over more than one sitting, burning from your hard disk image file is faster than from multiple sources in the layout. Just keep in mind that these image files do get pretty big.

The Least You Need to Know

➤ You can burn two types of multimedia CDs that contain both audio and data. The preferred method to use is CD-extra. This is because ordinary audio CD players can play these kinds of CDs. With mixed-mode CDs, most old and some newer audio CD players can't read the discs at all.

➤ Easy CD Creator is not a multimedia authoring program. You'll need one of those to create a multimedia presentation. After you have it, though, Easy CD Creator is ideal for burning that presentation to disc!

➤ To create multiple copies of either kind of CD over time, have the files and tracks ready and create a disk image on your hard drive that you can use as needed!

Part 4

It's Always Better to Look Good: Creating the Jewel Case Covers and Disc Labels

If you are just going to use your CD burner to make backups of data from your computer, you probably don't care what they look like when you get done, so long as they are readable. You can always use an ink pen (with a soft touch!) to write on the CD. If you want to make things fancier, though, use Easy CD Creator's Jewel Case Creator application to produce a truly quality product.

The Jewel Case Creator application lets you design your own jewel case inserts and CD labels. You can also use built-in templates that can be great time-savers if you don't care much about the formatting. The program even allows you to automatically download information about most CDs from the Internet. Presto! The artist's name, album name, and track names magically appear in the layout ready to print.

For both data and audio CDs (and combinations thereof) you can create professional-looking CD labels and jewel case inserts using an ordinary laser or ink jet printer. The large variety of label and insert manufacturers mean that you can find just the right kind of label or card stock to make your CDs look great!

Chapter 11

Using Jewel Case Creator to Create Labels and Inserts

In This Chapter

➤ Using Jewel Case Creator for audio CDs

➤ Using Jewel Case Creator for data and other CDs

➤ A quick look at several kinds of labels and inserts

➤ Do-it-yourself inserts!

➤ Creating the label and jewel case inserts

The CD labels and jewel case inserts that come with most recordable discs are pretty plain and usually littered with manufacturer logos. As you'll find in this chapter, there's no need to subject your CD burns to such inartistic treatment. Roxio Easy CD Creator 4.0 comes with an application called Jewel Case Creator. Using this program and the appropriate paper stock or pre-cut labels, you can print out customized disc labels and jewel case inserts to suit whatever project you have on your plate.

So Many Programs, So Many Labels

When any new device is created for use with a PC, you can be sure that a new market will be opened up for other products to support the new device. The recordable CD drive is no exception. Indeed, several companies have jumped in to provide supplies for you to use with your CD-RW drive.

Between Tracks

Labels and Software

Many, if not most, of the major CD label products come with their own software, which you can use to print your custom labels. The usefulness of this software depends on the package, but generally, Jewel Case Creator is still your best option.

The most obvious example is the blank, recordable CD itself. These are made by many manufacturers, and their usefulness on your system will depend on a myriad of factors, such as your drive model and your particular media. However, we've already discussed recordable media in Chapter 2, "The Machine Behind the Curtain: How CDs and Recordable CDs Work."

The other "expendables" you should think about are paper jewel case inserts and label stock. You can pick up these labels at any office supply store and most consumer electronics stores as well (like Best Buy and CompUSA). Some of the major brands include Farrow's Neato, Memorex, Stomper, and Avery. There are also new brand names and varieties coming into the market even as this book is being produced. The big advantage in using these products is that the CD labels (not the inserts) need an adhesive to "glue" them to your recordable CD. These packages come with that adhesive so you don't have to worry about buying it separately.

Depending on your budget and the number of labels you want to make, the cost of these packages can get pretty significant. There is another option, though, and we'll quickly dig into that before starting in with the Roxio Jewel Case Creator program. Why put the stock before the program? Because Jewel Case Creator supports any label/insert type you want to use.

Don't Get Burned

These Colors Run

If you are using an ink jet or other similar technology, you should probably give the label or inserts a little time to dry so you don't smear the ink when applying them. I recommend at least a half an hour.

Card Stock and Jewel Case Inserts

For those who don't want to get soaked paying for expensive brand name inserts, you can use Roxio's software to print to *card stock*, which can be found at any office supply store. It's usually near the stationery section. This kind of stock has many uses, but if you can find it in the 50–65 lb range, you've got about the same thing as what comes in the expensive packages CD label vendors try to sell you. Most card stock also comes in colors. If you are using a black-and-white printer instead of a color ink jet, this can spice up your inserts. Heck, color stock is useful even if you have a color printer because it could save you some ink! After all, why soak white paper stock in red ink if you can just buy the paper in that color to begin with?

Besides cost, the trouble with most label and insert packages is that they don't come with enough jewel case inserts to match the number of CD disc labels you get with them. Who knows why they do this. I blame it on that secret society, led by Elvis Presley, that runs the world. On top of that some products only print to one side of the front cover. This is a drag when compared to brands like Stomper, which enable you to print the front and inside covers on the same sheet of paper. Printing these two inserts on the same sheet (and folding it in half) makes the insert thicker and much less likely to just slide out of the jewel case like the flatter one-side inserts often do.

Although you might not have any issues with spending a few extra dollars on brand-name labels, just remember that the only difference between card stock and prepackaged inserts is that card stock doesn't have the prescored lines that make taking it apart after you print it an easy job. Of course, recent studies suggest that a special pair of cutting instruments called scissors could actually serve this purpose!

Between Tracks

No Label Required

You don't need to label everything, do you? Remember that you can always use a felt-tip pen (with water-based ink, not oil-based) to write a brief description on the label side of a recordable disc. And, of course, most blank CD-Rs come with jewel case labels you can write on, as well.

Using Roxio's Jewel Case Creator for Audio CDs

After you've got your labels or paper stock, all you need is an easy way to print the right information on them. Enter Roxio's Jewel Case Creator. This program is an excellent one that does just about everything the other programs, which come with some brand name labels, do. For most purposes I think you'll grow to like Roxio's Jewel Case Creator for its ease of use. It also has a huge advantage over some other programs I've looked at in that it can automatically look up and insert artist, title, and song names onto your labels using the layout you used to create the disc. That can save you a lot of typing!

Starting Jewel Case Creator

You can start up the Jewel Case Creator the same way you start up most other Roxio applications. Click Start, Programs, Roxio Easy CD Creator 4, Features, and finally, click Jewel Case Creator.

Or, if you allowed Easy CD Creator to place its icon on your desktop during installation, you can just double-click the Desktop icon named Create CD. This brings up a menu dialog box from which you can select Jewel Case Creator. Either of these methods will get you to the main window of this application, as you can see in Figure 11.1.

Quick Start

After you successfully burn a new CD from Easy CD Creator, you can jump directly to the Jewel Case Creator. The Success dialog box that appears when the burn is done has a button labeled Jewel Case on it. If you click this button, you go directly from creating the CD to making the jewel box case and label for it.

Figure 11.1

The main window of the Jewel Case Creator.

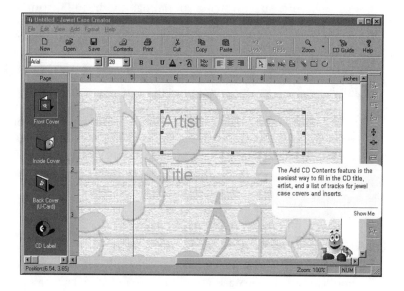

A close look at the screen shows that it's not going to be a difficult program to operate. There is the usual menu at the top, starting with File and including standard menus such as Edit and Help. Under this is a toolbar that can speed up many tasks.

Most of the window, however, is taken by the drawing space where you can construct the printouts that can be used to line the back and front of a jewel case. Using this program, you can also print a label that can be applied, by one of several popular applicators, to the CD. Assuming that the Front Cover icon on the left of the window is selected, this drawing space shows an editing field outline in which you can insert the name of the artist of the CD. The field under it enables you to enter the title for the CD. Off to the left side of this front cover is an area that can be used to add song tracks. Ignore that one for now as we'll look at it in just a minute.

Cross Reference

This section focuses on using Jewel Case Creator to make audio CDs. Even though the process is very similar for data CDs, you can get data CD specifics by setting your sights on the section called "Using Roxio's Jewel Case Creator for Data CDs," on page 166 of this chapter.

Off to the bottom right is a pesky little creature that looks like a dot with a face. This is the help wizard, and he will follow you around unless you right-click him and then click Hide. If you aren't familiar with using many of the Jewel Case Creator's functions, the wizard might be useful to you. When you get comfortable, however, he'll mostly just take up screen space, so send him packing.

Adding CD Info and Contents Automatically!

Because the little dot-boy in Figure 11.1 is telling you that an easy way to add tracks to a CD exists, we might as well start there. If you are currently connected to the Internet and are making a label for a copied music CD, or if you have downloaded the information for this particular CD previously, you can simply click the Add menu and then select Add Contents from that. If you have not downloaded the disc's information yet, you'll next see a dialog box telling you that a music service is being contacted on the Internet to get the album information. This, of course, is why you need that Internet connection. Regardless of whether the information is coming from the Web or is already stored on your hard drive, it should take just a few moments to complete the process.

The CD I'm using for this example was identified properly as *Mister Heartbreak* by Laurie Anderson. Because Jewel Case Creator uses that nice folded cover technique I mentioned earlier, it puts information about each song title and its length on the inside cover. Clicking the Inside Cover button on the window's left toolbar brings up this information (see Figure 11.2).

Figure 11.2

You can see the inside portion of the folded cover.

Now, if only doing your taxes could be that easy! All you had to do was click Add and then Add CD Contents, and instantly you've got yourself a jewel box cover. It gets even better. In addition to the front and inside cover icons on the left part of the Jewel Case Creator window, you'll see icons for the other things you can print for the CD or jewel case.

Timing Is Everything

An important thing to note about the Add CD Contents feature is that it works only for commercially available CDs. If you use Easy CD Creator to put together a best hits CD of your own design, you won't be able to use this feature because your CD won't be listed in the Internet database! You can get around this, though. Simply use the Internet to identify the individual discs of the compilation before burning the disc in Easy CD Creator. When the burn is complete, you can click the Jewel Case button mentioned earlier, and Jewel Case Creator will have your CD inserts ready to go.

If you click the icon labeled Back Cover, you'll find it looks similar to the inside cover (see Figure 11.3). Indeed, they are similar in that they both list the song titles and the play times. This back cover, which is also called the U-card, has a subtle difference. On each side of the cover you'll see text written in a vertical mode. This portion of the printed card will be folded so that when you insert it into the back of the CD jewel case, it will show the song titles on the rear of the case, and the album artist and title on both edges.

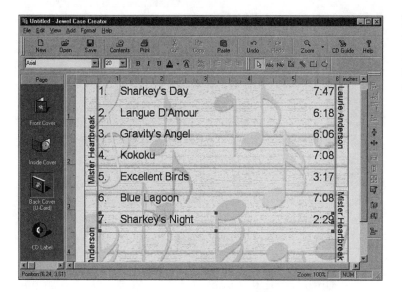

Figure 11.3

The U-card is where information for the back and sides of the jewel case comes from.

Don't Get Burned

Brittle Plastic

Inserting a U-card requires that you first pry up the plastic portion of the CD case that holds the CD in place. Although it's a simple process, it is very easy to snap off the pegs that hold it in place. This, of course, pretty much hoses any further use of the case. I find the easiest way to avoid this is by opening the jewel case and laying it on a flat surface. Then, use your fingernails to pry up the center portion of the holder that is located where the front and back sides of the jewel case join.

The final button on this toolbar is for the CD label itself. As you can see in Figure 11.4, Jewel Case Creator places the album artist and title on the CD label.

Figure 11.4

In addition the case inserts, Jewel Case Creator lets you print labels for the CD, too.

Entering Info the Hard Way: By Hand!

Unfortunately, it's not always possible to create all the components of the jewel case with just a few clicks. It can be a little more difficult if you're using a compilation CD or if the album is not found in the Internet database. I've personally tried a wide variety of CDs and have yet to have one that wasn't found, but as many of us found out in high school chemistry, nothing is an exact science. If you do run into this problem, you'll have to enter the information manually.

Handles?

Handles are little boxes that appear in each corner and halfway between each side of a selected field.

However, if you were smart enough to edit the track names manually when you used Easy CD Creator for the CD layout, then Jewel Case Creator should pick these up and you won't have this problem!

The good news about typing in information yourself is that once you're done, you can save the label information, just like you saved Easy CD Creator layouts. This way, if you need to print a new copy or modify the inserts in some way, you can open it back up whenever you need to. To save the layout, just click the File menu and choose Save As. From here, you can give the layout file a name, clicking OK to save it on your hard disk.

Entering the Title and Artist

As you saw in Figure 11.1, Jewel Case Creator has two boxes, called *fields*, that you can use to enter information. As the field names imply, one is for the CD's recording artist or group, and the other is for the name of the CD. You can select one of these fields by clicking it. After it's selected, the border around the field turns dark and several *handles* appear around it, which you can see in Figure 11.5.

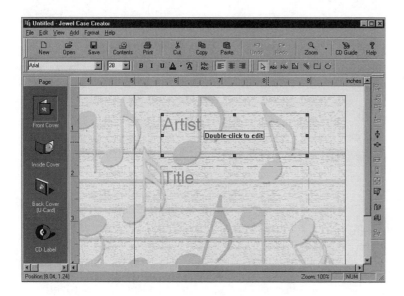

Figure 11.5

You can manually enter the information for the jewel case cover.

When you position your cursor over a handle, it turns into a double-arrow symbol. You can then press and hold down the mouse button while you drag that particular handle to change the size of the field. The handle you click determines in which direction you can move when resizing (horizontal, vertical, or diagonal).

Similar to a painting on a wall, you also can move a field to a different location on the cover. Just place your cursor inside the field, and then click and hold. It turns into cross hairs, enabling you to drag the field to any part of the cover.

Obviously, you aren't going to jump through all these hoops if you don't want to give these fields appropriate names. To add text to a field, just double-click it. This opens the selected field for editing. If, for example, you double-clicked the Artist field, you would find that the word Artist is now highlighted.

Because the field is highlighted automatically, all you have to do is start typing in the artist's name. As soon as the first key is pressed, the word "Artist" disappears, replaced by whatever you're typing. You can change both fields as often as you want. Figure 11.6 shows a completed front cover, with the artist name and CD title filled in.

157

Figure 11.6

The finished cover with both artist and title filled in manually.

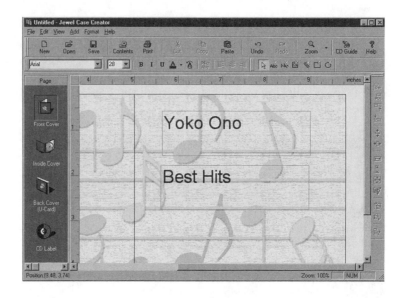

Numbers Are Optional

Keep in mind that if you don't care to know the length of a track, you don't have to enter anything for the duration. If you've put together a compilation from various CDs, you can even use this field to enter other information, such as an artist's name.

One nice feature about using the built-in templates Jewel Case Creator supplies is that certain fields are linked. For example, the CD title appears on the front cover, the edges of the U-card, and the CD label. Obviously, having to enter the same exact information for each field is a waste of your time. However, because Jewel Case Creator links these fields together, what you type in one automatically appears in the others, too.

Adding the Titles of Each Track

Adding the artist and title were easy—they were short and didn't take much time! The next thing you have to do is the most tedious part.

Entering in each song title, in order, and, if you want, adding the play times for each song can take a bit of time if you've got a lot of tracks or type using the time-honored "hunt and peck" method. To add this information, click the Inside Cover icon on the left side of the Jewel Case Creator window to bring up that view. The view, like the rear end of a horse, isn't much. Because each track gets its own field and, at this point, Jewel Case Creator doesn't have a clue how many tracks are on your CD, the Inside Cover (and Back Cover) is blank.

To start entering the track titles, click the Add menu at the top of the window and then select Track. In Figure 11.7, you can see that a new dialog box, titled Insert New Track, appears. Here you can enter the track number (which always defaults to the next new track number), the song title, and the *duration*, which means the time it takes to play the track.

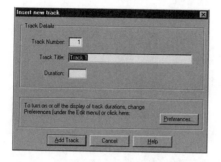

Figure 11.7

The Insert New Track dialog box enables you to enter information for each track on the CD.

Note the Preferences button in Figure 11.7. This brings up the Preferences dialog box, which has several tabs that can help make your label designing fun, but much more complicated. This is the same Preferences dialog box that pops up when you select Preferences from the main program's Edit menu. For now, don't worry about it. We will discuss the preferences you can set for the program in just a few more minutes.

Entering information in this window is no different from any other generic Windows dialog box. You can move between the fields with a click from your mouse or use the Tab key to jump through them all in order. You can give the track names any title you want, but generally speaking, naming a track Celine Dion's "My Heart Will Go On" when it's actually Metallica's "Enter Sandman" is only good for practical jokes.

When you've entered all the information you need for the first track, click the Add Track button and the track information appears on the main program window. The Insert New Track dialog box does remain on the screen, though, advancing the track number to the next track; you can continue to add tracks until you are done. Take note when entering track information that Jewel Case Creator sizes the text you enter according to the number of tracks you use. This helps ensure everything fits on the label appropriately. When you have finished, click Done. You can then see the results in the main window of Jewel Case Creator (see Figure 11.8).

Figure 11.8

When you have finished adding each track, they all appear on the jewel case insert.

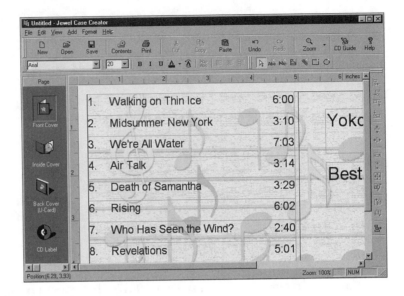

Choosing Your Theme and Background

Up to this point, we've covered how to get the CD information onto the various pieces that make up the CD insert and CD label. One thing we've completely ignored is the background art that accompanies the jewel case parts. For those who find Jewel Case Creator's default background for labels to be about as pretty to look at as Linda Blair in *The Exorcist*, there is good news. These "background" elements can be inserted several ways. In the following sections, we look at themes and backgrounds. In the next chapter, we'll cover how to incorporate your own artwork into the cover.

Unwanted Changes

Because clicking OK with a theme selected changes your labels to that theme, be sure that it's the theme you want. If you're only browsing the themes for the moment and don't want to change, click Cancel instead.

What Is a Theme?

With Jewel Case Creator, you get a small selection of *themes*. In the examples shown so far in this chapter, the musical notes background, meant for audio CDs, is called the music theme. The application comes with many themes, both for audio and data CDs. We won't cover them all here, but instead just tell you how to change them. For those who regularly visit the Internet—and who doesn't nowadays—visit Roxio's site at www.roxio.com for daily updates that enable you to download new themes from its site.

When you click the Format menu in Jewel Case Creator and then select Change Theme, it brings up the Change Theme dialog box shown in Figure 11.9. You can see the current theme displayed, for the folded front cover/inside card, the U-card, and the CD label. You can also see titles of other themes to choose from. If you make a lot of copies, you might want to vary the themes a bit, so that all your CDs don't look alike! Unfortunately, the theme titles in the left window pane don't give you clue one about what they actually look like. Clicking one of these titles, however, enables you to use the right pane to view the various themes. To change a theme, just click it and then click OK.

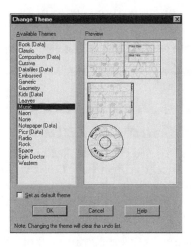

Figure 11.9

You can change the theme for the jewel case art by selecting Format/Change Theme.

Notice that a small check box is also near the bottom of this window called Set As Default Theme. If this box is checked when you click OK, any new labels you create will start out using the current theme.

Changing Backgrounds

This is similar to changing themes, but instead, you can vary the background by selecting a picture or color. To open the Backgrounds dialog box, click the Format menu and select Change Background. If you click Select a Color from the box that comes up, you will see the familiar (to regular Windows users) dialog box that enables you to select a background color. Note that you'll need a color printer, such as an inkjet, for this to work properly. If it's only black and white, this selection is about as useful to you as a bowling ball in a game of ping pong.

No Themes

Choosing a background color overrides whatever theme you are using.

If you decide to change the background color, just click that color and then click OK. When choosing a background color, it's important to keep in mind what color the text is for your CD. Even the best eyes aren't going to pick up black text on a black background!

Cross Reference

To learn about changing text colors, inserting pictures, and other ways to manipulate graphics and text in Jewel Case Creator, check out Chapter 12, "You've Got the Look: Using Graphics and Other Advanced Stuff with Jewel Case Creator."

Don't Get Burned

Paper is King

Before you even think about starting the printing process, make sure you have the correct kind of paper or label stock in the printer first!

Finally! Printing the Jewel Case Inserts and CD Label

After you've used the Add CD Contents or the manual-entry method to finish your CD covers or label, you can print the results. If you thought adding the titles and artist information was easy with Add/Add CD Contents, printing is just about as easy.

To get started, click the Print icon on the toolbar or select Print from the File menu. The Print dialog box pops up to enable you to make some changes before you print. In addition to selecting the printer (if you have more than one), there are some other options on this dialog box, shown in Figure 11.10, that you also need to pay close attention to.

Figure 11.10

The Print dialog box gives you many options.

Line 'em Up

When printing to precut inserts, it's a good idea to print to a regular sheet of paper first. If you place the test page back to back with the labels page, you can make sure that the printer is printing inside the labels and not slipping off the edge. If it is off a bit, you can use the Adjust Printer option to remedy the problem.

The most important button on this dialog box is the Page Setup button. This opens the Page Setup dialog box where you can select the kind of stock you are printing with (see Figure 11.11). If you are using labels from one of the firms mentioned earlier in this chapter or from one of the myriad of others, this is where you make sure Jewel Case Creator knows it.

Figure 11.11

The Page Setup dialog box enables you to select to which kind of label or jewel case insert stock you are printing.

Clicking the drop-down box labeled Current Paper Type brings up the list of paper options you can choose from. Jewel Case Creator supports the majority of the big names and, if you go with my suggestion at the beginning of the chapter and use generic card stock, includes a generic output option.

After choosing the type of paper you're using for each of the labels, click the OK button on the Print dialog box to return to the print window.

Finally, you need to select which of the label types you want to print. Near the bottom of the Print window (shown in Figure 11.10), is a dialog area with three tabs (again, for each of the label types). Each of these tabs has a check box on it that enables you to select which labels you want to print. If you want to print just the front and inside covers, you can. If you want to print all the covers, but not the CD label, you can. If you want to become the leader of the free world ... you're reading the wrong book.

After you've selected what to print and what you plan to print it on, you're finally ready to put an end to the insanity and print! Click the OK button at the bottom of the window and await the results.

Let's Talk About Preferences

A subject that fits neatly between this introduction about how to create CD inserts and labels for audio CDs and the next section that talks about the same for data CDs is the Preferences dialog box that enables you to control certain aspects of how the Jewel Case Creator program works. To bring up the Preferences dialog box, select Preferences from the Edit menu in Jewel Case Creator. Figure 11.12 shows this dialog box and the tabs you can use.

Figure 11.12

The Preferences dialog box contains tabs that let you control some aspects of the program.

Under the first tab, named Assistance, I have two check boxes selected. The first simply tells the program to pop up one of those reminder boxes when your cursor falls on an object, such as when you pass over a field you can edit and the text "Double-click to edit" appears. These reminders can be very useful if you don't use the program frequently. The second option is how you turn on or off that little CD guide guy who appeared at the beginning of this chapter. If you truly need to be guided, step by step, through some tasks, leave this check box selected so he will appear when you first start up the program.

Even if you turn off this little guy, you can still invoke him because you'll find on the toolbar a mini-picture of him labeled CD Guide.

The Internet Tab

The Internet tab is where you can control the download of information about a CD from an Internet source. The first check box on this tab allows you to enable or disable Internet downloads.

The second and third check boxes refer to how this is done. The second simply makes the program prompt you before performing the download.

The last check box, if selected, opens up two fields that you can use to specify the name (or numerical Internet address) of a proxy server and the port to use on that server. This is typically useful only if you are using the program from a work environment where most networks are connected by a security firewall to the Internet. Ask your supervisor or network administrator, if you don't already know, for the proxy server and port information.

The Printing Tab

This very important tab—from my cheap point of view—is an important one. It is on this tab of the Preferences property sheet that you can instruct the program to print the necessary lines on the output that show you where to cut the generic stock and where to fold it. For premade labels, this feature won't really help you out much. However, if you're using the Generic (Plain Paper) print option and must cut out the inserts yourself, this is actually quite helpful.

In addition, I must add that my fingers got very tired using scissors, trying to cut a straight line. Those of you who have also joined the, "I'm not young anymore" club and expect to cut out a lot of inserts may want to invest in a paper cutter!

The Tracks Tab

This tab enables you to select several things relating to how track information is displayed on the finished printed copy:

➤ **Show Track Number**—If selected, the track number appears on the jewel case inserts right before the audio track title.

➤ **Show Track Time**—This field might or might not be useful to you. It is simply used to show the time occupied by the current track.

➤ **Single/Double Column**—Each of these radio buttons is exclusive of the other. If you have only a few tracks on the CD, choose to print them in a single column. If this is a more voluminous CD, choose two column.

The Units Tab

This tab enables you to specify the method used for measurement in CD jewel case layout. You can select inches or centimeters.

Using Roxio's Jewel Case Creator for Data CDs

Using Jewel Case Creator to make data CD labels isn't much different from making them for audio discs. One thing is different, however—the list of available themes. Although some overlap does exist, many of the themes are geared specifically for use with either an audio or a data CD, but not both. For example, the music theme you saw in previous figures in this chapter consists of a musical note design. Another theme looks like an old-fashioned radio. These aren't available for data CDs. This is done on purpose. For example, whereas an audio theme might need a field to represent the playing time of the track, a data CD does not. Fortunately, no guesswork is involved for which themes work with which CD types. Data-only themes have the word "data" next to them!

Adding the CD Contents

Adding the contents of a data CD to the jewel case inserts of a CD can be an ominous task! It's not likely that you're going to store just two or three files (unless you're creating artwork with high graphics resolutions or working for NASA). Instead, you're likely to store a large number of files, and probably folders, on any CD-R you record.

If you have chosen a data theme, the program attempts to fill in the contents of the CD, as you can see in Figure 11.13, by simply listing the directories and files it finds until it runs out of room. If it doesn't happen automatically, you can force the issue by clicking the Add menu and then selecting Add CD Contents, just like you did with an audio CD insert.

Figure 11.13

The Jewel Case Creator starts a list of the folders and files it finds on your disc if you click Add and then CD Contents.

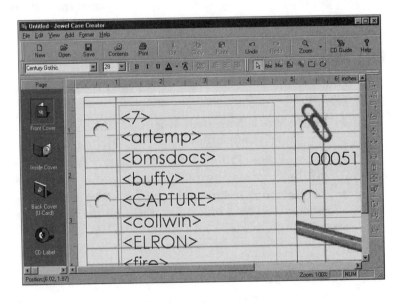

Obviously, using the Add Contents method won't be useful to you unless you have a very small number of files (that also have very descriptive names). Also, if you don't need to list the files or folders, you can do away with a U-card for this CD and just print the CD label and the front card piece. For that, all you need is a descriptive title. Choose Front Cover from the left toolbar; you see just a single field, similar to the one in Figure 11.14.

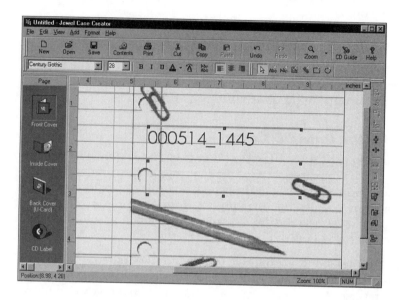

Figure 11.14

The front view of a data CD shows only one field in which to place information.

In the example shown in Figure 11.14, Jewel Case Creator inserted the label my computer assigned to the disc when it was written. If anything, it looks like a bizarre locker combination and is not particularly useful. Changing this field is no different from changing the title of an audio CD. If you double-click inside the field, the existing name becomes highlighted. Enter a useful new name, press Enter, and that's all she wrote.

Should you run out of room entering the name or description for your disc, remember that you can resize the field by clicking it once to select it and then clicking and holding one of the handles to stretch or shrink it as necessary.

Between Tracks

Data Backups

If your data CD is part of a periodic backup of important information on your computer, you should include a date as part of the disc title.

Editing Text on Jewel Case Inserts for Data CDs

As you saw in Figure 11.14, only one large field, by default, is on the front of the CD cover. When you choose Add CD Contents, the inside insert and the U-card insert automatically get a listing of the directories and files on the CD, space permitting. Only a single field, however, is used for this listing. This differs from the track listing produced for audio CDs. In that case, each track becomes a separate field you can edit. Here, you have only one field.

You can easily edit this field any time you want. To replace the existing text, just double-click the field; the text in the field turns blue. You can press the Delete key to delete the text and then enter your own. Remember, in addition to using the handles to resize a field, you can move the entire field around on the page by placing your cursor inside it, holding down the left mouse button, and dragging it.

Using Add Tracks for the Data CD Cover

Oddly enough, you can also use the Add Tracks option from the Add menu when using a data CD jewel case theme. Because we covered using the Add Tracks process earlier in this chapter, we won't go over it again here. Using this capability, you can add a numbered list of items that describe the purpose of the CD, or even a list of the major programs or data files. Because the disc doesn't really contain any audio tracks, you can just leave the time field blank.

There is one pitfall to this method: It is exclusive to the Add CD Contents method. If you've already used the Add CD Contents option, Add Track is no longer available. This rule also works in reverse. After you use the Add Track option, you can no longer click Add CD Contents.

Label Do's and Don'ts

There are a few things you must keep in mind about CD labels and inserts. First, the label side of the CD-R disc is actually closer to the data layer of the disc than the data layer is to the bottom of the disc. The other side, where the disc is read, has a protective layer about a millimeter of distance between the surface and the data layer.

Because no such protection is on the label side where you are going to be sticking CD labels, you have to be very careful after you place the label. First, under no circumstances try to remove a label after you've stuck in onto a CD-R disc. You can damage the reflective surface and render the CD unusable.

Second, if you print with an ink jet printer, remember that water causes the printing to run. Don't leave CD-R discs with ink jet–printed labels lying around on the coffee table!

Finally, if you do use a ballpoint pen to write on the label surface, whether it is directly onto the CD's label surface or onto a sticky label that you've attached, do so very carefully. Remember, the reflective surface is just a short distance away, and it doesn't take much pressure to push the ink into the data layer (destroying the disc). To be safe, use a water-based felt-tip pen instead.

The Least You Need to Know

➤ You can use premade labels, generic print stock, or even plain paper to create custom labels for your CD.

➤ Although it's not terribly powerful, using Roxio's Jewel Case Creator is an easy way to quickly create audio or data CD labels and inserts!

➤ You can use Jewel Case Creator's Add Contents option to automatically try to identify the names and lengths of tracks on your CD. If that doesn't work, you can use the Add Track option to enter them manually.

➤ Even though Jewel Case Creator comes with a variety of themes, some of them can be used for only a data or an audio CD, but not both.

Chapter 12

You've Got the Look: Using Graphics and Other Advanced Stuff with Jewel Case Creator

In This Chapter

➤ Get more out of your text in Jewel Case Creator

➤ Use categories to link text fields and save yourself from repeatedly typing the same information.

➤ Use graphics to add pictures and backgrounds to your CD labels and covers

In the last chapter, we created simple jewel case inserts and labels by using predefined fields for the artist, CD title, track titles, and so on. However, you can do a lot more to manipulate text with Jewel Case Creator. In this chapter, we'll go over some of the program's more advanced features that can add a more professional look, or at least a snazzier one, to your CD labeling fun.

Other Ways to Play with Text

To kick off this graduate program in Jewel Case Creator, we'll deal with some of the ways you can manipulate text to give your CD labels a better look. In the first place, you don't have to stick with the fields that are predefined for each template as we discussed in the last chapter. In true Jesse Ventura style, you can create your own independent fields and edit them as you see fit.

Predefined Fields Are Still Useful

Although you can do a lot in terms of creating your own fields, don't forget that predefined fields still have their advantages. Their biggest asset is that they can be linked so that, for example, when you fill in the artist's name on the front jewel case cover, it is automatically filled in on the U–card and CD label as well.

To quickly recall, all you have to do to edit a text field, whether it is predefined or one you create, is to double-click the field. You can then change the text's font or size and add, delete, or modify the text.

Adding a New Text Field

The most basic aspect of adding your own flavor to a jewel case layout is to add your own new text fields. For the purposes of this example, I'm going to make it easy to add text by starting out with a blank format. That is, instead of using one of the predefined themes that already contains text fields and graphics material, I have selected the theme called None, which basically starts with a clean slate with which to work. To change the theme to None, follow these steps:

1. Click the Format menu.
2. Click Change Theme.
3. In the Change Theme dialog box, select None.
4. Click OK to complete the change, and you'll find yourself back in the main program.

Working with no theme means that no grayed-out text fields are waiting for you to click them. The true artists among you can work free from the interference of Jewel Case Creator's handholding. Of course, that means you need to create some new fields yourself. To add a simple text field, just click the Add menu and then Text. In Figure 12.1, you can see that a very small text field shows up in the center of the layout. Some kind of text is already in the field, but the frame is so small that the text is unreadable. Why would Jewel Case Creator make a frame this small to start out with? Because nothing is ever supposed to be easy when using computers, of course!

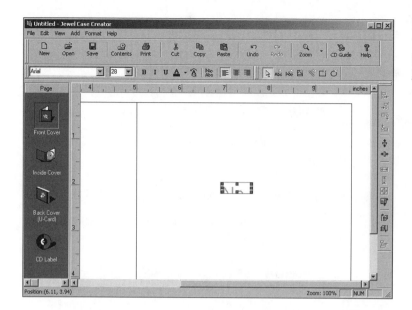

Figure 12.1

When you add a text field, you must size it to your needs.

You can make the text box larger by using the handles that appear as small boxes on each side of the field when you click it. When your cursor turns into a double arrow, you can click the left mouse button and move the handle to shrink or enlarge the box. However, in this case, shrinking it probably isn't an option. To place your own poetic prose in it, just double-click the field and type whatever strikes your fancy.

Cross Reference

Be sure to check out Chapter 11, "Using Jewel Case Creator to Create Labels and Inserts," if you need more help with using fields.

You can choose to create several text fields on any part of the jewel case inserts or the CD label. For example, you could make one large text box that could be used to enter both the artist and title of a music CD. Or, if creating a data CD, you could use the large box to enter a title and a paragraph explaining the contents of the disc.

Text Fields Have Properties!

You can change many things about the text that appears on your CD jewel case or label. After you've double-clicked a field to put it into editing mode, you can use the drop-down menus on your toolbar to change the font or point size. If you use a word processor such as Microsoft Word or Notepad, you're probably used to working with this stuff.

Between Tracks

Editing Shortcut

In addition to double-clicking, you can also put a field into editing mode by right-clicking the field and selecting Edit.

Arcane CD Speak

What's Your Point?

Points and fonts are printer's terms that define the kind of character you'll see on the printed copy—or in today's terms, on the computer screen. A font is a typeface that has a distinctive style or look. The point size, which is measured in 1/72 of an inch, represents the size of the characters as they appear on the screen or printed page. Increasing the point size increases the size of the font.

You can change properties for the text box itself by right-clicking the text field. A small menu pops up with the usual editing commands, such as edit text, cut, copy, and delete.

Other options, which we'll get to shortly, are also available here. The one we're interested in right now is called Properties, so give it a click and take a gander at Figure 12.2.

The dialog box that pops up enables you to modify both the font and size for the text, along with other attributes for the text box itself:

➤ **Text Style**—You can select the check boxes labeled Bold, Italic, and Underline to change the style of the text.

➤ **Positioning**—You can select the check boxes labeled Left-justified, Centered, and Right-justified to position your text in the box.

➤ **Text Type**—This option gives you two radio buttons that determine whether the text will be displayed in a straight line or in a curved format. Select Straight or Curved for this option. Straight text is the ordinary text you usually type on a page. Curved text makes the text box curve so that it can, for example, conform to the shape of a CD label. Figure 12.3 shows you a text box that started out as a rectangle and then was changed to have the curved attribute.

➤ **Color**—This option uses a drop-down menu to enable you to select the color for the text you'll enter into the text box.

➤ **Rotation**—You can rotate your text box by using the radio buttons for 0, 90, 180, and 270 degrees. Figure 12.3 shows an example of several text boxes that have be configured like this.

When you've finished making your selections, just click the OK button. Of course, you can also click Cancel if you change your mind.

In Figure 12.3, you can see that a curved text box fits around the CD label perfectly. Just because it's a curved text box doesn't mean that you can't continue to do other things with it that you can do to an ordinary text box. Figure 12.3 also shows that you can still grab the handles to resize the box and it will still keep its curved shape. When you double-click to edit a curved text box, however, another straight text box appears to make your typing easier. When you've finished adding or modifying the text, press Enter and the text you've edited will appear in the curved box.

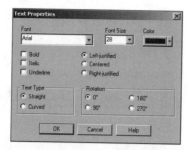

Figure 12.2

The Properties sheet for the text box enables you to specify a wide range of options for the field.

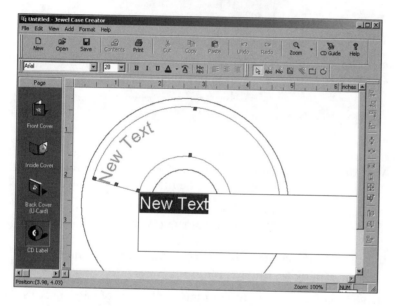

Figure 12.3

A curved text box is ideal for a CD label.

As you can see in Figure 12.4, each text box can be configured using a different angle of rotation. Although the uses of this might seem limited, those who want to design elaborate jewel case covers can be a bit more creative with these options.

Linking Text Fields

When you used a predefined theme to start your jewel case layout, you probably noticed that some fields were linked to others. For example, if you enter the artist's name on the front cover, it also appears on the CD label. This is because these two fields are members of the same category. All fields in the same category contain the same text. Even though themed labels select the categories for you, that doesn't mean you can't set them yourself, too. If you have information that needs to be repeated in several places, you can just create the appropriate fields and then place them in the same category.

Figure 12.4

You can use the Properties sheet for a text box to change the angle of rotation as it will appear on your jewel case layout.

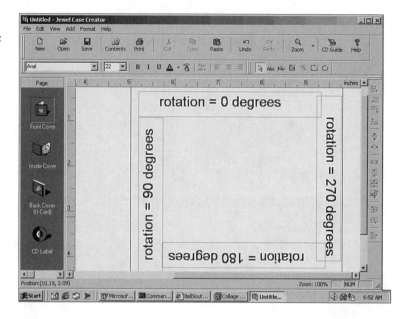

To get to the category option, highlight the first text box (so that the sizing handles show up) and then give it the mighty right-click treatment. From the menu that appears, select Categories. In Figure 12.5, you can see the many categories available.

Several categories are available here to choose from. Although not shown, because it is scrolled out of view, you can also select None so that the text box can stand alone. Just click the category type with which you want the field to be associated and click OK. After you repeat this process, using the same category type, for other fields in your layout, you will find that changing the text in one changes it for all.

Just remember, if you have linked text boxes in your layout that are of varying sizes, such as a CD title on the front insert with it repeated on the spine of the jewel box, you must size the text for each one appropriately. You don't want to waste a precious jewel case label because you're trying to squeeze in a 24-pt. font on the spine!

Figure 12.5

You can assign a category to each field. This links the fields to make text entry much easier.

Adding Background Graphics

One of the niftier Jewel Case Creator features discussed in the last chapter was for adding themes to your jewel case. Although the program has a number of themes—for both data and audio CDs—that you can use, you can also toss them aside like used garbage and add your own.

For those who haven't worked much with graphics files, the various formats and types can seem a little overwhelming. With Jewel Case Creator, you have to worry about only two because they are the only ones the program supports. Fortunately, they are also the two most common. One is Windows *bitmap*, recognizable in File Explorer by the .bmp extension. The other is *JPEG*. JPEGs come in a couple different flavors, but have either a .jpg or .jpeg file extension. If you have a graphics file in one of these formats then you can import that picture into your jewel case layout and make minor edits to it.

If talk of graphic file formats only serves to make you dizzy, don't worry! If you're not sure whether the application will support it, just try it and see. The worst you'll get is Jewel Case Creator complaining that it can't read it. If that happens, you're still not left out in the cold. Windows has a program called Imaging (click Start, Programs, Accessories to find it, depending on your version of Windows) that you can use to convert the file to the appropriate format. Just open the file, click the File menu, and select Save As. In the dialog box that pops up, use the drop-down list labeled Save As Type to choose either bmp or jpg. If, by chance,

Between Tracks

Making Your Own Categories

You should keep in mind that, generally speaking, categories in Jewel Case Creator really don't mean anything in terms of what kind of text or numbers you can enter in them. Even though you can't create your own categories, if you want to use a category not shown in the list, just select any one and use it however you see fit. For example, you could enter the artist name in a field categorized for track length and it wouldn't make a lick of difference to Jewel Case Creator.

you've got some wacky graphic file from the fifth dimension that Imaging doesn't recognize either, you'll need to look for other options. Many other graphics programs can be downloaded from the Web for free (or as shareware), and they can handle more files types.

Between Tracks

Getting Graphics

If you're going to be producing your own CDs and are taking the time to read this chapter then you're probably serious about creating good-looking covers. But, where do you get them?

If you have a scanner, you can scan in old album covers (my vinyl past is showing again). The same goes for CD covers. You also can download a lot of graphic files, both those relating to the CD's topics and those that are just simple pictures and other backgrounds from the Internet.

Heck, the way things have been going with MP3, Napster, and others, you might want to start downloading graphics now, before someone gets sued for using a patented color and they're not available on the Net anymore!

Two methods can be used for importing a graphics file into Jewel Case Creator. First, you can import the picture itself into a field and then size and position it somewhere in the layout, as you would a text field. Second, you can select the graphics file to be the background for your jewel case and label. In either case, you must make sure you know where the file is stored on your hard disk. Usually, it's best to use one folder, such as My Documents or My Pictures, to store these files. There is an advantage to using the first method in that you can add more than one picture. As always, you can still add text no matter what graphics you're using.

To import one or more pictures (not as a background), first select the view, such as Front Cover, U-Card, or Label, and then do the following:

1. Click the Add menu.
2. Click Picture.

3. A dialog box appears enabling you to locate the picture file. When you find the correct file to insert, double-click the filename or highlight it by clicking once, and then click the Open button.

4. The picture then appears on the layout. You can move the picture around to place it where you want it by holding down the left mouse button inside the picture field and dragging it to a new location. The picture file, similar to text boxes, also has handles you can use to resize it.

Figure 12.6 shows an example of a picture that has been imported to the front cover.

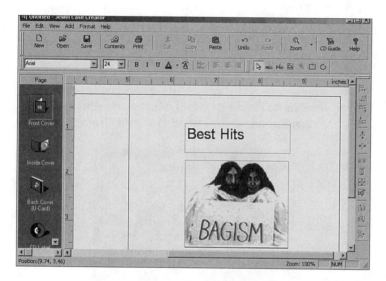

Figure 12.6

You can add pictures in addition to text for your jewel case layout.

To add a background picture, which can be used to cover the whole front cover, back insert, or label, use the following steps instead:

1. Click the Format menu.

2. Click Change Background.

3. The Change Background dialog box that appears enables you to select a background color or a picture. Note the other options available in this dialog box. You can choose where the background is located. It can be placed on any part of the jewel case insert or CD label, and can even be spanned across the front cover and inside cover. Click Select a Picture.

4. A standard Open dialog box appears from which you can locate the directory and file that contains the picture you want to use. When you've made your selection, click the Open button.

Thumbnail?

The term *thumbnail* is often used in graphics programs to refer to a miniature representation of a graphics file that can be previewed much more easily and quickly.

5. You should now find yourself back in the Change Background dialog box. However, for the views you've selected, you'll see thumbnails of the picture you selected (see Figure 12.7).

6. You can continue and select a different background picture for each of the major components of the jewel case and label. You do not have to use the same picture for each part of the package.

7. Click OK when you are satisfied with the picture(s) you've selected. The background picture(s) will now be displayed when you select those views in the main program.

After you've added one or more background pictures, you can still add text boxes, circles, and squares to continue composing your jewel case and CD label artwork.

Figure 12.7

You can add pictures to be the background of part or all of the jewel case and label printout.

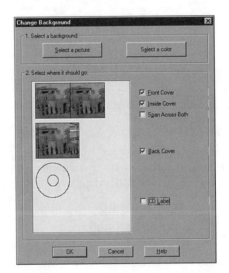

Adding Circles and Squares

If adding text and pictures isn't enough for you, you can also add circles or squares to the layout in the same manner you do the background figure. Just click the Add menu and select Square or Circle. For each circle or square you include, you can select certain properties for it. These shapes are manipulated in the same way you would a normal text field. However, a few options unique just to shapes are available, which you can find using the shape's Properties page (see Figure 12.8). Like any other object on the Jewel Case Creator layout, just right-click the shape and choose Properties from the menu that appears.

The options here are pretty self-explanatory. For both circles and squares, you can select the background color and a variety of patterns that can be used inside the boundaries of the circle or square. You also can vary the color and width of the lines that draw the object or change the pattern lines. All these options have drop-down lists that enable you to select whichever one suits your needs.

Now, when you want to put this all together, an important thing to remember is that each of the items we've worked with, whether they be text boxes, circles, or squares, can be moved around from foreground to background—top to bottom or vice versa. In the example shown in Figure 12.7, I created a square. Because Jewel Case Creator places new fields on top, any text I might have had behind the square would now be hidden. If computers had any common sense, they would understand that hidden text isn't of much use. But let's face it: For all that computers can do, they're really still pretty dumb. Fortunately, Jewel Case Creator lets you set your computer straight.

To change the order of these kinds of objects, just right-click the field in question and select either To Top or To Bottom from the menu that appears. Even though To Top works great if you can see at least part of a hidden object, if it's totally hidden there's nothing you can click to bring up the menu. Instead, just keep clicking away on the objects and fields hiding what you want to see, sending everything to the bottom, and eventually your missing item will pop to the top!

Editing Help

If you're like me, you like to see things in detail when making important changes. The Jewel Case Creator program enables you to perform a few standard chores that can help make creating CD labels and covers much easier.

One of the more useful options you can use is to zoom in or out to get a better look at whatever masterpiece you're creating. While you're working on a particular object, just select Zoom from the View menu. Then, select how much larger (or smaller) you want the perspective to be. The values in this menu range from 75% to 200%, but you can select the Custom option to choose your own zoom size. Zooming in and out can help you better judge the finished object, as well as fine-tune your art during its creation.

Don't forget that the standard Windows editing commands are also available under the Edit menu. These include the great lifesaver—Undo—and other favorites such as cut, copy, and paste.

Undo enables you to erase the last change you made to a layout. This is a lifesaver that can bring you back from the abyss if you make a critical mistake. If, for example, you deleted a field by accident, you can bring it back with just a couple of clicks (or by pressing Ctrl+Z on your keyboard).

Anyone who has used a Microsoft Office program has probably used cut, copy, and paste. In the case of Jewel Case Creator, copy is particularly useful if you want to, well, copy an existing field to another part of the case cover or CD label, but you don't want them to be associated with categories. Cut is handy if you merely want to move the field from one part of the layout to another. In either case, you select the object you want, use the cut or copy command, and then use paste where you want that field to appear.

The Least You Need to Know

➤ When creating text fields, Jewel Case Creator enables you to customize the type of font, its size, and its orientation on the CD and jewel case layouts.

➤ You can link text fields by associating them with one of several available categories.

➤ Jewel Case Creator can do a lot more than just add song titles to your layout. It also includes basic graphical capabilities that enable you to insert your own pictures, backgrounds, and shapes.

Part 5

Other Nifty Programs and Tools for Your CD Recorder

As if what we've gone through so far isn't enough, now comes even more fun things you can do with your CD recorder. Use the extra programs that come with Easy CD Creator to create photo albums. Using the Sound Editor, you can take those files you extracted from your record collection and modify them to suit your recording taste buds.

If fun and games aren't what you're looking for, turn to Chapter 15 on troubleshooting which is placed, appropriately, near the end of this book! If you've read all the rest and are having a problem, here's where you can look to find some pointers about determining the cause or producing the remedy.

Finally, the Easy CD Creator application was used throughout most of this book as the sample application. That doesn't mean it's the only product out there. For the price, Roxio is great when you consider the features it offers. In the last chapter of this book, we look at two more products: MusicMatch Jukebox and Windows Media Player. These applications can burn CDs—in some cases not as well as Roxio's entry—but they also have other advantages. You can use them to store and sort music on your hard drive, using your computer as a jukebox when you need some company browsing the Web or writing up that essential report!

Chapter 13

Other Roxio Utilities

In This Chapter

➤ Using the Sound Editor

➤ Using the Session Selector

➤ Using Take Two for backups

This chapter digs into some of the miscellaneous utilities that come with Roxio Easy CD Creator 4.0. Editing a book can be a difficult job; just think back to the term papers you had to write in school! However, the Sound Editor is an easy to use tool that can help you fix up some of the problems that come with burning CDs. For example, if you record using Spin Doctor from an LP, you can use the sound editor to remove that little bit of unwanted silence from the beginning or end of a track. The Session Selector program allows you to select which session on a multisession CD you want to make active. Finally, Take Two allows you to make a backup of your system that can be used, in most cases, to completely restore your system.

WAV Only

Sound Editor can use only files recorded in the WAV format. It cannot open MP3 and Windows Media Audio files.

Using the Sound Editor

One of the best things about being able to put WAV files on your hard drive is the fact that you can edit them to suit various needs. After all, if you're recording In-A-Gadda-Da-Vida, you might not want to eat up a quarter of your CD time on a drum solo. The Sound Editor packaged with Easy CD Creator Deluxe 4.0 is used to modify WAV files that you have extracted from other sources.

The Sound Editor enables you to add special effects, cut and paste sound clips, and perform a host of other features. To get to the Sound Editor, click the Edit button in either Easy CD Creator or Spin Doctor.

Getting WAV Files

To extract a CD track to a WAV file using Easy CD Creator, open that program, right-click the track(s) you want in the Explorer pane, and click Extract to File. Remember that a WAV file, although bigger than an MP3, is almost exactly the same as the CD-DA format that is recorded on the CD, whereas MP3s are a small step down in sound quality.

If you prefer to start the Sound Editor from your desktop click Start, Programs, Roxio Easy CD Creator 4, Features, and then the Sound Editor icon. Figure 13.1 shows you the opening window for this application.

At this point, you can use the File menu to open an existing WAV file on your hard drive for editing.

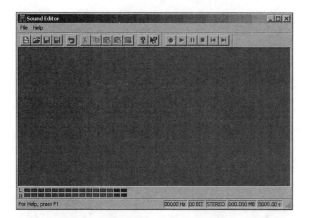

Figure 13.1

The Sound Editor enables you to make changes to WAV files before recording them to CD.

Opening WAV Files So You Can Make Edits

To open a WAV file that you have just recorded or saved to your hard disk, use the File menu and select Open. Then, navigate your computer's directory structure to find the file you want.

Working with Multiple Files

You can open multiple WAV files at the same time, but you have to open them one at a time. Unfortunately, the Shift+Click method won't allow you to select more than one file. So, if you plan to mix and match stuff from different audio files, just open the first, then the second, and so on. Each appears as its own window within the main program. You can cut and paste portions of the wave form from one WAV file window to another.

In Figure 13.2, you can see the Open dialog box that is used to select the track(s) you want to work with in the Sound Editor. If you're not sure whether you've selected the correct file, click the Preview button to give it a listen. When previewing a song, the Preview button changes to a Stop button, which you can use to stop listening when you've heard enough.

Figure 13.2

You can select to preview each track before you edit it using the Open dialog box.

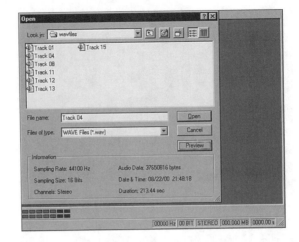

Notice in this dialog box that there is an Information section at the bottom showing a lot of technical gobbledy-gook about the quality of the WAV file you are about to work with. In this example, the file is recorded using a sampling rate of 44,100Hz, with a sampling size of 16 bits. The only thing you need to know about these numbers is that this is approximately CD quality. If you see lower numbers then this would be something of slightly poorer quality.

After you have found the file you want, click Open. As you can see in Figure 13.3, this opens the audio track in the main program window.

Figure 13.3

After you've opened an audio track, the editor brings up a window for it so you can start editing.

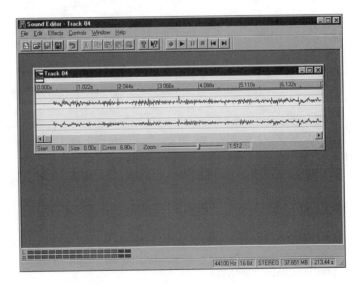

Arcane CD Speak

Amplitude?

I'll bet you've heard the word *amplitude* many times before and never given a second thought as to what it means. Basically, it's the volume of the sound track. In Sound Editor, you can actually "see" the amplitude of the audio in the file. The sound track is a continuous line that goes up and down as the volume changes. The greater the distance between the high and low points, the greater the amplitude, or volume.

As you can see in this figure, two jagged lines are drawn—one for each channel for the stereo effect. The lines are a graphic representation of the audio track, showing the amplitude of the audio signal. At the bottom of the window, you can see the data we just talked about concerning the WAV file. You can see the 44,100MHz, 16-bit stereo information here, along with the length of the track and how much space it takes to store this song. Although this 37.6MB file doesn't take up a large chunk of space on modern hard drives that often hold 10GB–20GB, I can still remember, back in the days when the wheel was still a pretty nifty idea, when PC hard drives couldn't store more than 5MB of data. The march of progress, 2001 style!

Navigating the WAV (File)

When you first open a WAV file, you'll notice that a slider bar appears at the bottom of the window. Unless your audio track is only a few seconds long and fits in this small editing window, you can use this slider bar to move to various parts of the file. If you want to edit a portion of the song that is, say, halfway through the track, just move the slider bar to about halfway. Of course, unlike text editors, this can be a little tricky. After all, it's not like you can look at a waveform and understand what it "says," like you can with text. To ensure you've gotten to the part of the file you want to edit, you can click a part of the graphic representation of the WAV data and then use the Preview button on the toolbar to actually hear the selected portion. You also can click and drag across a selection, like you can with text, to preview a specific portion of the track. If you're not where you want to be, move the slider bar around (or use the arrows you find at both ends if you want to move only a little to fine-tune your location).

Another interesting feature you can use is the Zoom feature. The Zoom feature also uses a slider bar, but its function is radically different! Zoom, predictably, expands or compresses the visual representation of the audio track onscreen. In the last paragraph, I told you that unless your song was just a few seconds long, the whole thing will not fit into the window and you must move to the part you want to edit.

Suppose all you want to do is chop off a little silence at the beginning of the track and a little at the end? Wouldn't it be nice to simply collapse the whole track so that it *does* fit in the window to enable you to see the whole file at once? Well, that's what Zoom does. If you move the slider bar the Zoom feature uses to the far right, the graphic representation of the WAV file is compressed and—usually—the whole thing fits within the space the editing window provides. Of course, you wouldn't want to do this if you're trying to just find one little annoying pop or click to delete. If you compress the track display too much, you'll have a much more difficult time trying to locate a tiny portion of the file.

Cutting and Pasting Audio Data

The two basic functions used for any kind of editing—cutting and pasting—are done easily in the Sound Editor. You can simply place your cursor where you want to start selecting the sound clip, hold down the left mouse button, and drag to the point where you want the selection to stop. In Figure 13.4, you can see that part of this WAV file has been selected using the cursor method.

Figure 13.4

You can select part of the WAV track just like you can text when you are editing the file.

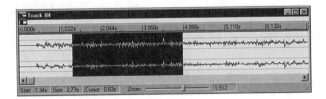

Selecting Shortcut

If you want to quickly select the entire track without having to use your mouse, just use the Edit menu and click Select All. This highlights the entire track so the effect you apply is for the entire file.

Consider the Edit menu your holy grail for making changes to a WAV file. If you want to cut out the selected part of the track, just select Cut from the Edit menu. To copy text, click Copy after you've selected part of the sound track. To insert a cut or copied piece of audio, place your cursor elsewhere in the track (or in another WAV file, for all that matters) and then use the Edit menu to click Paste. If you're unhappy with the results, the Undo command can turn back the clock, erasing your most recent change. From there, you can use Undo to remove the change right before that, too. Finally, you can put an undone change back in place using the Redo command.

Between Tracks

Just Sing, Darn It!

At the start of this chapter, I told you that you could use Sound Editor to chop out parts of the audio file you don't need, such as too much silence at the start or end of a track. Those of you with a lot of "live" recordings should consider that you can use Sound Editor to remove some of the junk usually found on these albums, like the artist talking, long applauses, and so on.

In addition to the normal paste command that you would expect, the Edit menu also has a command called Mixed Paste. This feature enables you to merge the sound clip with the other data at the point at which it is pasted. In effect, this is like having two tracks playing at the same time.

Using Special Effects on Sounds

Even though you're not going to find yourself using Sound Editor to create sound effects for the next *Star Wars* epic, you can apply some basic special effects to all or part of a clip. If the audio track you are working with is in stereo format, you can apply some effects to just one channel of the stereo track. You can find the different special effects you can use in the Effects menu. The effects that can be created using the Sound Editor are

➤ Amplify—The Amplify effect changes the volume of the track when it is played back. To use this effect, select part or all of the audio track using your cursor. Then, click Amplify on the Effects menu. A dialog box pops up and enables you to change the volume level for each track if this is a stereo track, as you can see in Figure 13.5.

Figure 13.5

The Amplification Settings dialog box enables you to change the volume of the audio data.

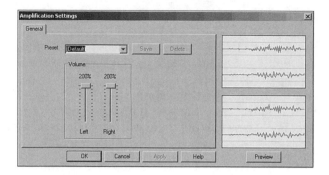

➤ DC offset—There are times when you might have hardware or other problems that cause an audio WAV file to be created with the waveform shifted from the baseline. This might be noticeable to you as a hissing in the background when you play the track. You can correct this using the Direct Current (DC) Offset effect.

➤ Echo—This is an audio effect that everyone is used to. It's just as easy to implement as the others. Select the part of the track you want to be echoed and then select Echo from the Effects menu. In Figure 13.6, you can see the dialog box you can use to control how this effect is applied.

Figure 13.6

The Echo Settings dialog box has several parameters to configure for the effect.

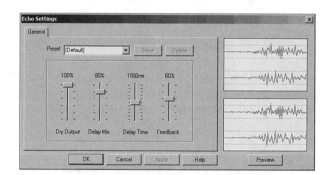

➤ Fade—this effect enables you to slowly increase or decrease the volume of the clip. You can specify a fade-in at the beginning of a clip and a fade-out at the end. There are two sliding bars for the fade effect. The one labeled Initial can be used to determine a fade-in at the beginning of the clip, whereas the one labeled Final enables you to control the degree of fading out at the end of the clip.

➤ Flange—This is a strange audio effect. It works much like an echo, but the delay times are not fixed as in an echo effect. In Figure 13.7, you can see that the controls for a flange effect are also more complicated than those for the echo effect.

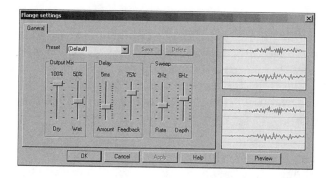

Figure 13.7

The Flange effect is similar to an echo effect.

➤ Format Conversion—This Effects menu selection, which is best left alone if you don't understand things such as sampling rates, applies to the entire WAV file with which you are working. It can be used to change the format of the WAV file, such as the rate at which sound is sampled and whether or not the track is in stereo or mono. To use this effect, just select Format Conversion from the Effects menu; the dialog box shown in Figure 13.8 pops up to enable you to make the appropriate format changes.

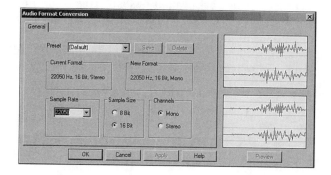

Figure 13.8

The Audio Format Conversion dialog box enables you to change the format type of the WAV file with which you are working.

➤ Graphic Equalization—This effect gives you a graphics equalizer on your desktop that can be used to manipulate the amplitude (amplification) of selected frequencies in the audio file. You might want to amplify a bass sound or lower the volume of a high-pitched sound.

➤ Invert—The Invert effect causes the waveform of the audio sound to be inverted vertically. This means that, if the original sound was increasing in volume, it will be decreasing after it is inverted, and vice versa. If you are pasting clips together into a single file, this might help by making one clip more compatible with another.

➤ Pitch Shift—This effect enables you to raise or lower the pitch of the track. This means you can take the audio track and change it from one musical key to another. If you are mixing two clips together into the same file, this can be useful by letting you match their pitches so that they blend together well.

What Are Effect Presets?

When you spend a lot of time fine-tuning something, isn't it nice to be able to save your settings so you don't have to go through that process all over again? For effects, some with complicated controls, this is accomplished by using *presets*. In all the dialog boxes for sound effects you've see so far, there has been a field called Preset near the top, and it has always said Default. Of course, that's because if you haven't changed anything, the dialog box pops up with the default values for that effect.

After you make changes to a particular effect, you can save those settings so you can recall them and use them again on another file. This does not save the audio information you are working on, though, just the positioning or selections made to the controls. To save a preset, place your cursor in the Presets field and enter something other than Default. After you've changed the text, the Save button becomes available; click it. The next time you use this effect, you can use the drop-down menu where the Default text appears to recall a particular preset you have created before.

Using the Session Selector

If you'll remember from Chapter 9, "Understanding and Using Multisession CDs," you can add data to CD-R discs in groups of tracks called *sessions*. This recording method enables you to write some of the CD at one sitting and add another session later. The problem with sessions is that, for audio players, only the first session will be seen. For CD-ROM drives, you can read any session on the disc, but the default session to read when opening such a disc is the last one.

Whether the sessions are audio or data, you need a way to select which session your computer CD-ROM uses. If you want to use a session other than the default, the Session Selector program can make it available for you. This is, perhaps, one of the easiest programs you can use in Easy CD Creator 4.0. To start the program, click Start, Programs, Easy CD Creator 4, Features, and click Session Selector.

Figure 13.9 shows you the main program window for this application. In this window, the disk drives installed on your computer show up in the left pane, whereas the contents of the CD drives you select show up in the right pane.

Figure 13.9

The Session Selector can be used to designate which session on a CD is to be used.

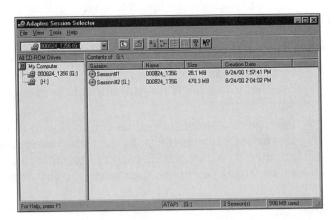

In Figure 13.9, you can see that a CD is inserted into a drive in this computer, which has more than one session burned into it. These sessions are listed as sessions #1 and #2. Notice also that the cryptic serial number–style label for session #2 is the same as what is listed next to the drive letter for this CD. This is because the last session is the default session when the CD is first read, and we've just opened the CD!

To change to another session, click the session you want, highlight it, and then use the Tools menu to click Activate Session. Now, when you use Windows Explorer or one of your other programs, such as Microsoft Word, the session you activated will be the one these programs see when they access this drive.

Making a Backup of Your Hard Drive Using Take Two

Roxio's Take Two application can be used to create a backup of your computer system on a CD-R or CD-RW disc. The program is simple to start. Just click Start, Programs, Easy CD Creator 4, and select System Backup CD from the menu. This launches the Take Two program, which operates like a wizard, prompting you through the process.

The Whole Disk or Nothing

Remember that this is a backup program for entire hard disks. If you just want to copy individual or groups of files and folder to a CD-R, see Chapter 4, "Using Easy CD Creator to Make Data CDs," or Chapter 8, "The Easiest Way to Pillage—Copying CDs Using Easy CD Copier."

In Figure 13.10, you can see the three-step process involved in a backup procedure. You select the backup's source and destination devices and then start the backup. For each procedure, click the appropriate icon, labeled well enough 1, 2, and 3.

Figure 13.10

*The Take Two interface is
straightforward and easy
to use.*

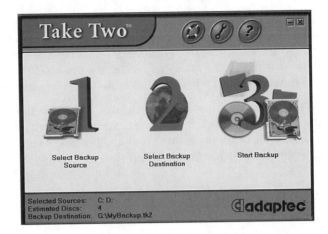

Each of the choices in the main menu brings up its own dialog box to prompt you for what it needs to continue. Clicking number 1 brings up the screen shown in Figure 13.11, which shows all the drives on your computer that Take Two can back up. Click the drive(s) you want to back up.

Figure 13.11

*You can select the logical
drives or the entire physical drive to be backed up.*

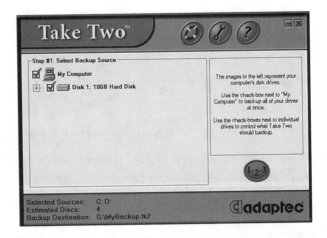

After you have selected the drive or drives to be backed up, click the 123 icon in the right part of the application. This button takes you back to the main part of the program where you can select the next step to continue. To select the destination for the backup data, of course, select step number 2. A dialog box similar to the one used for the source drive pops up, but instead of displaying all the disk drives on your system, it just shows the recordable CD drives (see Figure 13.12). If you only have one, like most people, this is an easy choice!

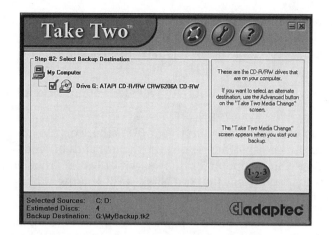

Figure 13.12

Next, you select the desti-nation for the backup, usually your CD-RW drive.

After you've made the oh-so-difficult selection of which drive you want to record to, click the 123 icon again and you're back to the main menu.

Between Tracks

It's Not Just for CDs

Those of you who have high-capacity removable storage, such as Zip or Jaz drives, also have the option of backing up to these devices. When you select the second option in the main Take Two window to specify the destination of the backup data, you can click the Advanced button to get to another dialog box. This Advanced dialog box allows you to specify writing your backup to another type of drive (even another hard disk).

Can you guess what you should click next?

Why, it's door number three, of course! Clicking the third option starts the count-down process leading to the backup.

Remember that Take Two can be used to back up one drive or all the drives on your computer. If you want to make a Take Two backup of only the main system disk, the program pops up a message telling you that you're forgetting about the other drives! It's just Take Two's way of telling you that you'll create a backup that can be used to restore the system disk and boot the system. If you have other disks, and you have

197

not selected them for this Take Two backup, you should be sure you have some other program you use regularly to back up those drives. Otherwise, the applications or data on those drives will not be recoverable using this Take Two backup CD if your computer's disks get fried.

Click the OK button to dismiss this box and continue, provided you understand what this message is telling you!

The next dialog box to pop up reminds you to limit your file activity on the drive while the backup is being performed—in other words, keep your hands off your computer during the backup! Using your computer, or more specifically, the drives you're backing up, can create errors that you won't find out about until you need to use the backup disc, only to find it doesn't work!

If you have open files on the backup disc, another pop-up dialog box tells you to close them, so that they can be backed up properly. After they are closed, click the Yes button to continue.

If you haven't already inserted a blank CD-R disc in the drive you've selected for the destination, the Take Two program tells you about it right away. Insert that disc!

The backup process takes some time to complete, depending on the amount of data you are recording. If the backup spans more than one disc, you'll be prompted to insert another disc when the current one is full. Remember that standard CD-R and CD-RW discs can hold only about 650MB, and that doesn't include any of the necessary overhead the program needs to write to each disc so your computer can recognize it when you go to use it later!

Between Tracks

What Gets Recorded?

One important thing to consider here, though, is that a backup made by Take Two doesn't create an exact duplicate of the disc you are backing up. The Take Two program creates an image file, which spans as many discs as are required to record the entire backup. This image file contains all the information necessary to restore data to your drive or, in a worst case scenario, a completely new drive.

While the backup process is proceeding, you can click the More Status button on the Take Two window to find out how much more there is to burn. Figure 13.13 shows a backup in which only 7% of the data backup has been written so far.

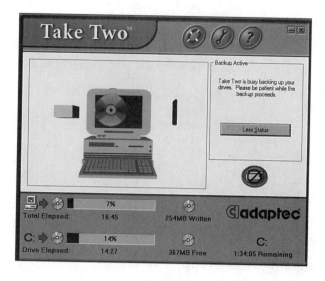

Figure 13.13

The More Status and Less Status buttons enable you to watch, if you want, the progress of the backup.

When backups are made to a CD-R or CD-RW, remember that the recording takes a lot longer than copying to a hard disk, so be patient. If the backup does use more than one disc, Take Two prompts you to insert the next disc, and so on, until the backup is complete.

Creating the Bootable Emergency Floppy Disk for a Restore

Back in Figure 13.10, you can see that, in addition to the bold numbers 1, 2, and 3 that are used to walk you through the backup program, there are also three icons at the top of the program window right next to the Take Two logo. These three icons provide important functions. The first icon, shaped like an ocean liner life preserver, creates a bootable floppy disk you can use to boot the system and restore a Take Two backup.

After you click this button, you are prompted to insert a blank floppy disk. Do this and then click Next. In Figure 13.14, you can see the dialog box that comes up next. It has a few arcane options you can choose from, but unless you know differently, use the defaults for these fields.

Figure 13.14

The format dialog box enables you to give a label to the emergency boot floppy disk.

Formatting New Floppy Discs

Although even new discs are usually formatted, occasionally you might buy a set of discs that didn't go through this prep treatment. If that's the case, clear the Quick Format check box where the dialog box lists the Format options. It'll make the format take longer (just a minute or two), but it's, unfortunately, necessary for a "virgin" disc.

When you are ready to continue, click Start. You might think that clicking a button labeled Start would actually make the computer start formatting the disc. But you would be wrong in this case. Before the format finally gets going, a dialog box pops up to tell you that formatting the disc will get rid of all the data that might be on it. There's a great big "DUH!" for you. Click OK to get this annoying and redundant message off your screen and start the format.

When the format is complete, another small dialog box pops up to let you know. Just click OK to keep going.

After the floppy disk has been formatted, Take Two copies files to the disc that are necessary to make it bootable. Between this disc and the backup you've burned to CD, you're now in good hands. If your system ever comes so unglued that you can't even start Windows, put the floppy disk in your floppy drive when starting your computer. When you boot from the Take Two floppy disk, it boots your computer and then prompts you through the restore process.

The Least You Need to Know

➤ The Sound Editor is used to edit or add special effects to WAV files on your hard drive.

➤ You can select all or part of a sound clip for editing purposes.

➤ You can cut and paste between various sound clips.

➤ The Session Selector is used to change the active session on a multisession disc (see Chapter 9, "Understanding and Using Multisession CDs").

➤ The Take Two program can be used to back up your hard disks and create a bootable floppy disk for emergency restores.

Chapter 14

Extra Delivery!
Using PhotoRelay

In This Chapter

➤ Using PhotoRelay to create digital photo albums

➤ Adding audio to each picture in your photo album

➤ Using basic editing tools to touch up your pictures

➤ Various ways to burn your photo album to CD using PhotoRelaxy

Most people I talk to who have CD burners use them to make copies of CDs they already own or to store important files on CD for long-term storage. However, a lot of other fun programs are out there that you can use with your burner, which you might not have ever thought about. For example, you already know, if you've read this book from the beginning, that you can take all your graphic files—family photos and stuff like that—and store them on a CD. However, when you want to go back and use them, you must go through all the trouble of finding specific pictures and cranking up some graphic editor to look at them. After all, these picture files don't look different from any other data file you might store on the disc.

PhotoRelay enables you to create photo albums on your computer's hard disk and, if you want, burn those favorite albums to a CD and bypass having to use another program to view them. When you make a PhotoRelay CD, all you have to do to view your digital photo album is stick it in your CD-ROM drive and it does all the rest! This is really a great idea when you want to send some photos to friends who know nothing about imaging editors and so on. Just make a PhotoRelay CD and mail it to them!

Creating Electronic Photo Albums on CD—Using PhotoRelay

If you have lots of disk space on your computer, you can use PhotoRelay to create photo albums that can hold both photographs and audio files. Why audio? One of the niftier PhotoRelay features makes it possible for you to attach an audio file to any particular picture. So, when the picture is viewed, the accompanying audio file gets played, too. If, for example, you happen to have a picture of yourself in the Rocky Mountains, would there be anything more appropriate than having Van Halen's "Top of the World" play when you view the picture?

PhotoRelay can be used sort of like a word processor—you can start creating the album, and when you get bored, you can save it. Later, you can come back and add more to the album or delete stuff that you've changed your mind about. In contrast to a real photo album, however, you won't run out space for your pictures (unless your hard drive fills up). You can also burn the album to CD when you have finished fine-tuning your project so that you don't have to waste that valuable real estate on your hard drive.

However, you must create the album before you can create the CD; so, let's start with creating an album first.

Starting PhotoRelay

To start the PhotoRelay program, you can select it from the Features menu in the Roxio Easy CD Creator 4 folder, or you can double-click the desktop icon Create CD. Using the icon method, select Photo and Video from the first menu and then select Photo Album from the second menu.

The PhotoRelay application window (shown in Figure 14.1) pops up, and you are ready to create a new photo album. Note that the Album field in this figure says New. You can use the pull-down menu for this field to open albums you've already created.

Notice also that next to this field is a series of icons, each of which represents a tool you can use with PhotoRelay. These tools are as follows:

➤ **Add tool**—Adds files to the album you are creating.

➤ **Acquire tool**—Use your scanner to "acquire" a new photo to add to the album.

➤ **Save tool**—Enables you to save your work on the current active album.

➤ **Print tool**—Prints all or part of an album.

➤ **Sort tool**—Sorts your images.

➤ **Delete tool**—Deletes an image in an album.

➤ **Make CD tool**—Burns your album to a disc.

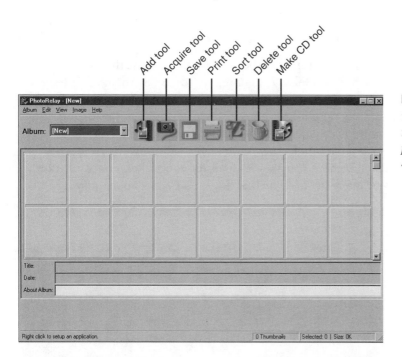

Figure 14.1

The PhotoRelay applica-tion enables you to create photo albums that can be stored on CD.

Adding and Removing Photographs from the Album

To add a picture to an album, click the Add tool—the first icon in the toolbar after the Album field. The Add to Album dialog box appears and enables you to select the disk and directory that contains the photographs with which you want to work.

To select an image for the album, just double-click it in the dialog box or click once to highlight it and then click the Open button. A thumbnail for the picture is created and appears on the application window. In Figure 14.2, you see PhotoRelay with an assortment of images ready for recording.

What the Heck Is a Thumbnail?

When you need to see several pictures on the computer screen at the same time, such as when working with PhotoRelay, it's impossible to display them all in their full-size format. This isn't just because of limited screen space, but because a large number of picture files takes up a lot of memory, too, which slows down your computer. A *thumbnail* is basically just a miniaturized version of a picture that takes up less screen space and considerably less memory. Although it has much less detail than the actual picture, it makes it easier for you to keep track of your work when dealing with many pictures, such as, say, in a photo album, maybe?

Figure 14.2

Thumbnails appear on the PhotoRelay window for each picture you select.

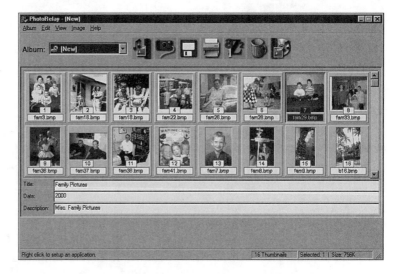

As you continue to add photographs to the album, you can use the scrollbar on the right side of the program to run through the album's contents.

Note that three fields are at the bottom of the PhotoRelay main window: Title, Date, and Description. You can fill in these fields for each picture as you add it. Or, later you can go back and click any picture to change this information.

Removing an image is just as simple as adding it to the album. Just right-click the image and select Cut from the menu that appears. You can also use the other standard editing commands that appear in this menu, such as copy and paste. Another method for removing a picture from the album is to select the thumbnail by clicking it once and then selecting Cut from the Edit menu found at the top of the application window. You'll find the same capabilities in this Edit menu that you do when you right-click the image, along with a few others.

Adding Audio to a Photo

You easily can add an audio clip to any picture or to the whole album that you create. If you add an audio clip to an individual picture, that audio clip gets played when the picture is displayed, such as in a slide show (which we'll get to later in the chapter!).

Simply select the picture on the workspace area and, on the Image menu, select Attach Audio. You are prompted to locate the file using the typical Open dialog box you see everywhere in Windows programs. Find and select the file; then, just click OK and you're done.

Another handy feature is that you don't have to create your audio files in advance. If, for example, you've just put together an album of pictures from your recent vacation, you can get the family around the computer, plug a microphone into your computer's sound card, and then record narrative to the audio file for each picture on the spot. To do this, select the picture and again use the Image menu. This time, though, select Record Audio from the menu instead of Attach Audio.

Editing Photographs

PhotoRelay comes with an editing program that enables you to crop (explained in the next section) and otherwise manipulate the images in your album. To edit an image, just double-click the thumbnail you see in the album or right-click the thumbnail and select Edit from the menu that appears. In Figure 14.3, you can see the dialog box that pops up to handle the editing chores.

Figure 14.3

You can double-click any thumbnail to bring up an editor to edit the image file.

Remember that we are editing the actual photograph image file, not the thumbnail. If you have only one copy of the image, you might want to make another before editing. It's always good to have things backed up when you're using a computer!

Don't Get Burned

Alter at Your Own Risk

As I just pointed out, make sure you have a backup copy of your photograph before you start editing and making changes. If you really screw up the only copy you have of a photo, *do not* save it! The editor will prompt you about whether you want to save your changes when you decide to exit. Yell, scream, and, most importantly, click the No button. After you've saved changes to a photo, you can't undo them without a backed up file.

Cutting an Image Down to Size—Cropping an Image

Cropping an image means removing part of the image that you don't want to appear in the final output. It works great if you have good-looking photos of yourself but need to get rid of that ex-significant other standing next to you. After you've brought up an image in the editor, click the first button on the toolbar—the scissors—and you can then start to crop.

To crop the image, just place your cursor where you want to start, hold down the left mouse button, and drag your cursor. A box forms showing you the outline of your cropped photo. When you are satisfied, let go of the mouse button. A red box is drawn around the area you have selected. If you like the way the cropping looks, just right-click inside the red area and that portion of the photograph becomes the image.

Using cropping, you can remove extraneous elements from an image—such as ugly people standing off to the side—or just make a picture look better by focusing on the principal subject of the photograph.

Other Image Editing Tools

The editor enables you to use several tools that can change the way the photograph looks. Each of these tools is represented by an icon in the toolbar that runs across the top of the editing window. These tools, in order left to right, are

➤ **Crop**—We just talked about this one in the last section. Use the scissors icon to start cropping an image.

➤ **Rotate Image**—This is a fun one. The icon, which looks like a circular arrow, enables you to rotate the image around an axis. Just click the tool, place your cursor over the image, hold down the left mouse button, and drag your cursor in a circle. As you can see in Figure 14.4, the image itself rotates around its center.

Figure 14.4

You can rotate a photograph around its central axis for a special effect.

➤ **Adjust Brightness**—Use this to adjust the brightness in your picture. This tool's icon looks like the sun. When you click it, a sliding bar appears at the far right of the toolbar. Move this sliding bar and watch the photograph as it gets lighter or darker.

➤ **Adjust Contrast**—The icon for this tool looks like a circle, half-black, half-white, and works similar to the Adjust Brightness tool, except that it makes various colors more or less distinguishable. When selected, a sliding bar appears at the far right of the toolbar that you can use to adjust the image's contrast.

➤ **Adjust Saturation**—This colorful icon, which appears in the toolbar as a circle with multicolored vertical stripes, enables you to adjust the color saturation of the image. Again, similar to the last two tools, a sliding bar is used to effect the changes. Slide until you are satisfied.

Saturation?

Saturation is a graphics term that refers to the depth of the color you see. The greater the saturation, the more of the color you see. When selecting to make a color appear with a lower saturation value, it appears as though it has been through the washing machine a few times!

➤ **Sharpen Image**—This tool, whose icon looks like a face with a vertical line drawn through it, is used to sharpen the image. The original file must be at least a 24-bit image or you can't use this tool.

Pixels, Bits, and Colors

When a graphic image is displayed on a computer screen, it's nothing more than a pattern of dots called pixels. Each pixel can be set to its own color, which is basically a mixture of the basic colors of light. Because the data for each pixel is stored in a digital format—bits and bytes—each particular color can be represented in digital format by a number. The more numbers you have, the more colors you can store. Thus, when you hear things like using 24-bit (16+ million colors) or 8-bit (256 colors) picture files, those terms refer to the number of bits used to create pixels onscreen. For most computer monitors, 24-bit (16+ million colors), also called true color, is the norm.

➤ **Center Crop Area**—After you drag your mouse to create a cropped area, using the cropping icon, you can click this tool and the boundaries of your cropping are automatically centered over the image. Suppose you used the cropping tool to select just a section of the image at the bottom left of the full image. After you've selected the part of the image you want, click this tool and that part of the picture becomes centered on the workspace area and the remainder of the picture disappears.

➤ **Zoom In and Zoom Out**—The next two icons on the toolbar look like magnifying glasses with a + and - sign next to them. Use these to zoom in and out so that you can inspect smaller portions of the photograph or reduce it to a manageable size.

➤ **Undo**—My favorite tool, which looks like a fat circular or bent arrow. It lets you undo the last change you made to the picture. Unlike some programs that let you undo until the cows come home, it can undo only one edit, so be careful as you go!

➤ **Play Audio**—The icon for this tool looks like a speaker. If you've attached audio to this file, you can use this to play the audio.

➤ **Record Audio**—The last icon on the toolbar is also audio related. It looks like a microphone and is used for recording audio to attach to the image.

Although it's no $500 professional product, as you can see, you can still do a lot with the editor. *It's very important to remember that these changes are made to your original file when you save the picture*. If you want to crop a picture just for this album, but want to save the original, be sure you make a copy!

Saving the Photo Album

You can save the photo album at any time during your work by clicking the Save tool (the floppy disk icon on the toolbar). You can also select Save Album from the Album menu. Either method brings up a small dialog box that enables you to give a filename to the album. After you've saved it, the "New" text in the Album field is replaced with this album's title.

Note that saving the album *doesn't save all the photographic image files you've selected*. It just saves the thumbnail that was created of the photo and other information you might have entered into the album, such as the title. When you recall an album to look through or to edit, the original files should still be present if you want to burn the CD. Just remember that until you do burn the CD, don't touch any of the photographs you've selected for the album! Even moving them to a new folder on your hard disk makes it so your album can't locate them.

You can tell that PhotoRelay has a problem locating an image when you reopen the album. It indicates this by putting the universal symbol, the red circle with a line through it, at the upper-left edge of the thumbnail.

One very important thing I should also say here is that—in addition to using the Save option to save an album so you can work on it at a later time—until you save the album, you cannot proceed to the next step of burning the CD! You must "save" the album; otherwise, the CD burning option barks at you and tells you to do so first!

Burning an Album to CD

When you've gotten together an album of photographs, and perhaps some audio to go with it, that you want to put to CD, all you need to do to start the process is bring up the album in the PhotoRelay application and click the last icon in the toolbar—Make CD. In Figure 14.5, you can see the dialog box that pops up. Here, you can select to make a slide show, a Web album, or a video postcard.

Figure 14.5

You can choose from three types of CDs to create.

A slide show CD shows the images in the order you decide and autoruns when inserted on a computer that supports that option. The Web album option, on the other hand, lets you create a CD that enables you to view thumbnails of your album in a Web browser. When you click a thumbnail, whatever default program Windows uses for viewing images pops up to show the entire image. Finally, a video postcard enables you to record a video using the AVI format on a CD. We take a look at each of these in more detail in the following sections.

Creating a Slide Show

After you click Create a Slide Show a dialog box titled Select File pops up and prompts you to select the images from the album that will be recorded onto the CD. You can pick and choose using the Add or Remove buttons, or you can simply select the Add All button if you want all the pictures in your album on the CD. After you've selected what you need, click Next to continue.

The next dialog box (shown in Figure 14.5), is titled Audio Options and it enables you to do the following:

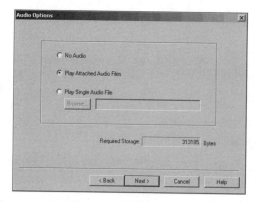

Figure 14.6

You can select how audio files are used when creating a slide show.

➤ Select that no audio be used on the CD.

➤ Play audio files attached to individual images. Just because you attached audio to the image when creating the album doesn't mean you have to record these audio tracks to the CD.

➤ Play a single audio file. This option enables you to play one audio file, and the slide show is timed to fit within it. Of course, as you can see in the Figure 14.5, you must select the audio file you want to add if you use this option.

Click the Next button to keep going. If you've selected audio, it might take a few seconds or even a minute or two before the next dialog box pops up. This dialog box, titled Select Destination, enables you to copy the slide show to your CD burner and create a CD, or to copy the slide show to a hard disk location if you want to further edit or work with it (see Figure 14.7). If you choose to first try out your slide show by storing it on the hard disk, you can also use the Directory field to tell PhotoRelay where you want it to place the files. If you are ready to burn a CD then you also can specify a directory name. This can be handy if you want to give a descriptive name to the directory on the CD so you can tell what is on the CD when you view it using tools such as Windows Explorer.

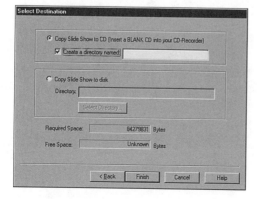

Figure 14.7

You can select to burn the CD or to store the slide show in a hard disk location.

Because this book is about burning CDs, that's the option we'll take now; then, click the Finish button.

The CD Creation Setup dialog box that you're used to seeing if you've read up on Easy CD Creator then pops up and enables you to make changes to several options. See Chapter 4, "Using Easy CD Creator to Make Data CDs," for more information about using this dialog box's advanced features. For our purposes, leave Create CD selected in the Create options section and then select Close CD in the Write Method section. To start the CD burning process, click the OK button.

If you haven't inserted a blank CD-R into the recorder yet, you are prompted to do so. The CD Creation Process dialog box shows you the progress of creating the CD.

Again, if you've used Easy CD Creator, you're used to this dialog box. It shows you which step the program is currently at in the creation process. When the CD has been successfully completed, it tells you so with the simple text "CD Successfully created".

Creating a Web Album

This CD burning option can be used to create a CD of photographs you can view using an Internet browser. If the computer supports the autorun feature, your browser pops up automatically and enables you to select from the thumbnails to see the full image. When selected, Windows opens whichever default program it's using to view graphic images (this will depend on what programs you have installed).

To create a Web album, make that selection from the dialog box shown back in Figure 14.5. The next dialog box that appears is the same as for the slide show, asking you to choose which images you want to appear in the Web album CD. Make your selections and click Next; you get to the Layout dialog box, shown in Figure 14.8.

Figure 14.8

You can customize the layout of a Web album using this dialog box.

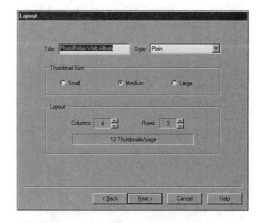

In this dialog box, you can select the size the thumbnails will be on a Web page (small, medium, or large) and the number of rows and columns for the display. Based on your selections, PhotoRelay tells you the number of thumbnails that appear on a page when it is displayed. You also can use this dialog box to give your Web album a title. Click the Next button when you are ready to continue.

Another dialog box asks you to select details you want to have displayed with each thumbnail. These include the title, date, and description of the image. Remember those three fields you had the option of entering information for each photo on the main PhotoRelay album window? That is where Web Album gets that information. Options are also available for including the picture's filename and file size. You can use check boxes to select which of these to display.

After you click Next, the Select Destination dialog box, which we saw back in Figure 14.6 appears and lets you choose to burn your Web album to a CD or to a directory on the hard disk. Make your selection and click, finally, Finish!

Once again, CD burners get the CD Creation Setup dialog box. Select to close the CD unless you plan to add more albums to the CD. Click the OK button, with a recordable CD already inserted in your CD-RW drive.

The CD Creation Process dialog box will keep you company and show you the steps being taken to create the CD, along with the number of files and tracks that have been written. When the CD is finished, the words "CD successfully created" appear on this dialog box.

Creating a Video Postcard

This option is a little different from the others in that it involves putting video data on a CD instead of still photographic images. Although creating a Video CD (VCD) is covered in Chapter 6, "Toss Your VCR: Using Video CD Creator to Create Video CDs," this is quite a bit different. To make matters even more confusing, whereas VCD Creator is adamant that files use the MPEG-1 video format, a video postcard uses yet another type: AVI.

Another difference between a Video postcard and the VCD is that, for a VCD, you must use an editing program to produce your video and then burn it to the disc. A Video postcard, on the other hand, is a much simpler type of CD that just plays back a short video clip you select, against a postcard-type of background. You shouldn't use PhotoRelay's Video Postcard feature to burn your favorite TV show onto a CD!

Because this is going to be a postcard, you can see in the first dialog box that you must select a template to use as the background for the video (see Figure 14.9). PhotoRelay comes with several images in the library portion of this dialog box.

Figure 14.9

You first select the background for the postcard and the size of the video window.

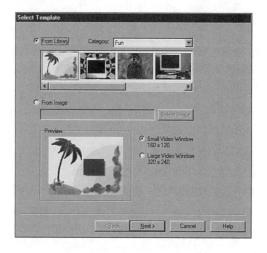

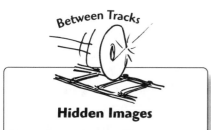

Between Tracks

Hidden Images

Note that in Figure 14.8 only a few images are shown in the library supplied with the program. Click the Category button, however, and you'll see that more libraries are available, with background images to choose from.

From this dialog box, you also can set the size of the window that is used to play back your video clip. Select small or large and then click Next to continue. You can experiment by simply clicking the small or large size radio buttons. The template image changes to show you the space your actual video will take up when it's played on top of the background you've selected for the postcard.

When you click Next, you get to the postcard section of this project you've gotten yourself into. Here, as you can see in Figure 14.10, the dialog box looks just like a postcard. What you enter here appears after the video has finished playing.

You can use the Select Font button to use another font for your text or to change the font size to enable you to get more text on the screen. To enter your oh-so-poetic message, just click in the area of the postcard you want to type into and click Next when finished.

The Preview dialog box pops up next, showing the background image you've selected. You can use the Select Video button to select the video clip you want attached to this video postcard. You can select from several video file formats, including MPEG and AVI. If it's not an AVI file, the postcard program converts it to one, as necessary. *After* you've located the file, click it once to select it. You can now use the preview pane on this dialog box to preview the clip.

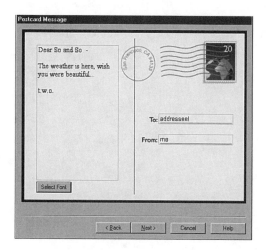

Figure 14.10

Fill in the typical post-card information, just as you would with the paper variety!

After you start previewing, the Play button turns into the Stop button, which you can use when you are satisfied that you've selected the correct video clip. When you've found your file, click the Open button, which returns you to the Preview dialog box. You can use the Play and Stop buttons found there to play the video again, or just click Next to continue.

Finally, the Select Destination dialog box appears, as was shown previously in Figure 14.6. To create the video postcard CD, select the option Copy Video PostCard to CD. Click the Finish button. The CD Creation Process dialog box appears and, as in the last two sections, shows you the progress of writing the CD. When it's finished, you'll see "CD successfully created" on this dialog box; you can then use the video postcard CD.

When your newly burned CD is inserted into a Windows computer, the postcard is automatically started up and your video plays, followed by your postcard message.

The Least You Need to Know

➤ You can use PhotoRelay to store pictures, along with audio files, on your hard disk or to burn a CD

➤ You can create simple postcards that play video clips against a postcard-like background to send to friends using PhotoRelay.

➤ You can use PhotoRelay to create a Web album that can be viewed using a Web browser.

We're Gonna Need a Bigger Boat: Troubleshooting CD Recording!

In This Chapter

➤ Nothing's perfect in a changing world, especially CD recording technology!

➤ Check your source first.

➤ If you source is okay, check the discs you are recording to.

➤ Is your software and hardware up to date?

➤ Check your vendor's site for help specific to your products.

Ready to throw your computer out a window, CD-RW drive and all? Okay, but make sure the window, is in fact open... or you can look to this chapter for a fix to your problem. Before you begin to troubleshoot, remember that any new technology is always prone to problems. With luck, and the use of this wonderful book, you are going to succeed.

When you run into any problems on the way, consult this chapter.

Hey, Nothing's Perfect!

No matter how good the technology, there's always going to be gremlins working themselves into the machinery here and there. In a field such as CD recording, where there are standards, but in which many companies produce equipment of varying capabilities, you can expect more gremlins. There'll be enough of them to have a party.

A typical example is the CD-R or CD-RW blank discs you use. Different dyes and metal alloys are used in various brands. Some might work better on your drive than others. Some might not work at all. As drive technology continues to improve, and as manufacturers keep working at getting the perfect media, these kinds of problems will go away. But I wouldn't hold my breath for that happening any time soon.

The remainder of this chapter is used to provide both a few tips and a few typical troubleshooting procedures that can help you as you exercise all the capabilities of the software you are using.

It Helps to Start with a Perfect Source

Whether you are making a simple copy of a CD or are undertaking a more complex project, such as creating a video CD, the first rule of thumb should always be to start with a good source. Although you can use the cleaning options provided by Spin Doctor, you won't get a crystal clear, brand-new–sounding CD from an old LP that has been treated badly.

The same goes for CDs. Although CDs have a nice protective coating on the bottom to help shield them from abuse, scratches can cause problems. CDs can tolerate some degree of fingerprints and other contamination before becoming noticeable when you play the CDs. So, before you even begin troubleshooting a problem with CD recording, make sure your sources are clean and in good condition. You can find all sorts of products at audio and discount stores that can be used to clean almost any kind of media. Don't forget that the media player itself might need some cleaning or tuning up. When recording from a phonograph LP, don't use a player that has a needle in it that's 20 years old. If you're recording from tape, clean those tape heads!

Between Tracks

Cleanup Time!

Like all recording media that has come before them, a new industry is forming to provide for the need to clean or repair CDs. Check the local record shop—forgive that slip of the tongue, I meant check the local *CD* shop—and you'll probably find a lot to choose from. There are even products that can be used to fill in scratches. In my opinion, if you have to go that far, just buy a new CD. Or, if you've made a backup copy and have been playing the backup copy, your new, barely used CD wouldn't have that scratch to begin with. It'd be stored safely in a closet somewhere!

Assuming that you start with a good source, you should get a good product at the end. So, in this chapter, we'll look at some specific problems that can occur and how you can avoid them.

Who Can Read What

One frequent problem is that you'll create a CD and give it to a friend and he complains that it doesn't do anything in his player. When using recordable CD media, remember that older audio players, and older computer CD-ROM drives, might not be able to use your CD-Rs. At this point, it's a hit-or-miss thing, because people tend to keep a working machine such as a CD player around for a long time until it breaks. Just about all the newer, and many of the older, audio players can read closed CD-R discs, and you shouldn't have any problems related to format if you buy a new audio player.

Whenever I hear from someone who can't play a newly created CD in his audio player I first tell him to insert it in his computer's CD-ROM drive and see whether he can play it from there. Most likely, his computer is newer than his stereo system, so he can quickly determine whether the problem resides in the CD or the player. There is always the possibility, too, that you forgot to close the CD! You can use Easy CD Creator to look at the properties for the CD to determine if this is the problem. If you did not close the CD then it's won't be playable in an ordinary CD audio player. Of course, the way this technology is changing all the time, that might not be true in the near future.

Also, remember that some kinds of discs can be read in only one kind of drive. For example, read-write discs that you can use over and over again aren't readable in CD-R drives. If you try to use a mixed-mode CD (as we talked about in Chapter 9, "Understanding and Using Multisession CDs") in your car CD player, you're going to get a big surprise when a loud grating noise comes blasting through your speakers as the player tries to interpret the first data track that comes before the audio! Note that this very kind of event has been known to actually ruin speakers, so be careful which CDs you place in your audio player!

Another thing to remember is that if you use multiple sessions on a disc then usually the last session is the one that's readable by a CD-ROM player, by default. To change sessions and access the data there, you'll need a product such as Roxio's Session Selector (see Chapter 13, "Other Roxio Utilities").

A Look at Common CD–R and CD–RW Recording Problems

Remember that although specific standards exist for the way data and audio is recorded onto CDs, there are many manufacturers and each might come up with a different method of creating a CD burner or a CD reader. Little differences between manufacturers can be significant problems for some people. For example, some people like using the 80-minute CD-R media instead of the standard 74-minute discs. Suppose you want to use these discs and find that your software says no way, can't use them. You upgrade your software to a version that does allow 80-minute recording, only to find out that it's your hardware CD burner that has a built-in 74-minute limit! It doesn't care what the software tells it to do, it's just a dumb machine!

This is a reminder of what I was referring to at the start of this chapter. The state of this industry is changing so rapidly that you can always expect the unexpected when you begin to troubleshoot. It could be the media. It could be the recording drive. It might be some silly program running in the background using up computer resources that you've forgotten about! For example, even if you have a large, fast system, be sure you disable things that start themselves up automatically. Such programs include screensavers, power management utilities, task schedulers, and the like. If you have a product like this, watch out! If it kicks in when you're burning, you might get burned, so to speak.

Disabling Background Programs

Although they don't all appear here, the easiest way to disable a background program is to look at the list of icons in your system tray (next to the clock on your desktop). Right-click each of these icons; you should see an option for closing or disabling them. Doing so prevents them from running and taking up resources your CD burning program might want.

To disable power management or a screensaver, right-click the desktop, choose Properties from the menu, and then click the Screen Saver tab in the dialog box that pops up. Here, you can turn off your screensaver and access any of the power management functions (which work a little differently depending on your flavor of Windows).

In the following sections, we'll look at some of the more common problems and some ways you can fix them.

Buffer Underruns: The Ultimate Coaster Creators

When we were looking at creating or copying CDs in previous chapters, we saw that the Easy CD Creator programs have a dialog box called CD Creation Process. This dialog box keeps you posted on the progress of the CD burn that is in progress. You can see a copy of this dialog box in Figure 15.1.

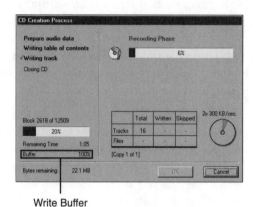

Write Buffer

Figure 15.1

The CD Creation Process dialog box is common to many applications and shows you the buffer usage.

The reason I mention this dialog box is that it has a field that shows you the amount of data available in the write buffer. Because the laser burner has to receive a constant stream of data telling it how to make burns through the dye layer of the CD-R blank, problems occur if an interruption of data occurs. For this reason, a buffer in the computer's memory is created to store part of the data stream. If the hard disk from which the file is coming is partially fragmented, there might be milliseconds here and there that are wasted while the disk heads look for the next block of data. During this seek time, the buffer is used to supply data to the laser. If the CD burner looks to the buffer for data and nothing is there, you'll get more use from your disc by setting a cold drink on it than you would trying put data on it.

Arcane CD Speak

Disk Fragmentation

The term *fragmentation* sounds kind of scary, doesn't it? No, it doesn't mean that part of your disk is broken! Instead, it is a condition that occurs naturally because of the way computers write data to the hard drive. If your computer just wrote one file after another to your hard disk and never deleted anything, you would (in an ideal world) have a disk on which similar blocks of data are located next to each other. This ordering would make them read more quickly because the computer wouldn't have to go looking to different parts of the hard disk for them.

However, when you delete a file, you leave a hole in your stored data. Because that space is now available, the drive eventually writes to this recycled space. When that space runs out, it just looks in its little index and finds some free spots elsewhere on the disk and continues writing the file at that location, and so on. Over time, you end up with a lot of data that's scattered, or fragmented, all over the disk! This, of course, can cause your data to take more time finding the files it needs. This includes files you want to write to a CD!

Most versions of Windows have a disk defragmenter utility, which examines how files are stored on the disk and attempts to rearrange them in a more orderly manner. Click Start, Programs, Accessories, System Tools to see whether your version of Windows has this program.

So a buffer underrun, as you can see, is a serious problem. Watch this indicator closely and be sure it stays near 100%. If it drops slightly, you should be okay, but you might start to see problems if the buffer drops even to the 75% mark. If you have a new computer that runs at least as fast as 500MHz, you probably won't have any problems with buffer underrun. If you do, the remedies you can try are varied. Some might work, some might not because the source of a buffer underrun is rarely perfectly clear. Here are some possibilities:

➤ Stop using the computer for anything else while the CD is burning. Don't use up the computer's resources while it's trying to keep that buffer full!

➤ If you're burning a disc on your work network or you have a home network then, for goodness sakes, don't use a network drive as your source! The network is gazillions of times slower than accessing your hard drive.

➤ If necessary, defragment your hard disk drive. If you are copying CD to CD, this won't help. But if you are copying WAV, MP3, or image files to your CD burner, a defragmented disk reads much more quickly, keeping that buffer full.

➤ Execute the Scandisk program (Start, Programs, Accessories, System Tools) to see whether it can locate and fix any problems that might exist on your hard drive.

➤ Check for viruses on your system! If you're on the Internet and you don't have a virus checker, you're just waiting around for trouble! A virus can hide in the background, unnoticed, using up valuable system resources.

➤ Turn off any background processes that might be running (as described in the previous section).

For Windows 98, you can defrag your hard disk by doing the following steps:

1. Click Start, then Programs, Accessories, and System Tools.
2. Click the Disk Defragmenter icon in the System Tools folder.
3. The Select Drive dialog box prompts you for the drive to defragment. Choose, of course, the one on which you have stored WAV or MP3 files (or disk images of CDs you want to create), and click OK.
4. A Defragment Drive dialog box keeps you company as the information on the drive is rearranged, block by block, to make as many like files as close to each other as possible. The larger the hard drive, the longer this will take, which can last up to a couple of hours.

For Windows Me and Windows NT/2000 users, the procedure is similar. If you have Windows 95 or some other operating system, you can always purchase a disk defragmenter utility, such as Norton SpeedDisk; however, it might not be an inexpensive proposition.

Pops and Clicks That Weren't on the Source

Sometimes the actual burning process produces pops and clicks in the output CD you create that sound as if you were recording from an FM radio station that was too far out of range. This can be due to many causes, such as a bad WAV file to begin with. If you extract audio CD-DA tracks to WAV files, be sure to listen to them using Spin Doctor, the Windows Media Player, or some other applicable program before you record to a blank CD. If these turn out to be the problem, try extracting the WAV files at a slower rate or try recording them using a different CD-ROM drive (for this, you could even record from your CD-RW drive).

Watch That Media!

The discs you buy to record on are a hit-or-miss kind of thing. Even some brand names you'd expect to be perfect use third-party manufacturers to make their discs and buy them in batches. That means one batch can come from one manufacturer and another batch from another. If I recall my high school days correctly, this is called capitalism, which is a pretty hit-or-miss proposition for us poor consumers.

You might think that recording at the fastest rated speed of your recorder drive might be the best thing. However, most media is rated as 1x through something-x. If you find it doesn't work well at the highest rate then back down. Even thought it takes a lot longer, almost everything works at 1x.

The reasons for failure can be numerous. Remember that on a CD-R disc, the laser is burning through a dye layer. It will do this differently at various speeds. If this dye layer acts differently at different speeds, so will go your recording abilities.

As a matter of fact, a general rule I always use when extracting audio tracks to WAV files is to do so at only 1x speed. I've got time to sit around and read while the extract takes place. Why extract at 4x—unless you're really sure your drive can handle it and you never have problems—when good old 1x still works just fine and can keep other problems from cropping up.

This problem can also occur when copying from a CD-ROM drive to your CD recorder. If your CD-ROM drive is an older one, and it passes the digital audio extraction test to see whether it can extract data at a fast enough rate to keep the recorder supplied, problems can still occur if you have a source CD that has minor errors on it. You might not be able to detect these sounds when you play the CD, but when the track is being extracted and the data sent to the recorder, these problems can become magnified. To find out whether this is the cause, try using your CD burner itself as the source, copying the CD image to a disk image file, and then burn the CD from that image. If this doesn't work, try cleaning the CD to eliminate the possibility of minor errors caused by a dirty disc.

The CD Recorder Drive Wants a Bigger Disc!

Sometimes we bite off more than we can chew! The same goes when trying to use an Easy CD Creator layout that goes past the 74-minute limit (weren't you watching the indicator at the bottom of the application window that tracked your time?).

Sometimes, however, it's because we want to use Easy CD Copier to make a copy of a commercial CD that was actually created at a length greater than 74 minutes. I've run into several of these *overburned* CDs myself during the copying process. CD burning fans of Frank Sinatra or Yoko Ono surely know what I'm talking about.

The solution? If your drive works with them, go out and buy a box of 80-minute blanks and try using those. Blank CD media doesn't come any larger than that yet, so if the 80s don't satisfy your burner's hunger, nothing will.

Another alternative is to look at the total time on the CD layout, if you're using Easy CD Creator, and try to remove one or more files or tracks to get back down under the 74-minute limit. If you are using Easy CD Copier, you might consider using the Easy CD Creator instead and selecting only the number of tracks that will fit onto a 74-minute blank. If it's a music CD and you're very close in time, you might even want to consider using Sound Editor to cut or fade out a few seconds of a music track or two.

Video CD Creator Doesn't Like My Video Files

The Video Creator program that comes with Easy CD Creator 4.0 Deluxe wants you to give it video files in a very specific MPEG format. As much as I'd like to avoid drowning you in file format semantics, that's the pain of using Video CD Creator. Don't confuse their MPEG Level-2 with MPEG-2. Video CDs (VCDs) use MPEG-1, *level*-2, and there are some very specific characteristics the file needs to have to work with Video CD Creator to produce a good VCD. There are variations within each specification, but you must follow the exact MPEG-1, level-2 VCD standard to create a VCD with Video CD Creator.

One caveat to note here is that I've not found a video editor yet that produces a quality product for a VCD. You see, you first have to get your video clips all arranged in the order you want them and then have some editor program spit them out in the correct format that the Video CD Creator can use. I find that, no matter which program I use, it's always at trade-off between video or audio quality when using the earlier MPEG-1 formats.

If Video CD Creator is rejecting your files, it displays a dialog box, similar to that shown in Figure 15.2, telling you what it is objecting to.

Figure 15.2

Video CD Creator tells you what's not right with your MPEG file.

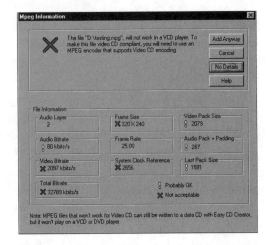

In Figure 15.2, the exclamation point next to an item means that it might work. The big X characters next to an item mean no way, forget it! This means you'll need to run the video file through an editing program that supports the correct MPEG-1 format.

Although you don't need to understand what these terms mean, the things you should check for in the output file format are as follows:

➤ MPEG-1, Layer 2

➤ Sampling frequency 44.1KHz

➤ Bit rate for audio and video tracks: 224Kbits/second

➤ Mode: Stereo, dual channel, intensity stereo

➤ Audio pack size of 23,304 bytes

For those of us in the U.S., a picture size of 352×240 also exists for the NTSC format, with a picture rate of 29.97Hz. Now, let me say that 30 is a more popular format on the Internet than 29.97. However, 29.97 is what a VCD wants, so check to see that your editor supports this output format.

As a last minute tip, here, you should know that I think it's worth going through the time and effort to record an important video, such as your family videos, using an MPEG-2 format. The higher the quality, the better. DVDs that you rent or buy use the MPEG-2 quality standard, usually along with Dolby sound and other extras. Experiment with VCDs; however, if you want a better quality, simply save the video input into an MPEG-2 file and *then use Easy CD Creator to burn that data file to a CD.* You will find that some CD players enable you to select tracks to play, as well as support playing entire CDs. At any rate, you'll at least have your valuable video collection in a good format that will be, hopefully, transferable to whatever becomes the next great thing! How much longer are those VHS or, if you were unfortunate enough to buy them, BetaMax tapes going to last? If not, you can always use Windows Media Player (or other similar products) to play MPEG-2 files. And, in the long run, you'll find you can convert your MPEG-2 files to newer formats because they are developed with more information than an MPEG-1 file. We're saving for the future, aren't we?

My solution is transfer now to the latest, higher quality, digital format you can and if something better comes along, you can always redo it later. The way computer technology is changing, you can expect to have to change to the latest and greatest media about every 10 years, if that.

I Put My Mixed-Mode CD in My Player and It Screams!

You're putting a mixed-mode CD into an audio player? What do you expect, you silly, CD-burning rebel! I told you in Chapter 10, "Best of Both Worlds: Creating CDs With Both Audio and Data," about creating these darn things.

CD-Extra formatted discs are more common, are more useful, and won't make your audio player scream because the audio session comes before the data. If you ruined your speakers because of a mixed-mode CD, it's not my fault!

I Used Spin Doctor's Morphing Options to Reduce Noise, and I Get a Dull Sound!

The cleaning options and pop removal that are part of Spin Doctor must be taken with a grain of salt. Although they do work, they're not the most perfect tools you could use to do this. And remember, when filling in a pop or a click in the record, the sound has to come from somewhere. When you take away some of the bad, you also take away some of the good.

The cleaning and pop removal tools should be used on WAV files on your hard disk so you can preview the output before committing it to a CD-R blank. I've found that when I've recorded some old LPs to CD, it actually doesn't sound that bad to have an occasional noise distortion here and there. To us old-timers, songs recorded with pops, hisses, and scratches is what nature intended! Besides, it brings back memories.

If you use the cleaning tool to its extreme value, which might be necessary for a record from the early part of this century, you get a very dull output. Experiment! However, light applications of this tool seem to improve some records significantly. Try it at your leisure, pretending you're cutting your latest album and trying to get that groovy *sound*, man! Can you dig it?

Another option is to try a more sophisticated sound editing program. Many are available; just check your local computer store and look for product reviews in magazines and on the Web.

These Discs I Just Bought Don't Work in My Drive!

There is the question of the blank CD-R media itself. Several kinds of blanks are on the market, using various chemicals for the dye layer that gets blasted by the laser during the recording process. Some seem to work fine in most recorders. However, some work better in one than another. The problem with trying to overcome this is that there are not really that many manufacturers of the CD-R blanks, but several vendors who put their names on the end product you buy in the store. So, although brand x might be just fine the first time you buy it, that vendor might go out and buy a large batch of discs from another company before you try them again.

Unfortunately, all you can do is go with trial and error. To solve the media problem, *find something that works and stick with it until it doesn't!* That might sound cynical, but that's the way to go right now. When you buy something and it doesn't work, take it back to the store for a refund. I've done this many times.

Don't Overlook Hardware and Software Problems

In the changing scene of technology that CD recording is, you should always check with your vendor(s) on a regular basis. If you are a hobbyist and are having great results from your computer and the applications you are using to make CDs, just skip this chapter (until the next Microsoft update, of course!). However, as new patches are issued for operating systems such as Windows and new devices are created and brought to market, the possibility always exists that, to get your parts all working together in unison, you'll need to download something from somebody.

The first place to start is your software vendor. You've already learned in Chapter 1, "The Digital Revolution!" that Roxio has a Web update feature you can use to check for new updates to its software. Just log into the Internet and then click Start/Programs/Roxio Easy CD Creator 4; then click Features. The last item in the Features menu is Web-Checkup, which is described in Chapter 1.

Next, check your other software vendors, and then go to the hardware sites for the manufacturer of your CD-R or CD-RW drive. You never know what you'll find. However, when new operating system patches or versions are released, shortly there-after you'll probably find a device driver file on your hardware vendor's Web page that should be downloaded and installed.

Another aspect of software as applied to hardware devices is *firmware*. This is software code, which usually is stored in your device's memory, that can be used to modify the operation of the hardware without having to actually change the hardware! In other words, firmware is the code that runs on the card or drive you've attached to your computer, but it's stored in a special kind of memory on the card or adapter, not the computer's memory.

Sometimes the update for hardware devices—such as CD recorders—are updates to firmware. Installing these kinds of updates varies based on who made your drive. Don't worry, these updates are usually very simple to apply and usually come with good directions. When you download them, just look for a file called Readme and open it up with Windows WordPad or Notepad!

Lastly, you might just have a drive that is either getting old or was defective from the start. For example, one common problem I hear about is the "power calibration area" error. When the CD burner starts to record a CD, it first performs a quick test near the very beginning of the CD (the center, remember!) to test how much power the laser will have to use to punch holes through the dye layer. Different blanks, different manufacturers, and different drives all add up to make this test necessary. If you get this error from the very start, try using a different brand of blanks. If that doesn't solve the problem, you might have a bad burner. If it's new, return it! If it's an older burner, the laser might simply be having trouble focusing the laser correctly. Either way, if changing blanks doesn't work, it's time to buy a new recorder. For the price a new one goes for now, it's really not worth attempting to repair the device.

Using Easy CD Creator's Built-In Tests

Ideally, this information would come right at the beginning of the book, but I wanted to get to the point of making your first CD as soon as I could, so into this chapter the material went. Now that you're near the end of this book, let's look at a few things Roxio thought fit to throw into their program to enable you to troubleshoot some aspects of CD recording.

Roxio's System Tests and Help Files

When you are in the Easy CD Creator program, you can select the System Test option from the Tools menu. In Figure 15.3, you can see the System Test dialog box, which enables you to test your drives to ensure they'll work for the applications Roxio provides.

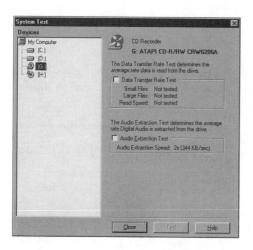

Figure 15.3

The System Test dialog box enables you to test your CD-ROM and CD recordable disc drives as well as your hard disks.

Note that you can use this for each CD-ROM or hard drive on your system, as well as your CD recorder. After all, even if your CD-ROM does not support digital audio extraction, your CD recorder can be used for that process, and you can still create CDs by using a your hard disk as a go-between. Use these testing functions if you are having problems with drives that used to work but are now having problems, or if you have just installed new equipment. If your hard drive doesn't pass the test then try defragmenting it. And, unless you really are an idiot, don't forget to insert a data or audio CD into the CD drive you want to test. Your CD-ROM drive won't read "air" very well.

The Data Transfer Rate test figures out the average speed it takes your drive to read information such as files and folders. The Audio Extraction Test, on the other hand, determines whether the drive can extract audio data from your music CDs and at what rate it can do so. Note that some older drives do not support digital audio extraction! If that is the case with one of your drives, that's why Easy CD Creator can't use it for audio CDs. Just use your CD-RW drive instead. Or, if you have one available, just plug a regular audio CD player into your sound card and use Spin Doctor to copy the music to your hard drive as WAV files and then burn them using the CD recorder.

You can also use Roxio's applications' online help files to determine whether you are doing things correctly. To check specific error messages, use the Index tab after you've brought up Help and enter the text **Error Messages**.

The Least You Need to Know

➤ Go slow if you have problems recording. Use the 1x speed for difficult discs or recorders.

➤ Clean up your sources before you record! A dirty LP vinyl album isn't going to improve in quality just because you transfer the dirty track to a digital format.

➤ Defragment your hard disk drive if you're using it as the source for WAV files being burned to CD.

➤ Update your software frequently by visiting the home pages of software vendors. The same goes for hardware vendors who might have to issue new driver software as operating systems continue to evolve.

Chapter 16

Other Neat Software

In This Chapter

➤ Try MusicMatch Jukebox free—it's on the CD!

➤ Try Microsoft's Media Player Version 7.0 free—it's on the Net!

➤ There's a heck of a lot of software you can get for free or next to nothing that can be used to assist you in creating CDs.

Throughout this book, we have used as an example Easy CD Creator 4.0 Deluxe, which is a great application. Earlier versions of this application are included with many CD burners. However, if you want to use some of the more advanced features of Easy CD Creator, you'll have to buy a copy of the full version, which is available for a very reasonable price. Of course this isn't the only software available for creating CDs. In just the last two years, there has been a boom in new software, such as Nero, Media Player 7, and MusicMatch, that can be used either to burn the CD or to help in the process in some other way, such as audio and video editing software.

In this chapter, we'll focus mainly on two applications. Both enable you to organize your audio files, and both enable you, in some ways, to burn CDs. These packages are

➤ MusicMatch Jukebox 5.0 Deluxe

➤ Microsoft's Windows Media Player 7

On the CD

Look on the CD that accompanies this book! You'll find a small treasure trove of some great software gadgets you can use. You'll find MusicMatch Jukebox, MP3 software, and more, including sound and video editors that can help you improve the quality of the CDs you create The demo version of MusicMatch Jukebox supports just about all the functions you find on MusicMatch Jukebox Plus. However, if you decide to purchase the Plus version, you'll find that you can create MP3 files much more quickly and burn CDs up to 12 times faster. Some features, such as preset equalizer settings and advanced printing features, aren't included on the demo, though.

The good news is you don't have to do much to get either of these programs. You can get Microsoft's Media Player 7 by downloading it free from www.microsoft.com. Just make sure you're running at least Windows 98 because this program is incompatible with Windows 95. You can get the demo version of MusicMatch Jukebox on the CD at the back of this book. A full version of this application can be had for about $20 at your local computer store or on the Web from www.musicmatch.com.

MusicMatch Jukebox Deluxe 5.0

MusicMatch Jukebox is an application you can use to find, create, organize, and play MP3, WAV, and even Windows Media files. You also can play CDs with the Jukebox and tune into the many radio stations that are now available on the Internet. I included this application in this book because it's a good one all around. And, of course, because this book is about gearing you up for a CD burning extravaganza, you can also use MusicMatch Jukebox to burn CDs!

To begin, MusicMatch Jukebox can work with the following file types:

➤ MP3 files

➤ Windows Media files

➤ Music CDs (CD-DA)

➤ WAV files

➤ Shoutcast

➤ M3U files

You don't have to worry about the details of what these formats are. The point is that, with this wide assortment of formats, you'll have no problem acquiring audio files from most sources. And several sources exist—including your local CD-ROM, Internet radio, Internet sites, and so on.

The install for MusicMatch Jukebox is pretty typical, so you shouldn't have any problems if you've ever installed an application before. If the installation program doesn't autorun when you insert the CD, click Start, Run. In the dialog box that appears, click Browse and navigate to your CD-ROM drive. From there, you just need to look for the file setup.exe and run it. Because of space limitations, we can't go into all the installation details here. However, one important question you do get asked during the install is whether you want MusicMatch Jukebox to periodically upload information from your computer to its site so that it can suggest other audio titles to help you. This dialog box, Personalize Net Music, is shown in Figure 16.1.

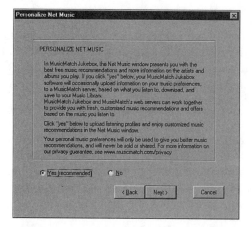

Figure 16.1

During installation, you can configure MusicMatch Jukebox to upload information about your preferences to its server.

Even though, as you can see in this dialog box, MusicMatch doesn't give or sell your personal information to anyone else, you can always select No during the install if you're the sort who doesn't even want the Post Office to know where you are. Of course, as the old saying goes, just because you're paranoid doesn't mean they're not out to get you. And because the Internet is still in its infancy, you might have a reason to be paranoid. But not me; my sins are all on public record, so I just checked the Yes radio button. I expect to be hearing from MusicMatch soon!

Learning About MusicMatch Jukebox Details

After you first launch MusicMatch Jukebox, you see an opening dialog box on top of the regular MusicMatch Jukebox window. It's titled Welcome to MusicMatch Jukebox. Use this if you want to quickly familiarize yourself with the program's features, some of whose explanation is beyond the scope of this chapter.

After you dismiss this screen, you see the main window of the program, as shown in Figure 16.2.

235

Figure 16.2

The main window for MusicMatch Jukebox enables you to perform many functions.

One important thing to note here is that the screen you see in Figure 16.2 is a compilation of three windows, all scrunched together. It might look like one window, but technically it's not. If you are familiar with Windows icons, you'll note that in this figure each window has a name. If you want to move all three windows as a single unit, just click and drag on the title bar of the top window. Otherwise, you can click and drag the other two separately by using their respective title bars.

The top window is called the Player. It sports the typical universal audio controls for play, pause, stop, and so on. It also has a Rec button you can use to record. When you click the Record button, the Recorder window opens. This is the bottom window shown in Figure 16.2. The window stuck in the middle of these two is the Music Library, which is where you organize your music. To bring up the Music Library window when it's not on the screen, you simply click the musical note icon on the left side of the Player window.

Between Tracks

Getting Rid of Unwanted Dialog Boxes!

You don't have to work with the full complement of MusicMatch Jukebox's dialog boxes. After you launch the program, you can use the Close Window (X) control to close any dialog boxes you don't need for the current session. Or, just move them around and arrange them as you want them to appear onscreen.

The Player, of course, is used to play music. Although you can play individual songs from wherever you find them, MusicMatch Jukebox uses the concept of a playlist to organize audio files into groups. You can create a playlist yourself and use it to hear any grouping of songs you want, in whatever order strikes your fancy.

Acquiring Audio Files

Before you can play any files, you must get them onto your computer in the first place! You can acquire the MP3 and other audio files you need from the Internet, by using MusicMatch Jukebox to rip them from a CD, or by using other available software to create these files. Technically, you can also acquire music from friends, although most of us know that the legality of that is in dispute in the courts and will probably be for many years as laws are updated to catch up with the fast-paced Internet revolution. Nobody has a problem with you lending a book to a friend to read, but it seems those international music companies don't feel the same way when it comes to music. With the noise they make about it, one would think these guys are living paycheck to paycheck in a studio apartment, sharing day-old pizza with the cockroach community.

Using the Recorder to Extract from CDs

Extracting tracks from your CDs is easy using the Recorder dialog box that was shown as part of the threesome back in Figure 16.2. Insert the audio CD and click the All button you see on the Recorder's toolbar, and you're in business. This is assuming, of course, that the artist produced a perfect album and you love every track. You also can select individual tracks instead of recording the whole thing. When you insert a music CD, you see the Recorder dialog box display a listing of that CD's tracks, which you can select individually using the check box located next to each one. Whether recording two tracks or twenty, click the Rec button on the left side of this dialog box when you're ready to start recording these files to your hard disk.

The default location the Recorder uses for the files it extracts from your CD is C:\Program Files\MusicMatch\Music. You can change this by clicking Options, Recorder, and Settings in the main player window. The Settings dialog box that pops up gives you the ability to configure many aspects of the Jukebox program.

The options in this dialog box are pretty self-explanatory, and because we're more concerned right now with choosing where to store your music, look to the dialog box's upper-right corner and click the Songs Directory button. This brings up yet another dialog box, which is shown in Figure 16.3.

Figure 16.3

*You can change the direc-
tory the Recorder uses to
store newly recorded songs.*

In addition to letting you customize where to store music files, this dialog box also enables you to decide how to name the new files. You can change the default direc-tory for new songs by simply highlighting the Directory For New Songs field and entering the path you want. If you want to have MusicMatch Jukebox automatically create subdirectories, based on the artist or the album title (or both), *under* this direc-tory, use the check boxes found in the Make Sub-Path Using section. Using these features, you can decide on a main directory path that is used to store all your music files.

Note that when you use the sub-path options, you see that, at the bottom of this dia-log box, the Sample Path field shows you what you've selected.

You can also see in this figure that you can further customize how music files are named and stored on your computer. For example, when you want to record a song from a CD, you can name the song in several ways:

➤ The actual song title (use the Track Name check box)

➤ The artist's name (use the Artist check box)

➤ The number of the track as it appears on the CD (use the Track Number check box)

➤ The album name (use the Album check box)

➤ Combinations of the above! (Select more than one check box)

For example, one of my favorite songs is "Walking on Thin Ice" by Yoko Ono. This song appears on several of her albums. If I wanted to name this song, I might want to use both the Artist and the Album check boxes, so I could look back and determine from where it was obtained. Perhaps you are like me and sometimes buy a CD just for one song. In that case, you might just use the Album check box.

If you do use more than one of these check boxes, MusicMatch Jukebox names the file accordingly and places a separator character between each of your choices when it creates the filename. The Separator check box allows you to select the hyphen or underscore character or, if you want, the space character. Just place your cursor in this field and type in whichever one you want to use. However, if you enter any other character, MusicMatch Jukebox goes back to the underscore character.

Click OK when you've finished viewing or modifying information in this dialog box.

This brings you back to the Recorder tab in the Settings dialog box. When you're happy with your settings here, click OK again to return to the main MusicMatch window.

When you've selected the tracks you want to record and have made any adjustments you want on the Settings dialog box, just click the Rec button on the Recorder to start the actual recording process. As each track is recorded, a green box appears onscreen next to the track if the song was recorded with no problems. If you see a yellow box then the song was recorded, but the quality will not be the best in the world. A red box, as you can guess, means that something went wrong and the track was not recorded.

Getting Music from the Net

Many sources of music exist on the Internet. To use MusicMatch Jukebox to look for music, you first must be connected to the Internet. Then, you click the Net Music icon, which looks like a globe of the world, on the Player window. This opens up the MusicMatch Web page in its own window (see Figure 16.4).

Figure 16.4

The Net Music window connects you to music sources on the Internet.

At the top of this window, you can use the Recommendations button to get a look at some recent songs. The Charts button, on the other hand, brings up a listing of the songs being listened to most frequently by MusicMatch customers. The Find Music button enables you to select from a variety of music categories, so you can refine your search in your quest for new songs.

Using the Music Library and Playlists

The two central themes around which this application is run are your music library and playlists. The *library* tells MusicMatch which audio files are on your hard disk and where they are located. The *playlist* is nothing more than a collection of audio files from your library that you want played as a group. This is similar to a collection of tracks from a music CD. The idea of libraries and playlists is a standard feature you'll find in most good media software. Because you can use playlists to burn a disc, they pretty much make you the producer of your own CDs. And, like Easy CD Creator, you can use a playlist to create and print jewel case inserts.

Before you can go making all sorts of wonderful playlists for the ages, though, you need to add music files to the MusicMatch library. To add a song to the library, simply click the Add button on the toolbar at the top of the Music Library window. The Add Songs to Music Library dialog box pops up, enabling you to browse your disks for the songs you want to add (see Figure 16.5).

Figure 16.5

Add songs to the Music Library so you can then create playlists.

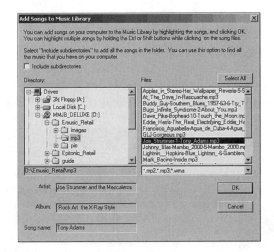

Use the Directory pane on the left to find the directory in which the files are located and then simply click the songs that appear in the Files pane on the right. Or, use the Select All button to add all the songs that appear in this pane. You can even use the standard Windows method of selecting multiple songs to add, by using Shift+click.

If you want to add songs to the library from a CD, simply place the CD in your CD-ROM player. In the Recorder window, information about the CD is displayed (if it's available; otherwise, you see track1, track2, and so on). Next to each track is a check box. You can select all the songs from the CD or just the ones you want to add to your library by using these check boxes.

Between Tracks

Adding Other Information to the Library

MusicMatch Jukebox can save and display on the screen all sorts of information about each song you put in its database. This can include the title, the artist, and even lyrics to a song! MusicMatch calls this information a *tag*. If you need to add the information manually, you can simply right-click the song in the Music Library window; the Tag Song File dialog box then pops up. From here, you can add the artist, song title, notes, lyrics, and more.

Besides adding information about the song, you can use other categories to classify a track. The AutoDJ feature (which I cover soon) can use these categories—sorted by genre, tempo, mood, situation, and preference—to select music from the library.

After making your selections, click the Record button in the Record window; the extraction process starts. The amount of time it takes depends on the speed at which your CD-ROM can perform digital audio extraction, so be patient if you select all the songs. MusicMatch Jukebox displays a small bar graph beside each track showing the percentage extracted for each song it extracts so you don't have to sit around wondering what's going on!

After you have music in your library, it's time to make some playlists!

Creating a Manual Playlist

A manual playlist is one in which you select each song individually. It might be time-consuming, but it does help ensure you get only the songs you want. You do this by dragging the song from the Music Library window to the Playlist pane in the Player application. After you've selected all the songs you want for a particular playlist, just click the Save button in the Playlist pane. The Save Playlist dialog box pops up and enables you to give a name to the Playlist so you'll be able to retrieve it at a later time.

To open a Playlist after you've created it, just click Open. Then, in the Open Music dialog box, click the Playlists button and select the list you want to open.

You can delete songs from any playlist by simply clicking the song in the list and pressing the Delete key on your computer. If you want to re-order the playlist, simply click the song in it and drag it to a new location in the list. To make this change permanent, be sure you use the Save button. This opens up a Save dialog box in which you can give the list a new name or save over the old one. If you choose the latter, MusicMatch Jukebox lets you know you're about to overwrite an existing playlist. Duh! Click OK and the next time you open the list, it remembers the changes you just saved.

Using the AutoDJ to Create a Playlist

If you don't want to be tied into selecting each song for your playlist, the MusicMatch Jukebox has an AutoDJ feature that can save you some time. To begin this process, click the AutoDJ button on the Music Library's toolbar. The dialog box shown in Figure 16.6 enables you to select the criteria that gets used to select songs for the playlist. Remember in the previous section how you could include genre type, mood information, and so on for each audio track you add to your library? For AutoDJ to work effectively, it needs this information!

Figure 16.6

You can select music auto-matically by specifying the criteria the AutoDJ should use.

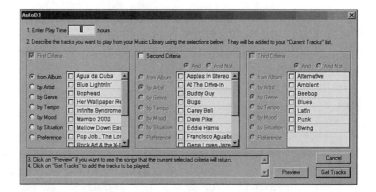

You can select tracks by artist name, album name, genre, and other categories, as you can see in Figure 16.6. You further subselect by using second and third criteria, if you want, to narrow down the playlist. When you're finished selecting criteria, click the Get Tracks button; the AutoDJ then makes selections for you and adds them to the current playlist window. You can then use the playlist to start playing the songs, or you can save the playlist and give it a name. You also can use the playlist to burn a CD.

Using the Playlist to Burn a CD

If you look at the player window, the buttons above the Playlist pane include one labeled CD-R. Guess what this is used for. That's right; you click this button to start the recording process. This brings up the Create CD from Playlist dialog box, from which you can do several things. First, you can add more songs to the playlist or delete songs if your playlist takes up more time than your CD has to give. In Figure 16.7, you can see this dialog box with the Options button clicked to show additional selections you can make when creating a CD.

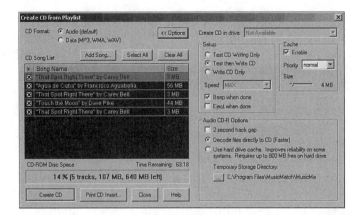

Figure 16.7

The Create CD from Playlist dialog box enables you to test or actually burn a CD.

You can use this dialog box to create either an audio or a data CD. An audio CD, of course, means the files are converted to the CD-DA format compatible with any music CD player and written to the disc. A data CD writes the actual audio files (MP3, WMA, and WAV) to the disc, should you plan to play it on a computer CD-ROM or compatible CD player. Many of the other options, including write testing and eliminating the two-second gap between tracks, are similar to what you saw in Chapter 3, "Using Easy CD Creator to Make Audio CDs," for creating audio CDs with Easy CD Creator. The Print CD Insert button prints a single page that contains a front cover insert and a back cover insert. You can specify the text for the spines (edges) of the back insert, and you can either browse to find your own cover art or let the program choose something for you. Unfortunately, there is no option to print a label for your CD.

Use the Cache Feature to Prevent Coasters!

Just like Easy CD Creator, Music Matchbox has a cache that can store information so it can supply a steady stream of data to the laser burner. In the Create CD from Playlist dialog box, you see the Cache section at the top right. Leave the Enable check box selected. The Priority feature determines the amount of system resources MusicMatch Jukebox can use when burning the CD. The Size slider bar feature enables you to set the size of the cache. Unless you find that you are creating lots of coasters, leave both of these fields at their default levels—Priority: normal and Size: 4Mb.

When you're finally ready, click the Create CD button to start burning. Similar to Easy CD Creator, you see a dialog box; this one is called CD Creation Progress. The usual Preparing Audio Data and Writing Music Tracks are shown here. When finished, MusicMatch Jukebox tells you, with a small dialog box, that the CD is complete. Click OK to dismiss this dialog box and you've got a new CD!

Forget Windows 95!

You can forget about using Windows 95 with version 7 of the Media Player. It is available at this time only for Windows 98 and higher versions of Windows, such as Windows NT 4 and Windows 2000.

Microsoft's Media Player Version 7.0

This application is included in this chapter because *it's free*. And, of course, it meets the other requirement for this book: It burns CDs—well, it tries to, anyway. This new version of the media player is similar both to its predecessors and to MusicMatch Jukebox. It helps you organize your music (using a Media Library) and enables you to gather music from different sources in a variety of formats. One important distinction that you can make between Microsoft's new media player and MusicMatch Jukebox is that the new media player handles video files as well as audio files.

As you can see in Figure 16.8, the program as it first appears on your computer has a toolbar on the left side. Note also the standard audio/video buttons on the display (Play, Pause, Stop, and so on).

Figure 16.8

The Windows Media Player has several controls that affect how you plan to use it.

The options on this toolbar enable you to switch between the various features the player offers. These are as follows:

➤ **Now Playing**—Shows you information about the media file (CD or otherwise) now playing. Here, you can also see *visualizations*, which are animated graphic thingies you can watch while you listen to digital audio tracks. They can provide a nifty visual treat for five minutes or so. After that, they're just distracting.

➤ **Media Guide**—If you are connected to the Internet, you can use the Media Guide to see content provided here by Microsoft, such as music downloads.

➤ **CD Audio**—This is the button you use to access CD-ROM drives on your system. This is where you see the listing of tracks on the CD. Similar to Easy CD Creator, Media Player can download CD title, artist, and track information from the Internet if you are connected.

➤ **Media Library**—Like MusicMatch Jukebox, the new media player enables you to organize all your audio (and video) files into a library, which gives you capabilities such as searching and creating playlists.

➤ **Radio Tuner**—Tune into the many radio stations that are now available on the Internet, by category.

➤ **Portable Device**—Upload audio files to your portable device.

➤ **Skin Chooser**—Change the way the media player appears on your screen. Skins are comparable to the clothes you wear. Although we all look pretty much the same underneath, clothes give us each a different look. Skins add a different look to the Media Player. You can download new skins from Microsoft.

Building Your Media Library

Like MusicMatch, you usually need to add media files to your Media Library before you can use them. Media Player is actually a little more helpful in this regard in terms of adding this information without your help. In the following sections, we take a look at making sure every media file you have gets in your library.

Searching Your Computer for Media Files

The Media Player can quickly look through your hard disks and find any files that are of a format it supports. To begin the search, simply click the Tools menu and select Search Computer for Media. A dialog box named Search for Media In appears. From this, you can select all drives on your computer or narrow the search to specific drives.

Several media files are on your computer that you probably don't want in your Media Library, such as the files used to create the sounds Windows makes during normal operations. If, however, you like playing with these sounds from the System folder, check the box Include WAV and MIDI Files Found in System Folders. Just be prepared for a lot of files!

After the program has found all the media files it can locate, it adds them to your Media Library, enabling you to use them individually or in playlists.

Copying Files from CD to Your Computer

Use the CD Audio button on the left toolbar to access audio CDs. As you already know, when you insert a CD into the computer's CD-ROM drive, the Media Player begins to play the CD—unless it's currently playing some other file. But, if you don't want your CD-ROM constantly filled with audio CDs, you can copy the tracks to your computer, just like in MusicMatch.

Note that the view you get when using the CD Audio button shows you information about the CD inserted in the computer. If the information is available locally or via the Internet, you see the name of the track, its length, and the artist name, along with other information. Otherwise, you get the generic Track 1, Track 2, and so on. If you want or need to enter the CD information manually, just right-click the track and choose Edit from the menu that appears.

Between Tracks

Get the Info from the Internet!

For almost every CD you have, a database exists on the Internet that contains the artist and song title data. You can automatically get the media player to look this up for you and save your fingers for better things than typing! Just use the Get Names button or the Get Album Details button near the right corner of Media Player and follow the prompts. Of course, you must be logged on to the Internet first! After you download this information, Windows remembers it automatically whenever you insert the CD.

To copy files from CD to your computer, follow these steps:

1. Insert the CD in the computer's CD-ROM drive.
2. All songs on the CD are selected by default. If there are any songs you do not want to have copied, click the check box next to them to deselect them. If you want only a track or two, click the check mark toggle at the very top of the list. This deselects all the check boxes (or adds them back, if clicked again).
3. Click the Copy Music button near the top of the application window.

As you can see in Figure 16.9, the Copy Status field (next to the track Length field) tells you whether a track has been copied, is being copied, or has not been copied to your hard disk. As files are copied, the percentage of the file copied so far is displayed in this field. In Figure 16.9, you can see that the first eight songs have been Copied to Library, while the "Now or Never" track is 92% complete, and the remaining titles are Pending.

Figure 16.9

You can watch as files from the CD are copied to the Media Library on your computer.

Once copied to your media library, you can select any of the copied songs to be part of a playlist.

Setting Options for Audio Recording

Copying audio tracks to your computer is a simple task, as you've just seen. You can manage settings for how the process is done, however, and the decisions you make can affect the quality of the music file that results from the copy process. To get to the Options dialog box, click the Tools menu at the very top of the application and then select Options. When the Options dialog box appears, select the CD Audio tab, as shown in Figure 16.10.

To select the location for storing audio files on the computer, just click the Change button at the bottom of the dialog box. It opens up a dialog box that enables you to select a new folder.

Moving up to the Copying Settings section, note that the slider bar labeled Copy Music at This Quality is an important one. If you have a lot of hard disk space, you can probably afford to give up the real estate necessary to store all your music at the highest quality. If not, you can use this slider bar to adjust the quality downward and the file size at the same time.

Figure 16.10

The CD Audio tab enables you to control the size, quality, and location of the music tracks you want to record.

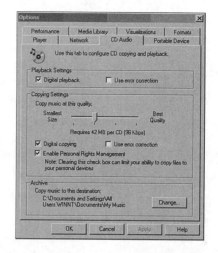

The best quality at which you can record to disk is 160Kbps (that's the number of bits per second), and it would take about 69MB of disk space to store an entire CD. At the other end of the spectrum, the smallest file will store an entire CD in only 28MB of disk space, and the file will play back at 64Kbps. A value of 96 seems to work pretty well for this, but it's up to you and your ears to decide what's best for you.

It's a tradeoff. If you own the CD, you can always make another copy later if you add a new hard disk. You might want to try the various quality settings to see whether a smaller size makes any difference in what you hear. For example, at work you're not likely to be blasting out Led Zeppelin, so using the highest quality probably isn't necessary!

After you have used the aforementioned check boxes to select the songs you want copied to your hard disk, it's time to start the copying process. Click the Copy Music button located on the same toolbar as the Get Album Info button. As the tracks are extracted from the CD, the Copy Status field shows you the percentage copied for the song it's currently transferring. Completed tracks have the text "Copied to Library" in this field. Completed songs are also automatically added to Media Player's music library.

The Microsoft Killjoys

Seeing as they provide Media Player 7 for free, Microsoft seems to figure they can tell you how you should record your music. Whereas other programs usually let you record to WAV or MP3 files (at the very least), Media Player requires that you copy them to WMA (Windows Media Audio) files instead.

Why does it do this? Well, unlike MP3 files, which you can freely distribute to anyone, WMA files have licenses that tell a computer whether you have the "right" to listen to the file. The Media Player gets the license for a track automatically if you purchase and download music from the Internet or burn it from the original CD. However, the license is a separate and hidden file, so if you send the WMA music file to a friend, he or she can't listen to it. Making matters even worse, if you lose the license (because you formatted your computer, your hard drive crashes, and so on) *you* lose the ability to play music you rightfully own! Gee... thanks.

When recording your own CDs to a hard disk, you should use a different program that records to MP3s. Media Player will use these files after you have them; it just doesn't record to MP3s itself.

Creating and Using Playlists

Similar to MusicMatch Jukebox, you can collect songs into playlists that can be used to either listen to the music or to burn a CD. After you've added audio tracks to the Media Library, you can organize them into one or more playlists. To create a new playlist, follow this procedure:

1. Click the Media Library button on the left toolbar.
2. Click the New playlist button, which now appears at the top of the Media Player.
3. When the New Playlist dialog box pops up, enter a name for the playlist and click OK. You can create as many playlists as you want. After you've created a plalist, it shows up on the left side of the Media Library under My Playlists.
4. To add a song to a playlist, click the song once in the right pane and then click the Add to Playlist button. You can also add several songs at once using the Ctrl+click method. The Media Player shows you a list of the existing playlists,

249

allowing you to choose which one to add the track(s) to. Alternatively, you can simply click and drag a song from the Media Library to the playlist folder on the left side of the Media Player window.

5. Keep adding tracks until you've added all the songs you want. After that is done, so are you! Remember, though, no playlist is permanent. You can always add more songs to any playlist in the same manner at another time.

Between Tracks

Removing Tracks and Playlists

To delete a playlist or an audio track from the library, click the Media Library button, and then right-click the playlist or song and select Delete from the left-hand pane. The item is moved to the Deleted Items section of the Media Library. From here, you can still restore the playlist by going to the Deleted Items folder, right-clicking the playlist or song, and selecting Restore.

When you are sure you no longer want the items that appear in the Deleted Items section of the Media Library, you can purge them by expanding the folder and selecting All Deleted Media (if you want to permanently delete everything in the folder). Otherwise, you can right-click individual items in the Deleted Items folder and press the Delete key. Media Player then asks whether you want to remove the song files permanently from your hard drive (as opposed to just removing them from your library).

You also can add a track to a playlist by right-clicking the track once and selecting Add to Playlist. A dialog box appears that enables you to select the playlist.

Playing Music Using a Playlist

Playing the songs in a playlist is simple. Start by clicking the Media Library button to bring up the playlists. Click the playlist you want to use once and then click the Play button at the bottom of the application window. You can also select a playlist from the drop-down list at the upper-right corner of the window and then select Play/Pause. Finally, you can right-click the playlist and select Play!

Burning a CD Using a Playlist

You can also copy a playlist to a CD. Even though Media Player records to only WMA (Windows Media), you can record files from MP3 and WAV formats. After you've created a playlist—and made sure that it doesn't contain more than 74 minutes of music—you can create a CD:

1. Click the File menu.
2. Select Copy to CD.
3. From the Playlists dialog box that pops up, select the playlist you want to copy to CD.
4. The Roxio CD Recording plug-in pops up and burns the CD (see Figure 16.11). Note that in this figure, you can see that, unlike Easy CD Creator, there are no options for you to select when burning the CD except to start recording or cancel a recording. You can't even set the speed at which your CD-RW drive burns the disc!

Between Tracks: More Wallet Gouging

When you look at Figure 16.11, you also might notice an Upgrade Now button at the bottom of the screen. Predictably, this is not for any bug-fixing patch program you might need. Rather, because this is an Roxio plug-in, it takes you to a Web page where you have the "opportunity" to buy the full Roxio Easy CD Creator software package. Gee... thanks.

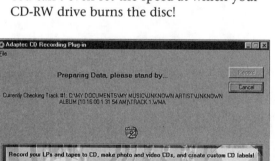

Figure 16.11

The Roxio CD Recording plug-in is used to burn the CD.

More, More, More!

Multimedia content on the Internet is booming. It's very likely that in a few more years you won't even be buying CDs at a store anymore—or going to the video store to rent a video. You'll be sitting on your sofa getting fat watching and listening as it's all delivered right to your doorstep (or your computer, I should say). What's covered in this book is just the beginning! Look at the CD at the back of the book for more fun audio/video files and applications you can try. Look on the Internet and you'll find dozens or hundreds of other applications. If you don't find what you want today, it'll likely be there tomorrow!

The Least You Need to Know

➤ As CD burners become more popular, you will see many more applications that can be used with them to burn your own CDs.

➤ You don't have to pay for software without trying it first. Grab MusicMatch Jukebox off the CD at the back of this book, or download Microsoft's Window Media Player 7.0 from www.microsoft.com.

➤ What we have covered in this chapter is just the tip of the iceberg. Try out both of these applications to see which one suits your media habits best.

A Quick Overview of the Book Standards

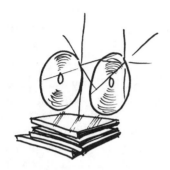

While those of use who grew up with phonograph records and black-and-white TVs never thought of the complicated technologies that were to come, we thought much less about standards. That is, until the famous VHS/BetaMax wars came along! Surely, some of you remember going to a video store and having to choose between the VHS and BetaMax sections? How horribly expensive Beta's death must have been for those who chose the wrong team. Compact disc manufacturers were wise enough to avoid this by creating standards for the various kinds of CDs you use today. This appendix provides a brief overview of the books that define these standards, all of which are known by the color of their covers. So, if you're ever in a conversation with some cyber geeks and someone mentions the "orange book" or the "white book," you'll know what he's talking about.

Because my aim here is really just to give you a basic idea of what these standards represent, you're not going to come out of this appendix a scholar in the field. In fact, you'll likely find that some of the numbers and specifications I'm bandying about are just way over your head. Don't worry about it—this is strictly an FYI for those who want a few more tidbits about the various CD specs. That's why this is just an appendix!

For more information on the contents of these specification documents, just call up your local international manufacturer and ask for a copy ... and expect a big bill! These aren't like Internet standards, which are developed by standards organizations comprised mostly of volunteers. These are the hard facts from the companies who developed the technology and now make it so "cheaply" available to us. If, for some reason, you do want the actual docs, be warned—they ain't cheap!

Philips and Sony, in cooperation with each other, developed many of the compact disc formats in use today. Some others were also developed, or adapted from the standard formats, by other companies. At the time Philips and Sony developed their audio formats, all records (as we old-timers sometimes still call CDs today), used basically one of two formats: mono or stereo. Most players for these records could play either format. A few other standards were also developed, but the majority of the records produced were recorded in one of these formats.

When it came to developing the compact disc, however, it was a reasonable decision to come to agreement about how the product would be produced rather than develop multiple standards. After all, as history had shown, why should a company have to develop a Beta Max version of a video production and a VHS version? Both systems meant that the manufacturer of a video had to go through processes that are not exactly cheap to produce master copies for two different formats and then hope that both would sell well enough to justify the development costs.

The first compact disc standard was designed with the music industry as its target. Today many standards exist, but these were not developed to satisfy the consumer's brand of a particular playback device; instead they were developed to include new kinds of data that could be stored on the disc. Of course, this doesn't mean that all CDs will work on all CD hardware devices. For example, although you can play an audio CD (more correctly called CD-DA), you obviously cannot insert a photo-CD into an ordinary CD player made for playing back audio recordings and expect to see your photos. Audio players don't have display screens or video out ports to your television! You can use that same CD, however, in a player meant to interpret the data as photographic images. The point is that when you buy an audio CD-DA disc, you can be assured, because of the standards, that it will play in your CD player.

So, for this discussion, we focus on the "book" specifications that were created to specify how certain types of discs should be created. Each book is used to define a different purpose for the compact disc, and each is identified by the color of the cover of the book.

The Red Book—The Audio CD Format

In 1982, Philips and Sony released the "Red Book," which set forth the specifications for creating audio CDs (also called CD-DAs). This is the CD with which most people are familiar. This type of CD uses an error-correction scheme called *CIRC*. When using Easy CD Creator, you can choose to record MP3 files in addition to the CD-DA tracks you can find on a Red Book CD. The program, however, converts the MP3 file to a WAV file, which is almost exactly the same as the Red Book CD-DA method. Either way, you won't be able to tell the difference.

The Yellow Book—The Computer CD-ROM Format

This standard was released in 1983. As you can probably figure out, the term CD-ROM stands for compact disc read-only memory. It would be years before we'd see the birth of a recordable CD.

At the time this standard was created, computer manufacturers had been creating faster systems with larger storage capacities (both in hard disks and in memory chips), which in turn led to software applications that grew in size. This process is still going on today! Installation files for an application that used to fit on one or two floppy disks now require many more. The first version of Microsoft Office that I purchased came on, I believe, more than twenty floppy disks! Yet, all that could easily be stored on a single CD-ROM today, along with a lot of other data.

The Next Storage Evolution

As computers continue to become more powerful, and as software developers continue to develop larger applications, it is easy to see that the typical business or home computer is already outgrowing the limitations of the CD. It is easy to see that just a few years down the road, the CD will be thought of much as we do the floppy disk today. If you don't believe this, look in your local computer store—or search the Internet—and you will find that already many software packages and applications are available on DVD as well as CD-ROM. Even the venerable Microsoft Office has outgrown the format. Have you seen the Premium Edition for Office 2000? It requires four CD-ROM discs!

The CD-ROM disc is the same size as a CD-DA disc, 120mm. However, the method used for storing data on the disc is different. Each data block on a CD-ROM disc is made up of 98 CD frames, with an additional 12 bytes used for synchronization for each block and 4 bytes used for header and timing information. With 24 bytes in each frame, this yields a block of data that is 2,352 bytes long. What do you really need to remember and understand about this? Just that despite being the same size, CD-ROM and CD-DA formats are, in fact, different!

Unlike computer hard disks or floppy disks, most of the header information (like a table of contents) is used to store timing information. For example, the first byte is used to store minutes. The second byte is used to store seconds, and the third byte stores a block number that is within that second. Remember that, even though the CD-ROM is not identical to the CD-DA, its format was adapted from it. Thus, they have these timing values rather than the typical block addressing found on other computer drive storage devices.

The last byte in the header is called the *Mode* byte. Two modes can be used. Mode 1 uses 2,048 bytes in each block for storing user data. It also uses 280 bytes for error correction and detection (EDC). Because the Red Book audio format uses only CIRC error correction, Mode 1 disks have this additional method for determining when an error has occurred and needs to be corrected. This additional error correction is one of the reasons why Mode 1 is used more often than Mode 2.

255

Mode 2 uses 2,336 bytes in each block for data. This allows for a larger amount of user data on the disc, but this format is not used very often by itself. Mode 2 also uses just CIRC for error correction.

The Green Book—Interactive Multimedia Format

Just as computer manufacturers realized that an immense amount of data could be stored on a CD-ROM, companies specializing in multimedia came to the same conclusion. Thus, the interactive multimedia (CD-I) format was released in 1987 to enable video, audio, and other files to be stored on the CD-ROM and to be used in special interactive devices or in a standard computer.

This kind of disc is usually found in those self-repeating product demonstrators found on kiosks in shopping malls. The ability to allow the user to interact with a program and incorporate multimedia features makes it ideal for this purpose. This reminds me, when was the last time you saw such a kiosk? This goes to show you that sometimes standards get developed for an anticipated usage that materializes only briefly, if at all.

The Orange Book (Parts I, II, and III)—CD-R

This kind of CD differed in its development from the others in that it was the first "recordable" CD. Actually, two kinds of CDs are defined in this book—called CD-WO (CD write once), which is now called CD-R, and CD-MO (CD magneto optical), which is usually found in high-end installations such as large computer rooms. These standards, which form parts I and II, were released in 1990. However, inexpensive recording devices did not start to come on the mass market until about 1995. At this time, they are now so inexpensive—you can get one on sale with a rebate at some computer stores for around $150—that they are becoming a standard feature on most newer computers.

Part III of the Orange Book was released in 1995 and takes the CD-R concept and adds the ability to erase and re-record on a CD-ROM. The actual CD-R and CD-RW (which started out being called CD-erasable or CD-E) discs are, however, not manufactured in the same manner, and the reflection of the laser light is different on the two discs. If you have a new model of CD-ROM disc drive, it might be able to read CD-RW discs on the CD-ROM drive, but the older models cannot. CD-RW drives, however, are backward-compatible with most other compact disc formats, so you will most likely be able to read any kind of CD on a CD-RW drive.

The White Book—The Video CD

This standard was defined in 1993 by Philips, Sony, and JVC to enable storing about 70 minutes of video on a CD-ROM. It was based partly on a karaoke CD that JVC had developed earlier. This was version 1.1 of the White Book. In version 2.0, released in 1994, Philips, JVC, and Matsushita developed a more versatile version of the video CD that could be used for standard video content, as well as provide support for interactive applications.

The drive used to read these kinds of discs is called CD-ROM/XA.

The CD-ROM/XA uses the Mode 2 format discussed earlier to allow for 2,336 bytes of data in each block. This means that this kind of disc must depend on only CIRC error-correction methods and is therefore less reliable than a CD-ROM disc that uses Mode 1. The *XA* in this disc's name stands for *extended architecture*. This kind of disc is an extension of the Yellow Book standards and enables several kinds of data to be stored on the same disc, including the following:

➤ Audio

➤ Video

➤ Computer data

➤ Compressed audio

This type of disc uses a subheader that defines the kind of block that follows. This enables the interleaving of various kinds of data on the same track. This disc is considered a *bridge* disc format between the regular CD-ROM and CD-I formats. However, you will usually need a special kind of player to read a disc that is of the CD-ROM/XA type.

The Blue Book—CD-Extra

This format was released in 1996 and has been known by other names, such as CD-Plus and Enhanced CD. It contains multisessions, each of which can contain various kinds of data. For example, most audio CD players can recognize only the first session, and the music recorded there will play just as if the CD were of the CD-DA variety. However, a second session could be added to contain computer data. Because most audio CDs usually contain only 50–60 minutes of music, a second session could be added that could store a few hundred megabytes of computer applications or data. When played in an ordinary audio player, you would hear the music. When played in a computer, you would listen to the musical selections *or* play with the multimedia applications stored in the second session.

Packet Writing Formats (Sorry, No Color)

In many cases, you either copy an entire CD or at least select data from several sources and write a CD-R disc during one session. A technology called *packet writing* enables you to write in much smaller increments to a disc over time. Two standards have been developed for packet writing. The CD-RFS format is a Sony-developed format, whereas the CD-UDF format is a more standard format for packet writing.

Cross Reference

➤ In Chapter 4, "Using Easy CD Creator to Make Data CDs" you can read about using Roxio's software to create and read this type of CD.

Index